"On March 18, the coup took place, led by General Lon Nol and Sirik Matak. A tiny Cambodian elite, hoping to win for itself a larger share of control in the economy and political life and resentful of Sihanouk's personal authority and prestige, plunged the country into civil war and set the stage for the American invasion that now threatens to turn Cambodia into another Laos or Vietnam."

—NOAM CHOMSKY
"Cambodia in Conflict"

Has Operation "Total Victory" backfired?
Did the United States back the coup that ousted Sihanouk? Did the Pentagon push President Nixon into the Fishook invasion?

Cambodia
The Widening War in Indochina
is the essential sourcebook on the Cambodian invasion and the transformation of the Vietnam War into an Indochina War.

CAMBODIA

THE WIDENING WAR
IN INDOCHINA

EDITED BY
JONATHAN S. GRANT, LAURENCE A. G. MOSS,
AND JONATHAN UNGER

COMMITTEE OF CONCERNED ASIAN SCHOLARS
UNIVERSITY OF CALIFORNIA, BERKELEY

WSP
WASHINGTON SQUARE PRESS · NEW YORK

CAMBODIA:
THE WIDENING WAR IN INDOCHINA

Washington Square Press edition published February, 1971

L

Published by
Washington Square Press, a division of Simon & Schuster, Inc.,
630 Fifth Avenue, New York, N.Y.

WASHINGTON SQUARE PRESS editions are distributed in the
U.S. by Simon & Schuster, Inc., 630 Fifth Avenue, New
York, N.Y. 10020 and in Canada by Simon & Schuster
of Canada, Ltd., Richmond Hill, Ontario, Canada.

PERMISSIONS

"From the Vietnam War to an Indochina War," by Jean Lacouture. Reprinted by permission from *Foreign Affairs*, July 1970. Copyright © Council on Foreign Relations, Inc., New York.

"The Syndrome of American Escalation," by Peter Dale Scott. Reprinted by permission from *The New York Review of Books*. Copyright © 1970 *The New York Review*.

Acknowledgments

In the wake of the American thrust into the Cambodian sanctuaries in the spring of 1970, universities and colleges shut down in a nationwide strike for the first time in American history. Many among the hundreds of thousands of students, teachers, and members of the greater community who joined in active opposition to President Nixon's decision sought out Asia specialists in their universities for information and analyses on the expanded war. Yet there was little appropriate material to offer inquirers. This book was written to help fill that gap.

On those campuses where scholarship on Asia is concentrated, the Committee of Concerned Asian Scholars provided a framework for coordinated research on Cambodia and the American escalation. The Committee was formed in 1968 by several hundred young Asia scholars who oppose America's role in Asia and their own profession's silent acquiescence, and who share the conviction that scholarly endeavor should be combined with political and ethical concerns. This book is edited by three members of the CCAS chapter at the University of California, Berkeley.

Many friends have helped in the creation of this book. The editors wish to thank the contributing authors, particularly those who committed their energies to an additional work load during the crisis. Douglas Sparks undertook the difficult task of securing and developing the information in the appendices. In this work he was aided by materials prepared by the Bay Area Institute and by the Cornell University chapter of CCAS. Darlene Jang drafted the maps. Luther Allen of the University of Massachusetts, Amherst, and Joseph Fisher, Arthur Mitchell, and Douglas Sparks of the University of California, Berkeley, assisted in the formulation of the contents. Carol Friedman, Carolyn Grant, Cynthia Hermes, Norma Montgomery, Jo Pearson, Suzanne Rogalin, Karen Tanaka, Frederick Wakeman, and others too numerous to mention gave generously of their time and expertise.

Berkeley, July 15, 1970

vii

CONTENTS

Introduction

This book analyzes the latest and most dramatic escalation of America's conflict with Asia—the spread of hostilities into Cambodia and the transformation of the Vietnam War into an Indochina War. The contributors offer no new solutions to the conflict in Indochina, but rather present information that reinforces an existing solution—immediate withdrawal.

The editors recognize the frailty of knowledge in the arena of human battles. Not only are words pitifully insignificant beside the enormity of the event, even their power of communication seems discouragingly meager. This is particularly true in the polarized society of the United States today, when those people receptive to informed argument are steadily diminishing. Nevertheless, the attempt to inform and rationally persuade must be made.

When President Nixon announced the American incursion into Cambodia, very few Americans knew anything about Cambodia or the invasion's relationship to the United States' military presence in Vietnam and Laos. Despite the subsequent news coverage devoted to the fighting in Cambodia, and despite the agonizing debate that ensued in the United States, most of us still have only a superficial knowledge of Cambodia and of the forces contesting her soil. Little has been said of the coup that deposed Prince Sihanouk, or of the conditions surrounding it. Sihanouk's policies and complex personality have been consigned to occasional phrases, and one hears less of General Lon Nol. Of the seven million Cambodian people, their history, and their politics, one hears even less. Yet these factors are essential to comprehending and forming rational opinions on the expanded war.

Facing the common enemy—the United States of America and its client governments—the revolutionary forces of the three Indochinese peoples have joined together in the United Alliance of Indochina. In one sense this is an ironic fulfill-

1

ment of the French colonial goal of forging the diverse peoples of the area into an integral unit.

To Peter Dale Scott and Noam Chomsky, this situation largely results from the expanded American presence. The extension of the war into Cambodia fits the pattern of the earlier United States escalations into Laos: a neutralist government is overthrown by a right-wing pro-American coup; the new regime launches a minor attack on a clearly superior revolutionary force and subsequently retreats while demanding anti-communist assistance from the United States; a crisis decision is made in Washington that precludes civilian review, and on the basis of military advice the United States is committed.

But the preconditions created by the American military must also be recognized. In Cambodia the numerous United States border violations, from bombing attacks to the use of defoliants on Cambodian rubber plantations, heightened the internal dissension that led to the overthrow of the neutralist Prince Sihanouk. However, as Banning Garrett points out, the long-term consequence of that coup and the American invasion will be the strengthening of the Left in Cambodia.

The situation within Cambodia is examined in considerable detail in the middle chapters of the book. From Roger M. Smith's portrayal of Cambodia's past, three experiences appear to have particular bearing on the present: the god-king tradition, French colonial rule, and the struggle for independence. According to the concept of the god-king, the Cambodian ruler is the intermediary between society and the supernatural. The legitimizing vestiges of this role were enjoyed by Prince Sihanouk who is directly descended from the ancient Khmer kings. The Prince combined this role with that of a nationalist patriot, as it was he who led Cambodia gradually to independence from France. Since Cambodia became a sovereign nation in 1953, Sihanouk controlled the government and politics of his country; his leadership has been based on skillful statesmanship, a charismatic personality, and the loyalty of the peasants. However, during the past few years opposition to Sihanouk's personal rule and economic policies became manifest in the army and among Cambodia's urban elite.

After the March 1970 coup, the new regime of General Lon Nol rallied support from the urban community. As

Jonathan S. Grant demonstrates, however, this government's programs for economic development and the persecution of the ethnic Vietnamese were in effect subverted by the actions of those to whom Lon Nol turned for support—the Americans and the South Vietnamese. The Allied invasion, which Richard Falk shows to be a violation of international law, drastically altered the situation in Cambodia. Six days after the invasion, Sihanouk, from exile in Peking, formed the National United Front of Cambodia, which rapidly gained support among the peasantry and launched a full-fledged civil war. This mobilization effort was assisted by the North Vietnamese and the National Liberation Front which had been forced out of the border areas by the sanctuary invasion. As Banning Garrett and Jonathan Unger point out, the Maoist concept of a people's war of liberation has significantly influenced the program of the National United Front. Conversely, the continuing presence in Cambodia of South Vietnamese ground forces and American air power has integrated the Cambodian conflict into strategic planning for South Vietnam and Laos.

The instruments of war being employed by the United States in Vietnam and Laos indicate what the future holds for Cambodia. The impact of saturation bombing, defoliation, and forced urbanization is examined by Laurence A. G. Moss, Zmarak M. Shalizi and Ngô Vinh Long. The combined use of these instruments along with more conventional ones amounts to ecocide—the destruction of the Indochinese peoples and the environment in which they live. Through the systematic devastation of the countryside, its inhabitants, and their ways of life, and the crowding of survivors into wretched urban slums or "relocation camps," the environment which supports "the enemy" is eliminated and theoretically "the enemy" will cease to survive. This is the essence of Nixon's Vietnamization program.

Not only is this strategy destroying Indochina, but it has also reaped a tragic harvest in the United States of America. The last section of the book raises questions about conditions in America, particularly the role of the military in American society. Franz Schurmann sees in the political decision to invade Cambodia a constitutional crisis over the power of the Pentagon, and Robert Jay Lifton gives us a glimpse of the veteran and the environment to which he returns. The severe distortion of the American economy caused by war expenditures is examined in the final article by Douglass B. Lee, Jr., and John W. Dyckman.

Asia scholars, like their fellow citizens, possess political axioms and ideological biases that affect their perceptions. But scholars often conceal these biases, sometimes even from themselves, beneath a "value-free" veneer of scholarship. The editors of this book maintain that a scholar should attempt to make explicit the assumptions, biases, and predilections that he brings to research. The editors believe that American policy in Indochina is criminal, both in conception and implementation, and that America must immediately cease her destruction of the lives, the culture, and the environment of the Indochinese peoples.

The critical words of Mark Twain apply as well to the United States in Indochina today as to the United States military interventions of seventy years ago.

> This Republic's life is not in peril. The nation has sold its honor for a phrase. It has swung itself loose from its safe anchorage and is drifting, its helm is in pirate hands. The stupid phrase [*Our Country, Right or Wrong!*] needed help, and it got another one: "Even if the war be wrong we are in it and must fight it out: *we cannot retire from it without dishonor.*" Why, not even a burglar could have said it better. We cannot withdraw from this sordid raid because to grant peace to those little people upon their terms—independence—would dishonor us. You have flung away Adam's phrase—you should take it up and examine it again. He said, *"An inglorious peace is better than a dishonorable war."*
>
> THE EDITORS

PART ONE

THE WIDENING WAR

1

From the Vietnam War to an Indochina War

by Jean Lacouture

I

During the last week of April 1970 the Vietnam war became the Second Indochina War. On April 24 and 25 representatives of the four movements of the Indochinese Left convened at a certain spot in south China to seal an alliance that had been contracted many years before by three of the movements—the North Vietnamese Lao Dong, the Pathet Lao and the South Vietnamese National Liberation Front (NLF) —and to which Prince Sihanouk, overthrown a month earlier by the Cambodian Right, was now adhering in a conspicuously unconditional manner. The *Indochinese* revolutionary front thus came into being.

Five days later, President Nixon announced the entry into Cambodia of sizable American contingents backed up by South Vietnamese units. This operation, dubbed "Total Victory," was presented in Saigon as an attempt to wind up the war and be done with it. In this manner a strategy was defined which confuses the idea of victory with that of extending the conflict outside Vietnam. In the light of the disclosures made two weeks before by a subcommittee of the Senate Foreign Relations Committee regarding American participation in the fighting in Laos, the conclusion is inescapable that on April 30, 1970, the United States embarked on what is now the Second Indochina War.

Thus Richard Nixon became the first Republican President to increase the responsibilities of the United States on that Asian landmass into which Washington's best strategists have so often insisted that no American army must ever plunge. And the operation was launched under conditions that the

Jean Lacouture is a distinguished French journalist. His many books include *Ho Chi Minh: A Political Biography* and *Vietnam: Between Two Truces.*

worst enemies of the United States might have hoped for.
"We must have two or three Vietnams!" Ernesto "Che"
Guevara had trumpeted in 1967 in the name of the worldwide revolution. And there they are, from Luang Prabang to
Kep: two or three Vietnams, that is to say, the whole of that
territory of Indochina which French colonization seems, in
retrospect, to have put together to serve as the framework
for a revolutionary undertaking—a framework that is more
open to Vietnamese energies than the restricted territory of
Vietnam alone.

The very word "Indochina" was created by colonization
and for colonization; the Danish-born geographer Malte-Brun
coined the term in 1852. In 1887, an Indochinese administration was set up, under the authority of a governor general
presiding sometimes in Saigon and sometimes in Hanoi, composed of the following elements—the colony of Cochin China
in the south; the protectorates of Annam in the east, which
retained a ceremonial sovereign residing in Hué, and of
Tonkin, in the north, where an "imperial delegate" resided;
and the kingdoms of Cambodia and Laos in the west, whose
monarchical systems were left intact by the colonizers. This
arrangement was a strange combination of three Vietnamese
countries strongly marked by Chinese influence and Confu-
cian historical tradition and the little kingdoms of the
Mekong, which belong, rather, with the cultural sphere of
India and are wholly dominated by the strictest form of
Buddhism.

In concocting this amalgam of nations and civilizations, the
French colonizers were, like their British rivals in Nigeria,
attempting to set up the most economical kind of operation,
one by which some of the colonized peoples are made to
exploit the others. And to a large extent they succeeded. In
Vietnam, they managed to maintain a class of mandarins,
which enabled them to develop an artful indirect kind of
colonization. In Laos and Cambodia, a class made up of
Vietnamese petty officials, small businessmen and artisans
served as the motor of French colonization. In this way, a
relatively economical system of exploitation was established,
and the three peoples to be dominated were, in appearance,
lined up against one another.

In fact, the French colonizers overshot their objective; in
spite of themselves they united, in a strange way, these three

different peoples, at very dissimilar levels of development, and in so doing imposed on them a single historical framework which the revolutionaries are now making use of for their own purposes. Of course, the Vietnamese intermediaries did inspire ill feeling and hatred of the kind which recently exploded in Cambodia. But this ill-will does not appear to be great enough to deflect the three peoples from developing together on converging courses in the years to come.

II

This Indochinese concept, intimately bound up with history and with colonial methods, was, indeed, very quickly seized upon by the revolutionaries, who retained the framework imposed by their enemy the better to struggle against him. This was what one of the founders of the Vietminh dubbed one day the strategy of "the glove turned inside out."

On February 3, 1930, in Hong Kong, the Vietnamese Communist Party was founded; Ho Chi Minh (then Nguyen Ai Quoc) immediately became its top leader. But six months later the leader called his comrades together in another conference in the course of which he gave the party a new name, rechristening it the Indochinese Communist Party (ICP). It was after consulting with the leaders of the Third International that the future president of the Democratic Republic of North Vietnam reached this decision, which in his eyes had the merit of giving the revolutionary effort he had just launched a more international character. It is worth noting, moreover, that the program which Nguyen Ai Quoc promulgated at that time included the following aims: (1) to overthrow imperialism, feudalism and the reactionary bourgeoisie in Vietnam; and (2) to achieve the complete independence of Indochina. Thus the first strategist of communism in this region restored a distinction consonant with the inequalities of the three countries in terms of development by calling for a *social* revolution in Vietnam and a *political* one in the peninsula as a whole.

It must be admitted that this Indochinese strategy was for a long time quite artificial, since the ICP remained for many years essentially Vietnamese. And it must be noted that when the Laotians and Cambodians truly embarked on revolutionary action they founded their own organizations—the

Pathet Lao for the first and the Pracheachon for the second.

It was on an almost exclusively Vietnamese basis that Ho Chi Minh and his comrades launched the revolution in 1945. In the two neighboring countries, the independence movement was sparked by very diverse forces: in Cambodia, they were, at first, two traditionally educated intellectuals, Hiem Chieu and Son Ngoc Minh, and in Laos a curious triumvirate of half-brother princes: the feudalist Petsarath, the liberal Souvanna Phouma and the Marxist Souphanouvong. Very quickly, moreover, the Vietnamese revolutionaries were to set up cells within the Laotian movement, while in Cambodia the local revolutionaries were to conserve a much greater degree of autonomy.

In 1951, six years after the outbreak of the colonial war against France, the three Indochinese movements concluded a Viet-Lao-Khmer alliance for the purpose of preparing to extend the fighting to the whole of the peninsula. Two years later, indeed, General Giap, pinned down by the French expeditionary corps in the key zones of the deltas of the Red River and the Mekong, suddenly decided to widen the theater of operations and entice his enemies onto new battle-fields. In April 1953, he drew the French general staff toward Laos, encouraging them little by little to think that that was the terrain on which they could smash him. Between November 1953 and May 1954 came the creation, then the resistance, and finally the collapse of the entrenched camp of Dienbienphu. In broadening the First Indochina War, Giap faced the loss of everything. (This was a lesson which American strategists do not seem to have remembered; I shall have more to say on the subject.)

The Geneva Conference in 1954 was to bring the First Indochina War to an end. The Indochinese front was not, indeed, much in evidence at those councils; since the revolutionary parties had not had sufficient time to coordinate their efforts, Laos and Cambodia were represented there by governments whose only wish was to separate their problems from those of Vietnam and to draw a veil over the existence on their territories of groups that were more or less Marxist. But these groups were to grow bigger in the course of the ensuing years, and at the second Geneva Conference, the one devoted to Laos in the summer of 1962, the Indochinese theme was invoked much more often. The delegate from

North Vietnam, Ung Van Khiem, hinted that a neutralization of the Indochinese region would be salutary. He specifically excluded the Democratic Republic of North Vietnam from this, but left the door open for the future.

This idea was taken up again in a much more precise and interesting form in various programs promulgated by the National Liberation Front of South Vietnam, founded in December 1960, which went on record as favoring an alliance of neutral nations comprised of Cambodia, Laos and South Vietnam. It seems astonishing today that observers at the time did not take greater note of the very great originality of this program and the audacity it took for those South Vietnamese underground fighters to place their future within a framework in which, at least for a time, Cambodia and Laos would be closer to them than North Vietnam. Of course, for most of the American experts the NLF did not exist except as an echo of hypocritical orders dictated by Hanoi.

It was at the beginning of 1965, on the initiative of Prince Sihanouk, that Indochina emerged clearly as the major theme of all struggle against the American intervention and for political and economic reconstruction. On February 14, 1965, a "conference of Indochinese peoples" met in Phnom Penh. For Sihanouk this was most importantly an opportunity to have his country's frontiers guaranteed by the North Vietnamese and the NLF, whom he saw as the eventual victors and thus as his future neighbors. For Hanoi and the Front it was a chance to demonstrate the solidarity against imperialism of the revolution and neutralism, of the national masses and the national bourgeoisies, of the Vietnamese and their neighbors.

Geopolitical front, socio-economic alliance: at Phnom Penh were to be found all the factions opposed to American hegemony, from the intellectuals, mostly bourgeois and Catholic, of Tran Van Huu's "Committee for Peace and for the Renovation of South Vietnam" to the guerrilla fighters of the Pathet Lao and the bureaucrats of the Cambodian Sangkum. The major theme of the Phnom Penh meeting was the search for a formula for the neutralization of the whole of Indochina, the first step toward which might be an international conference like that of 1962, broadened to consider the future of the three countries. But the delegate from Hanoi, Hoang Quoc Viet, opposed this idea of Prince Sihanouk's: the

bombardments of the North by the U.S. Air Force had just
stiffened Hanoi's attitude still further. The Phnom Penh
conference made no advance along the road to peace; but it
confirmed and made manifest the "Indochinese" theme, and
brought to light aspirations held in common by the most
diverse delegations. It was, on this level, a success.

The American bombing of North Vietnam also contributed
to the "materialization" of Indochina. It did this in three
ways. First, the Vietnamese revolution, attacked at the very
center of its strength, sought any and all means of hitting
back, and all fronts thereafter became acceptable for striking
a blow at the enemy. Second, this retaliation, with priority
targets in South Vietnam, required a step-up in the transport
of men and supplies from North to South by way of the
Ho Chi Minh Trail, which goes through Laos for several
hundred kilometers and through Cambodia for about a hundred. And finally, this aerial strategy gave an impetus to the
increase of flights by American aircraft over the most diverse
objectives—including, among others, frontiers; from this
to a multiplicity of aerial incursions, in 1965 and 1966, which
progressively nudged Cambodia into the war.

It was, however, in Laos that the greatest extension of the
war outside the frontiers of Vietnam occurred. Since 1964—
that is, since the actual dissociation of the neutralist coalition
government formed in 1962—a sort of modus vivendi had
been established, dividing the kingdom into two zones: in the
west, seven provinces, from Luang Prabang to Savannaket,
controlled (less and less) by the Vientiane government of
Prince Souvanna Phouma, and to the east, from Sam Neua
to the Cambodian frontier, five provinces controlled by the
Pathet Lao and traversed by the Ho Chi Minh Trail. The
double neutralization, both diplomatic and governmental,
imposed by the 14 powers participating in the second Geneva
Conference had thus given way to an actual partition.

After the halt of the bombings of North Vietnam in
November 1968, however, the American bombers stepped
up their raids on the Ho Chi Minh Trail linking North and
South Vietnam across Laos and part of Cambodia. The
frequency and amplitude of these bombings were described
in a report of a Senate Foreign Relations subcommittee published in April 1970. Testifying before this subcommittee,
Senator Stuart Symington declared that these raids had

Jean Lacouture 13

practically supplanted the raids over North Vietnam that had been halted, and revealed that the U.S. ambassador in Vientiane had the authority to order these bombings and specify where the bombs were to be dropped, which, according to the Senator from Missouri, made that diplomat virtually a "military proconsul." Directly challenged on this matter, former Ambassador Sullivan declared that since he had been replaced in Vientiane by his colleague Godley these bombing raids had doubled.

So Laos, where almost 40,000 North Vietnamese soldiers are permanently entrenched in a zone which covers almost half the country and against which the U.S. Air Force daily launches from 300 to 400 aerial strikes, has certainly been "in the war" for several years. But operations there took on a new dimension in February 1970, when the Pathet Lao, aided by its Vietnamese allies, overran the Plaine des Jarres, the strategic crossroads of the country, which the tacit partition of Laos had provisionally kept outside its sector. The strategic ascendancy of the communist forces was thus affirmed: it was becoming increasingly obvious that Prince Souphanouvong and his allies held the country in their hands, and that if they did not take either Vientiane or Luang Prabang it was in consequence of a political decision and not a strategic incapacity. (What is more, in spite of the redoubling of operations by the U.S. Air Force after the capture of the Plaine des Jarres, the Pathet Lao's military and political ascendancy grew still more, so that it was able, at the beginning of May, to take an important center in the south, Attopeu.)

But this strategic ascendancy has not been used (or not yet) by the leaders of the Pathet Lao in pursuit of "total victory." After his forces had seized the Plaine des Jarres, Souphanouvong sent his half-brother and rival Souvanna Phouma an offer to negotiate within the framework of the 1962 agreements, to the end of establishing a coalition government, restoring territorial unity and cutting short all foreign intervention. Obviously, the successes it had achieved in the course of the preceding months would enable the Pathet Lao to increase its demands and its share of power. But the situation of the Vientiane government was so bad that it accepted the principle of negotiation, with Washington's approval.

It will be up to future historians to find out whether or not this trend toward "appeasement" in Laos helped to set in motion the operation of March 1970 in Phnom Penh, and whether or not it was to prevent the initiation of a process which might have led to a generalized negotiation of Indochinese problems as a whole that led the "ultras"—South Vietnamese, Cambodians, Thais (and perhaps, but not probably, Americans)—to prepare and carry out the Phnom Penh coup d'état.

III

For it is, in any case, the Cambodian episode that has just given the war its true dimensions. We must inquire into the background of it, for the overlapping of strategic combinations and internal intrigue may throw light on the probable future evolution of Indochina as a whole. The affair began in the summer of 1966. Within a few weeks, the Sihanouk régime, which had managed until then to keep the kingdom out of the war and maintain a precarious balance at home between a feudal system adapted to the needs of a nascent capitalism and a progressive intelligentsia (very small in numbers but very active), found itself in a shaky condition at the very moment when the visit in August of General de Gaulle served to shore it up.

One may recall that General de Gaulle's speech at Phnom Penh caused a considerable stir. From then on, Sihanouk became the accomplice in what the entire anti-communist cause in Southeast Asia considered a most troublesome program. In their view, this outpost of Gaullist subversion had to go. In the end, it was to be gotten rid of more easily than they imagined because Sihanouk's great ally in Paris was eliminated, and because his successors would turn out to be less attached to the policy General de Gaulle had defined in Phnom Penh.

But Sihanouk found himself on dangerous ground both internationally and at Phnom Penh. He had allowed his relations with Peking to degenerate, thus weakening himself in dealing with the Americans. At home, a few weeks after General de Gaulle's visit, general elections were held—elections which the Prince had wanted to be "freer" than such events had ever been before in Cambodia. The result was to bring a majority of influential landowners into the parliament. Khmer society became represented by those controlled by money and by feudal relationships. Sihanouk had wanted to pay tribute to democracy: instead, he placed the noose of feudalism around his neck.

In the next four years, his personal power was steadily eroded by private interests and those friendly to the Americans. At the same time, neutrality was encouraged and a start was made in establishing state control of the economy. In 1967, one of the leaders of the Left intelligentsia, Chau Seng, who under Sihanouk had held almost all the high offices except the ministries controlling the army and the police, warned the comrade-prince that intrigues were being brought to a boil by the chiefs of the former party of "national renovation," the traditional Right. The names of two of these had already been singled out: Prince Sirik Matak and General Lon Nol. Sihanouk had long been wary of the former and had sent him abroad from one embassy to another. But Lon Nol? He was a soldier, therefore disciplined; and since he was not even a prince, how could he possibly be ambitious enough to think of substituting himself for a descendant of the kings of Angkor?

From 1967 to 1969 Sihanouk, more and more responsive to pressures from the Right, seemed to be letting his relations with Peking become strained, allowing private interests to regain complete control over foreign commerce and banking, and launching a "red hunt" and an anti-Vietnamese campaign.

But why, in the fall of 1969, did Prince Sihanouk go so far as to entrust General Lon Nol with power three months before setting off on a long sojourn in France? Why did he thus entrust his régime to a man he had been warned against, and whose friendly relations with the West had long been known? This can be seen as an overestimation of his own charismatic power, which he believed to be so vast that he could wield it from afar. Or it can be seen as a sign of lassitude. Or it may be considered a Machiavellian trick. Like everyone else, Sihanouk was aware of the growth of the Vietnamese presence in his country. It is possible that in order to avoid having a direct confrontation with his associates, who were beginning to threaten his neutrality, he wanted to stand aside, leaving to General Lon Nol the chore of "cleaning out" Cambodia of the Vietnamese presence, to come back later with his hands clean and his country freer. This is only an hypothesis, but it cannot be completely discounted. One can be too subtle and be mistaken, not so much as to the objective as to the means used. Sihanouk underestimated either the ambition or the convictions of Lon Nol, and the influence of the general's friends in Saigon, if not in Washington.

Sihanouk, who was on the point of slipping into the Western camp, thus found himself abruptly recaptured by the party of revolution. This did not come about wholly by chance. With all his sudden changes of fortune and his diplomatic acrobatics, Norodom Sihanouk had fought almost constantly for over 15 years for peace and neutrality—a neutrality frankly oriented to the East and much more favorable to the interests of Peking and Hanoi than to those of the West. So it was not altogether surprising to find him at the opening of that curious conference of Indochinese revolutionaries which, as I said, was one of the two most obvious signs of the extension of the conflict, both ideologically and strategically, to the entire peninsula.

IV

The inspiration for the Indochinese conference which convened on April 24, 1970, in a little village in southern China about a hundred kilometers south of Canton came as in 1965 from Norodom Sihanouk. But it was no longer 1965. And it was no longer the colorful, laughing leader, the "star" of Phnom Penh loaded down with unshared powers, the ironic virtuoso of diplomatic tightrope-walking between East and West, who met with the "serious" revolutionary chieftains of Vietnam and Laos. This was now an exile struggling to throw his rivals out of Phnom Penh, a leader flung back by a Rightist coup into the arms of the very same *Khmers Rouges* he had been hunting down three months before. He was now a revolutionary, and as such all the more radical for having been recently converted.

It was in a barracks guarded by soldiers in coarse blue uniforms and surrounded by barbed wire emplacements, a barracks which the Chinese hosts entered only to find out whether the visitors needed anything, that the four groups of Indochinese leaders met for two days. The atmosphere of

these sessions, one of the participants informed me, was
"brotherly." The chosen language was French, which is
spoken perfectly by the lawyer Nguyen Huu Tho, president
of the NLF, by the engineer Souphanouvong, the leader of
the Pathet Lao, by the militant Marxist Pham Van Dong
(the son of a mandarin) and by Prince Sihanouk. It was,
another witness said, a meeting of "old Indochina hands," a
phrase that is all the more colorful for being the same one
used by aging French ex-colonials when they get together in
some dusty, sunny café in Marseilles or Nice for nostalgic
chats about the good old days.

The greater part of the conference was given over to
drafting the final communiqué, a mixture of threats to the
United States and its "lackeys," optimistic proclamations of
"final victory" and rather prudent or moderate reminders of
the concluding texts of the Geneva conferences, denounced
long since by Peking as null and void. An amusing (or significant) incident occurred at the last session. Prince Souphanouvong was in the chair: he called in turn upon his Cambodian
and South Vietnamese colleagues to speak. He was preparing
to wind up the proceedings himself when Pham Van Dong
protested: "You've forgotten me!" "Our friend has anticipated
the unification of Vietnam," Prince Sihanouk remarked, making everybody laugh except the delegate from the NLF.

The most interesting themes developed at that conference
seem to have been three. First came the affirmation of a very
firm *solidarity* among the four movements—but a solidarity
sufficiently flexible not to have led the chiefs of "red Indochina" (or those who aspire to being such) into creating a
common combat structure. Second, there was the proclamation of the *original nature* of the different struggles and their
diversity, from Hanoi to Phnom Penh and from Saigon to
Vientiane. Clearly, Pham Van Dong and his delegation wanted
to avoid the impression of being imperialists, or even exces-
sively forceful federators. "They were very diplomatic," a
witness told me, thinking perhaps that this diplomacy was not
necessarily, in the long run, disinterested. And third, there
was the reminder of the *neutralist* themes explicitly or im-
plicitly formulated in the Geneva texts of 1954 and 1962,
and in the political platforms of the NLF and the Pathet Lao
(not to mention, of course, the Sihanouk "line")—theses
which could be of use in later negotiations. So in proclaiming

themselves certain of military victory the Indochinese leaders were careful to leave out any form of political settlement. Militant Indochina is, then, not just a war cry: it can also be a program for peace.

V

In the meantime, the war is spreading and wreaking havoc. What is most startling in President Nixon's decision of April 30 is its suicidal aspect. I am not speaking here about the consequences of this move for internal American politics, or about the effects it will have on relations between Washington and Moscow. I do not even wish to comment on the obvious contradiction between the two aspects of a strategy which claims that it will rapidly reduce the number of men fighting in the Asian war while it enlarges the field of battle. I prefer to confine myself to a more specifically Indochinese aspect of the question.

There is, first of all, what might be called the gift that has been made to General Giap. In all his steady stream of writings over the last ten years or so, Hanoi's commander-in-chief has never ceased to assert that every extension of the field of battle serves the revolutionary interests. This is so, he explains, for two reasons: (1) because it is to the advantage of the side with the greater firepower and superior heavy equipment on the ground to concentrate the fighting, while it is obviously in the interest of the side with the greater mobility and lighter armament to break up the fighting and seek to enlarge the combat zone; and (2) because the revolutionaries basically count on the complicity and support of the people, whereas a foreign force has to devote a great deal of time and effort to winning over or controlling by force the people among whom the fighting is going on.

For months, observers had been wondering whether Giap would dare apply his own doctrine and himself extend the front and the battle-zones outside the areas of Vietnam within which he had been more or less held in check since the counterblow that stopped the Tet offensive of February 1968. Now it is his enemies who are spreading the fighting to all of Indochina, under conditions which, in Cambodia, are uniting the masses behind a prestigious political chief who is entering the fray against these enemies. Thus the operation launched on April 30 seems to me to be contributing to the revolutionary unification of the old colonial Indochina.

Will such a united Indochina become the satellite of China? Mao's speech of May 20 gave many observers the impression that Peking was finally ripping off the mask and proclaiming China's right to control the Indochinese area, much as the Soviet Union held Eastern Europe in thrall after World War II. In my view, this interpretation is wrong. Of course the Chinese leader took the opportunity the Cambodian operation afforded him to attack in the harshest terms the American role of world policeman, and to rejoice in seeing American power entrapped in the Asian rice paddies. But it is noteworthy that his speech did not mention any precise threat or specific action. His appeal was to world revolution, for moral aid and approval, not a call for military escalation. It was a song of triumph rather than a warlike gesture.

The evolution of the Indochina war is the fulfillment of Peking's hopes. The character of the conflict more and more clearly illustrates the validity of the warning of Lin Piao regarding the strategy of countryside versus cities, *i.e.*, what is happening in Laos and Cambodia is as it was in Vietnam. The Chinese strategists do not predict complete victory. Revolution in Indochina does not mean Chinese domination. But while a united Indochina, more or less inspired by Hanoi, cannot oppose China, it can limit Chinese expansion. At present, Indochina is fighting under a Chinese banner but its aim is to survive under its own colors.

2

The Syndrome of U.S. Escalation

by Peter Dale Scott

Though the U.S. invasion of Cambodia itself was unprecedented, all of the prior elements in the scenario were of a timeworn pattern, from the initial military overthrow of a popular leader by a right-wing pro-American clique, to the announced response to an enemy "invasion" at a time when the prospects for ending the war seemed to be increasing. Most characteristic of all is the likelihood that Nixon was pressured by the Joint Chiefs of Staff to authorize the Cambodian adventure in great haste and in such a way as to bypass or overrule most of his civilian advisers, as a response to an "emergency" for which U.S. intelligence agencies and perhaps the Joint Chiefs themselves were largely responsible. The Cambodian adventure has confirmed yet again what some of us have been saying for years, that the U.S. military apparatus in Southeast Asia will work to reject a new policy of de-escalation as certainly as the human organism will work to reject a transplanted heart. The formula to neutralize this rejection process has unfortunately not yet been discovered.

In other words, one cannot understand what has happened recently in Cambodia without understanding the whole history of the Second Indochina War. One cannot, for example, appreciate Lon Nol's expectations in overthrowing Prince Sihanouk on March 18 without recalling the antineutralist military coups of late 1960 and April 1964 in Laos, or of January 1964 and June 1965 in Saigon. U.S. personnel were involved in (or at the very least were cognizant of) every one of these coups.[1]

Each coup was followed by, and helped to facilitate, an escalation of the U.S. military effort which the overthrown

---

Peter Dale Scott is Associate Professor of English at the University of California, Berkeley. A former member of the Canadian foreign service, Mr. Scott is co-author of *The Politics of Escalation in Vietnam* and author of the forthcoming *The Covert Origins of the Indochina War*.

regime would not have tolerated. As my colleagues and I tried to demonstrate in our book, *The Politics of Escalation in Vietnam,* the result (if not the intention) of every one of these escalations was to nullify a real or apparent threat of peace at the time.

Further, Lon Nol's deliberate breach of the accommodation hitherto established between the NLF troops in Cambodia and the troops of Pnompenh, followed by a precipitous retreat back to the outskirts of Pnompenh itself, in the face of what seem to have been only light enemy probes, will be seen to have its own Machiavellian logic when compared to similar events in the Second Indochina War. By the same combination of absurd provocation and precipitous withdrawal in previous springs, Laotian troops (and/or their American advisers) secured the first commitment of U.S. combat troops to Thailand in May 1962—the first in Southeast Asia, for that matter—and the first bombings of Laos in May 1964, which *Aviation Week* correctly reported to be "the first U.S. offensive military action since Korea."

Thus Lon Nol's actions, far from being irrational, followed a recipe for U.S. support which by now has been tested many times and never known to fail. The monsoon season and the U.S. budgetary process encourage an annual cycle of escalation which by now can be not only analyzed but predicted.[2]

The third, and the most frightening, of the timeworn patterns is the phenomenon of the artificially induced "crisis," used as a pretext for hasty executive actions which preempt the rights of Congress to declare wars and advise on foreign policy. The military pressure on Nixon to escalate hastily in Cambodia recalls the pressure on Kennedy to escalate in 1962 and on Johnson to escalate in 1964, first in response to Laos and later in response to the alleged Tonkin Gulf "incident" of August 1964. In all cases, including the present one, a key role was played by our intelligence agencies, who first helped to induce a crisis which they subsequently misreported to the President. For example, Nixon informed the American people on April 30 that the enemy "is concentrating his main forces in these sanctuaries where they are building up to launch massive attacks on our forces" and that in these sanctuaries were concealed the Communist "headquarters."[3]

If the President was told this, he was not only misinformed

but probably lied to. Robert Shaplen, among others, knew of "reliable reports" that the famous COSVN Headquarters had in fact been moved *out* of the sanctuaries area "at the time of the [March 18] coup against Sihanouk"[4]; field reports soon confirmed that NLF forces, far from being concentrated, had fanned out westward. U.S. military sources in Saigon are reported to have had no knowledge of a Communist buildup in Cambodia (despite Lon Nol's public claims that their numbers had been trebled).[5] Such evidence raises as many questions about the performance of our senior officers and intelligence agencies during this "emergency" as during the "emergencies" of Nam Tha in 1962 and the Tonkin Gulf incidents of 1964. At the very least, it illustrates yet again the old maxim that the objectivity of official intelligence tends to vary inversely with its relevance to impending strategic decisions.

Furthermore, all but the most rudimentary forms of civilian review within the executive branch were suppressed. When the first U.S. arms shipment to Cambodia was announced on April 22 by White House Press Secretary Ronald Ziegler, his counterpart Robert McCloskey at the State Department admitted that he "knew nothing about it."[6] On April 23, the very day that "emergency" meetings of the Special Action Group began to consider the Fishhook invasion, Secretary of State Rogers told a House Appropriations subcommittee that if U.S. troops went into Cambodia "our whole [Vietnamization] program is defeated," and that "we have no incentive to escalate into Cambodia."[7] In the wake of the Fishhook decision ("Operation Prometheus"), it was suggested that the Joint Chiefs of Staff had

> . . . pulled an end run in their effort to get the attack against the border areas approved. . . . Some believed Mr. Laird found himself in the final stages of planning for the invasion without being fully consulted and informed during the preliminary planning stages.[8]

Congressional consultation under Nixon, professedly a "strict constructionist" on constitutional matters, has clearly deteriorated a long way since 1954, when Dulles had to inform Bidault of France that even a single U.S. air strike to relieve Dienbienphu (which they both desired) could not be authorized by the U.S. President "without action by Congress because to do so was beyond the President's Constitutional powers."[9] Here the Tonkin Gulf incidents have set an unfortunate precedent, not only for unilateral executive action before Congress is consulted but, above all, for compressing the review procedures of the National Security Council into a few brief hours.

On April 20, in announcing his projected withdrawal of 150,000 U.S. troops over the next twelve months, Nixon had assured his audience that "Vietnamization" was stabilizing the situation beyond anyone's expectations: "We finally have in sight the just peace we are seeking." Yet the April 28 decision to invade Cambodia was clearly reached by *emergency* procedures, through meetings of a "Special Action Group" which originally had been created after the United States had failed to respond swiftly to the shooting down of an electronic intelligence spy plane by the North Koreans in 1969.[10] Convened by a National Security Council meeting of Wednesday, April 22, the Special Action Group was chaired by Henry Kissinger, the man who as early as the spring of 1969 had "got Nixon to order bombing strikes against communist bases in Cambodia."[11]

The Special Action Group met on April 23 to consider a range of options including the Fishhook invasion plans, of which Secretary Rogers was apparently still unaware, at a time when two of the Joint Chiefs of Staff, apparently worried about the "imminent collapse" of the Lon Nol regime, were reported to

> . . . contend that the President now controls the fate of the new Cambodia Government, and that the allies' military success in South Vietnam depends on its survival.[12]

The Special Action Group's recommendations were expected to be discussed at the National Security Council meeting scheduled for Friday, April 24. One indication of the haste in convening the Special Action Group is that the NSC Friday meeting did not originally list Cambodia on its agenda. (Similarly, the August 4, 1964, meeting, which authorized air strikes against North Vietnam less than two hours after flash reports of a most improbable "attack" had been received

in Washington, had been convened to discuss not Southeast
Asia but Cyprus.)

To his credit, Nixon waited four days before finally sub-
mitting to the pressure from the Joint Chiefs and (apparently)
his own White House staff. The National Security Council
meeting was postponed to Saturday, April 25, and then took
place on Sunday. Decisions at a third meeting on Monday
were not made final until Tuesday, April 28, apparently after
both Laird and Rogers had voiced their misgivings about an
American invasion. It appears that Nixon chose "what appeared to be the middle option" on Cambodia, rejecting a
more ambitious proposal supported on April 27 by two of
the Joint Chiefs for an amphibious invasion to take control
of Sihanoukville.[13] The Joint Chiefs had wanted to pursue
this plan even though they knew that for nearly a year
Sihanouk, in an effort to improve relations with the U.S., had
cut the NLF off from virtually all supplies from Sihanoukville.[14]

Nixon's delaying action was consistent with his earlier
resistance to pressure from two of the Joint Chiefs before he
responded on April 22 to the April 11 request of the Lon Nol
regime for aid. One reason for his delay, according to *The
New York Times,* was

> . . . the lingering hope that the Soviet Union might be
> able to persuade North Vietnam and possibly Com-
> munist China to participate in a broad peace conference
> on Indochina.[15]

This "lingering hope" for a peace conference had been
rekindled during April by the obvious impasse which the war
had reached. As in previous "critical periods" of the U.S.
military effort in Indochina, the inefficiency of its military
strategies had led doves to take more seriously the hope (and
hawks, the risk) of a diplomatic solution. In this context of
uncertainty about the war, the idea of a peace conference
had again been put forward by French Foreign Minister
Maurice Schumann on April 1. And on April 16 the Soviet
delegate to the United Nations, Yakov Malik, was quoted as
saying he favored the idea of convening such a conference
as the only way to bring about a new solution of the Indochina conflict. The next night, in a radio interview, Malik

appeared to reject the French idea, though in qualified terms, calling it "unrealistic *at the present time*." This same qualification (suggesting that in the future a conference might be more propitious) was echoed and to some extent amplified by Madame Binh, the NLF delegate to the Paris talks. Attacking the recent massacre of Vietnamese in Cambodia by Lon Nol's army, Madame Binh went on to say that

> . . . *in these conditions,* we think that the proposal of the French Government cannot contribute to the settlement of these problems.[16]

That diplomatic prospects existed or were likely to be profitable is less important than the fact that, by all accounts, the President seems to have taken them seriously enough to delay decisions being pressed on him by his Joint Chiefs. Furthermore, the French proposal for a conference was only one of the diplomatic options being explored at this time. Though the Paris talks on the subject of Vietnam itself had been at a standstill since the departure of Lodge in the fall of 1969, there had been talk for a year of a step-by-step disengagement in Laos, which if matched by the other side could be enlarged to include Vietnam as well. More recently in Washington there had been discussion (with bitter opposition from American military leaders) of

> . . . halting the bombing of the [Ho Chi Minh] Trail in Laos—in return for which Hanoi and . . . the Pathet Lao have indicated their willingness to limit military operations in that country and to start political negotiations there.[17]

Since the NLF forces in Cambodia have been cut off from their coastal supply routes through Cambodian ports, they have predictably taken steps to increase their hold over southern portions of the Ho Chi Minh Trail in Laos; and U.S. and South Vietnamese operations (the former in violation of a Congressional budgetary prohibition) have also escalated there. Thus,

> Unfortunately, whatever chances existed for halting the bombing of the Ho Chi Minh Trail—even for a trial

period—have been diminished as a result of our intervention in Cambodia. To stop the bombing now, the American military argue, would give the North Vietnamese total freedom to pour supplies and troops not only into Laos and South Vietnam but also into Cambodia.[18]

The Cambodian escalation also cut off the prospect, announced April 27, of renewed U.S.-Chinese ambassadorial talks at Warsaw on May 20. Even before the Chinese announced that they would not attend the talks, giving Cambodia as the reason, U.S. journalists had reported that

> . . . the American military operation in Cambodia has crushed any hope the United States may have had for a significant improvement in relations with Communist China.[19]

This diplomatic casualty may well prove the most serious of all, in view of General Gavin's recent warning that the United States "incursion" into Cambodia carries the risk of a war with Communist China, and his fear expressed to the Senate Foreign Relations Committee that some American generals may want such an "ultimate confrontation":

> There is always a military officer somewhere who wants to win a battle by taking one more hill or dropping one more bomb. . . . But what deeply concerns me now is that out of the . . . inability of our tactical commanders to realize victory, there may be those who would be tempted to the ultimate confrontation, the war with Red China.[20]

It is hard to escape the conclusion that for years some U.S. generals and intelligence agencies in Southeast Asia have been working in collaboration with Nationalist Chinese to frustrate an improvement of relations between Peking and Washington. This alarming fear was raised in 1966 when U.S. planes first bombed and strafed Chinese vessels in the Tonkin Gulf, both times within days of two important Warsaw meetings (the 130th and 131st) on May 25 and September 7, 1966. It was revived in early 1969, when the prospect of the first Warsaw meeting in thirteen months came to nought, after the CIA, for unexplained and probably inexplicable reasons, decided to give unusual publicity to the defection of a minor Chinese diplomat in The Hague.[21]

Last summer the United States cut back the Seventh Fleet's patrol in the Taiwan straits to a single radar ship, after broadcasts from Peking hinted that withdrawal of the Fleet (without reference to a concomitant dismantling of U.S. bases on Taiwan, as had previously been demanded) could lead to an improvement of U.S.-Chinese relations. But soon after, in October 1969, the intelligence community resumed the flights of "drones," or pilotless reconnaissance planes, over China, "at a time when the State Department was working to reopen the Warsaw channel."[22] The flights, which might seem redundant in the light of continued satellite surveillance, had been canceled by President Johnson in March 1968 as part of his strategy to start Vietnam peace talks. Their resumption suggested to at least one Washington observer, cited by Joseph Goulden in *The Nation,* that

. . . military and intelligence commanders in the Far East wanted a *quid pro quo* for dropping the naval patrol-drones for destroyers.[23]

The cumulative record suggests that personnel within the executive branch, and the intelligence agencies in particular, have over the years participated in a continuous effort, which so far has always been successful, to prevent any significant U.S. de-escalation in Southeast Asia, and above all any significant improvement of U.S.-Chinese relations.

It must be clearly understood that since 1950, the year of the Korean War and the China Lobby, there has never been a genuine U.S. de-escalation in Southeast Asia. Every apparent de-escalation of the fighting, such as in Vietnam in 1954 and Laos in 1961–1962, has been balanced by an escalation, either covert or structural, whose long-range result overshadowed America's previous war effort.

For example, in early 1961 Kennedy resisted energetic pressures from his Joint Chiefs to invade Laos openly with up to 60,000 soldiers empowered, if necessary, to use tactical nuclear weapons (Nixon also conferred with Kennedy and again urged, at the least, "a commitment of American air power").[24] Unwilling with his limited reserves to initiate major operations simultaneously in both Laos and Cuba, Kennedy settled for a political solution in Laos, beginning with a cease-fire which went into effect on May 3, 1961. On May 4 and 5, 1961, Rusk and Kennedy announced the first of a series of measures to strengthen the U.S. military commitment in South Vietnam. The timing suggests that the advocates of a showdown with China in one country had been placated by the *quid pro quo* of a buildup in another. In like manner the final conclusion of the 1962 Geneva Agreements on Laos came only after the United States had satisfied Asian and domestic hawks by its first commitment of U.S. combat troops to the area, in Thailand.

In 1968, finally, we now know that the "de-escalation" announced by President Johnson in March and November, in the form of a cessation of the bombing of North Vietnam, was misleading. In fact, the same planes were simply diverted from North Vietnam to Laos: the overall level of bombing, far from decreasing, continued to increase.

One has, unhappily, to conclude that there is simply no precedent for a genuine U.S. de-escalation in Southeast Asia, though there have been illusory appearances of de-escalation. This conclusion does not of itself prove that "Vietnamization" of the war is impossible or a deception to delude the American electorate. It does, however, suggest that a twenty-year search for a successful war in Southeast Asia will not be easily converted into a search for the means to withdraw. The Cambodian adventure is only one more proof, for anyone who still needs it, that our current crisis in Southeast Asia is only the outward manifestation of a continuing crisis of government at home in America.

It is symptomatic of the deep division within our country that Nixon's "Vietnamization" is in essence neither a simple escalation nor a simple de-escalation, but an effort, which in all likelihood is bound to fail, to pursue both courses simultaneously. Rather like Johnson during his first fourteen months in office, Nixon has tried to sound like an advocate of peace in Southeast Asia, while assuring us he will never let us lose there. In both cases this may be rather more self-deception than a conscious attempt to delude voters: Nixon, like Johnson before him, is still putting off the brutal choice between peace and "victory" through unprecedented escalation. Thus his "Vietnamization" policy is an attempt to balance certain partial withdrawals of U.S. combat and support troops (which are probably too limited to lead to peace) with a real escalation of the air war (an escalation which, though murderous, is probably too limited to lead to victory).

The full extent of the expanded air war is a closely kept secret. Congressional inquiries into the Laotian war have indicated that in Laos alone the United States is flying anywhere between 20,000 and 27,000 sorties a month, perhaps seven times the level of June 1968. For an indication of what this means, it is important to remember that in early 1968 there were roughly 1,000 to 3,500 sorties over Laos a month. At that time we had already generated several hundred thousand refugees in a nation of some four million inhabitants, and almost all the Pathet Lao villages which Jacques DeCornoy of *Le Monde* visited at that time were already flattened. (As for Vietnam, the United States intends to double the size of the South Vietnamese Air Force between early 1970 and late 1971, to some 40 squadrons or 800 planes; yet even after this expansion the United States will continue to fly half the combat missions in South Vietnam.[25])

Why do we thus escalate our punishment of a terrain already demolished? One answer, as Noam Chomsky has pointed out, is the conclusion of theorists like Harvard government professor Samuel Huntington that the enemy's base among the peasantry can be eradicated if there is "direct application of mechanical and conventional power . . . on such a massive scale as to produce a massive migration from countryside to city."[26] But we are also dropping strategic tonnages over sparsely inhabited areas as part of our tactical air support. The precedent for this lies in Air Force General Momyer's tactics of saturation bombing around the isolated Marine outpost of Khe Sanh in early 1968, a bombing unprecedented in the history of warfare.

It is not clear that the North Vietnamese were defeated at Khe Sanh—the United States was asking for a "sign" that Hanoi was ready for serious talks, and their withdrawal may well have been in reply. It is, however, clear that the Pentagon believes it won a decisive military victory. A senior Army general called Khe Sanh "probably the first major ground action won entirely or almost entirely by air power"; and even Townsend Hoopes, ostensibly an opponent of escalation, calls Khe Sanh "the one decisive victory for air power in the Vietnam war."[27] (Richard Barnet, a former State Department official, has charged in a recent speech that Johnson, under pressure from the military, considered using tactical nuclear weapons to relieve Khe Sanh.[28]) For six weeks, we dropped 100,000 tons of bombs around Khe Sanh, the equivalent of five Hiroshima atomic bombs.

It is uncertain whether the United States can win by converting more and more of Indochina into a landscape of splinters and bomb craters. One result, however, has already been accomplished. The so-called firebreak distinction, which opponents of tactical nuclear weapons had attempted to establish between "conventional" and "limited nuclear war," has been virtually obliterated, leaving the way open to an escalation that would be qualitative as well as quantitative.*

For the U.S. Air Force, "Vietnamization" is only one more step in a long history of U.S. escalation. It is evident from recent modifications in the conduct of our offensive operations in South Vietnam that the role of ground troops is now less to destroy the enemy than to locate him. Those who believe that major ground actions can be "won entirely or almost entirely by air power" can doubtless argue that Asian troops will suffice for this reduced role, while the United States can continue its air actions from Vietnam enclaves, from Thailand, or conceivably even from aircraft carriers.

It was obvious, however, that this strategy of air power would put a severe and probably intolerable strain on Cambodian neutrality. On the one hand, the NLF forces had little choice but to take shelter in this one part of Indochina which was relatively secure from our rain of death. On the other, it was predictable that local U.S. commanders would initiate or condone unauthorized operations against Cambodia, long before Nixon (on the urging of Kissinger) had ordered bombing strikes there in the spring of 1969. A U.S. heli-

---

* *Editor's note:* The "firebreak" distinction simply is a distinction between nuclear and conventional weapons on the basis of their degree of destructiveness. Thus, when you drop enough conventional bombs so that their destructiveness is equal to or greater than that of a nuclear bomb, any distinction on the basis of destructiveness is lost. And since this distinction, which has restrained the military from using nuclear weapons, is now lost in Indochina, the military can rationally turn to limited nuclear warfare.

copter pilot boasted in a letter to the San Francisco *Chronicle*, May 13, 1970, that

> I've been to Cambodia many times in performing my missions—each time I might add at the risk of a court-martial if caught crossing the border.[29]

It is also obvious that this modified ground strategy of "Vietnamization," largely devised by civilians, has met with stubborn resistance from elements in the U.S. Army. This has been evidenced in part by the Army's foot-dragging on the actual withdrawals of U.S. forces. Nixon's original hope in the spring of 1969 was to have almost all 250,000 U.S. combat troops out of Vietnam by the end of 1970,[30] but actual reductions have averaged only 10,000 a month for the last eight months (in mid-May, as I write, there are now 428,750 troops, as against 509,800 on August 31, 1969),[31] and Nixon's April 20 announcement of a large but postponed reduction no longer refers specifically to combat troops at all. It is clear, moreover, that even this latest announcement was as disappointing to many Army generals as it was to the antiwar movement; above all, it is by cutting back the Army that Nixon plans to achieve his "low profile."

Repeated allusions by civilian officials and advisers (from David Packard to Sir Robert Thompson) to the prospect of a "Korean" standoff in South Vietnam can only further alienate the Army generals whose recommendations for Asian strategy have for fifteen years been based on the slogan "Never another Korea." By this the so-called never-again school has not meant the avoidance of all Asian ground wars, as some columnists have suggested, but that U.S. ground troops should never again be committed without a prior decision to win with whatever weapons are necessary.

From the point of view of air strategy, the Cambodian adventure is indeed, as Senator Tower and others have argued, a logical extension of "Vietnamization," for it aims to get rid of the major enemy refuge from U.S. air power. The ground strategy of "Vietnamization" has just as clearly been negated: Westmoreland's tactic of attempting to "bottle up" the enemy has at last been revived, two years after its author was relieved of his command and made the present Army Chief of Staff. Hitherto the largest single allied war effort (and the most spectacular such failure) had been Operation Junction City in February 1967, with some 25,000 U.S. and South Vietnamese troops.[32] The Fishhook operation alone required the same number of troops.[33] Even as Nixon announced the Cambodian Fishhook operation, Administration spokesmen noted that the U.S. troop withdrawals announced on April 20 "will probably be slowed down." Although announcements of "future" withdrawals are likely to be escalated before the November elections, practice may be different: by May 14 there had actually been a troop increase, of 3,250 men, over the level of one month before.

On May 8, Nixon said he "would expect that the South Vietnamese would come out [of Cambodia] approximately at the same time that we do." On May 21, General Ky bluntly rejected this suggestion ("We will continue to maintain our military presence in Cambodia") in terms which prompted Senator Mansfield to recall that the South Vietnamese have long had territorial ambitions in this part of Cambodia.[34] In this way an Indonesian-style massacre of ethnic Vietnamese in Cambodia by our reactionary protégés in Pnompenh is likely to be followed by a permanent invasion by our reactionary protégés in Saigon. Viewed in the context of previous U.S. escalations, both the Cambodian adventure and the evolution of the "Vietnamization" strategy confirm an alarming thesis. There is not today, and indeed there has not been for some time, a civilian government in Washington with the will or power to enforce a cutback of our operations in Southeast Asia. On the contrary, in their intensity, those operations have already reached the upper limits of what can reasonably be called a "limited war," so that Washington's increasing hints and rumors about tactical nuclear weapons no longer seem fantastic. Far from having reached a level of stability, this heightened and enlarged war threatens to expand still further outward. In the wake of the first announcement of U.S. military advisers fighting in the Laotian panhandle, columnist Jack Anderson reported that "President Nixon had on his desk detailed contingency plans calling for U.S. troops to cross into North Vietnam."[35]

In the face of this crisis, it is not enough to repeat Acheson's observation to Johnson that "with all due respect . . . the Joint Chiefs of Staff don't know what they're talking about."[36] Even the Joint Chiefs realize the likelihood that any one of these escalations will sooner or later bring us into direct confrontation with Communist China. In their tendency to grasp at ever bigger solutions, they do not seem to face serious opposition from the President,[37] who on May 8 stressed that the Cambodian invasion was a "decisive move" and added that if the enemy escalated in the future "we will move decisively and not step by step."

We should watch for the first signs of the next "decisive" escalation. For the crisis we face at present derives not from a single mistaken adventure but from a settled strategy, a military effort that has twenty years of uninterrupted momentum behind it.

3

Cambodia in Conflict

by Noam Chomsky

In 1947, commenting on the rising tide of "anti-Communist" hysteria in the United States, John K. Fairbank made the following perceptive observations:

> Our fear of Communism, partly as an expression of our general fear of the future, will continue to inspire us to aggressive anti-Communist policies in Asia and elsewhere, [and] the American people will be led to think and may honestly believe that the support of anti-Communist governments in Asia will somehow defend the American way of life. This line of American policy will lead to American aid to establish regimes which attempt to suppress the popular movements in Indonesia, Indochina, the Philippines, and China. . . . Thus, after setting out to fight Communism in Asia, the American people will be obliged in the end to fight the peoples of Asia.
>
> This American aggression abroad will be associated with an increasing trend toward anti-Communist authoritarianism within the United States, which its victims will call fascism and which may eventually make it impossible to have discussions like this one today. This American fascism will come, if it comes, because American liberals have joined the American public in a fear of Communism from abroad rather than fascism at home as the chief totalitarian menace.[1]

These remarks have proved to be accurate. The Cambodian invasion and its aftermath reveal, once again, how the Ameri-

Noam Chomsky is Professor of Linguistics at the Massachusetts Institute of Technology. His numerous publications include *Aspects of Theory of Syntax, American Power and the New Mandarins,* and *America At War with Asia.*

can policy of "anti-Communism"—to be more precise, the effort to prevent the development of indigenous movements that might extricate their societies from the integrated world system dominated by American capital—draws the American government, step by fateful step, into an endless war against the people of Asia, and, as an inevitable concomitant, toward harsh repression and defiance of law at home.

The invasion of Cambodia by the United States and its Saigon subsidiary comes as no surprise in the light of recent events in Southeast Asia. Since 1968, the United States has steadily escalated the war in Laos, both on the ground, as the CIA-sponsored Clandestine Army swept through the Plaine of Jars in late 1969, and from the air. This American escalation provoked a response by the Pathet Lao and North Vietnam, who now control more of Laos than ever before, and led to devastation and population removal on a vast scale.

The destabilizing event in Cambodia—assiduously ignored by President Nixon in his speech of April 30 announcing the American invasion—was the right-wing coup of March 18 which overthrew Prince Sihanouk and drove him into an alliance with the Cambodian left and the mass popular movements of Laos and Vietnam, which are dominated by left-wing forces. The coup, and the events that followed, must be understood as a further step in the internationalization of the Vietnam war. However, the coup should also be seen in the context of developments internal to Cambodia over the past several years. These factors are, of course, interrelated.

During the 1960's, Prince Sihanouk tried, with much success, to save Cambodia from the spreading Indochina war. Nevertheless, the war spilled over into eastern Cambodia. Readers whose information is restricted to American government propaganda may have visions of an invasion of Cambodia by great North Vietnamese armies, but the truth is rather different. As American ground sweeps and aerial bombardment devastated much of the Vietnamese countryside, Vietnamese resistance forces took refuge in sparsely inhabited areas of eastern Cambodia, which increasingly were used as rest-and-recreation areas and, conceivably, command posts. At the same time, the armed forces of the

United States and its allies and collaborators carried out military attacks against Cambodia.

The earlier stages are described as follows by the British scholar Michael Leifer:

> From the early 1960's charges had been levelled from Saigon and later from Washington that Cambodian territory was being used as an active sanctuary for Viet Cong insurgents. Prince Sihanouk had denied the charges consistently and the denials had always been substantiated as a result of inquiries by the International Control Commission for Cambodia, by Western journalists, and even by Western military attachés stationed in Phnom Penh.[2]

In July 1966, an American study team investigated specific charges by the U.S. government on the scene and found them to be entirely without substance.[3] However, the team happened to be present immediately after an American helicopter attack on the Cambodian village of Thlok Trach; and its published report, relying on information supplied by Cambodian officials, also mentions specific attacks on other villages. The Thlok Trach attack was at first denied by the United States but was then conceded since eye-witnesses (including a CBS television team) were present.

Cambodia reported many other such incidents. For example, on February 24, 1967, "a large number of armed forces elements consisting of Americans, South Vietnamese and South Koreans entered Cambodian territory and fired heavily on the Khmer defenders of the village of Duan Roth. . . . On the same day . . . aircraft of the same armed forces heavily bombed the Khmer village of Chrak Kranh . . . [which] was then invaded and burnt by United States-South Vietnamese troops" who occupied the village until March 3.[4]

Up to May 1969, according to official Cambodian statistics, the United States and its allies were responsible for 1,864 border violations, 165 sea violations, 5,149 air violations, 293 Cambodian deaths, and 690 Cambodians wounded.[5]

Discussing the events of 1967, Roger Smith wrote that relations between Cambodia and the United States "were strained because of periodic South Vietnamese and American bombing of Cambodian villages along the South Vietnamese frontier, armed incursions from Thailand, and, late in the year, a reported South Vietnamese-imposed blockade of shipping to Phnom Penh via the Mekong River."[6] Additional problems were caused by the activities of the Khmer Serei (Free Khmers), which, in the beginning of 1966, declared war on Cambodia and claimed responsibility for incursions across the border.[7] The Khmer Serei is led by an adventurer named Songsak, who fled Cambodia by bribing a pilot of an aviation club (taking with him all its funds), and Son Ngoc Thanh, who was the head of the Cambodian government under the Japanese, and later switched his allegiance to the CIA—not an unfamiliar pattern. This group is made up of Cambodians who were trained by the American Special Forces in South Vietnam and carried out operations against Cambodia from bases in South Vietnam and Thailand.[8]

There have been many further incidents. The American biologist Arthur Westing, who was investigating American defoliation in Cambodia (see note 7), inspected the site of one such incident shortly after it occurred in November 1969. He describes this as a "particularly vicious" case. A village was attacked, and houses, a school, livestock, a hospital marked with a giant red cross on its roof, and a well-marked ambulance trying to retrieve wounded were all destroyed by bombs, rockets, and napalm. The International Control Commission reported no evidence of the presence of Viet Cong, nor could the United States produce any photographic (or other) evidence, despite daily reconnaissance flights. The U.S. chargé suggested that "our pilots must have lost their cool"—for about forty-eight hours.

Westing speculates that the attack may have been "a punitive or retaliatory measure following the destruction of a U.S. helicopter last October 24 and particularly of a U.S. F-105 on November 14, both shot down in the course of attacking Dak Dam in casual and callous disregard of Cambodian neutrality."[9]

It may be asked what the United States hoped to achieve by these repeated attacks on Cambodia, in which, so far as is known, no Viet Cong or North Vietnamese was ever killed and no damage was done to any Vietnamese military site. Again, it is possible that "faulty intelligence" is to blame. I suspect, however, that the aerial, naval, and ground attacks were for the most part capricious or vengeful, as appears to have been the case in the incident that Westing reported. The American military does not recognize the right of others to defend their own territory from American attack or over-flight, or to interfere with American plans by inhabiting areas that the U.S. government feels should be cratered or defoliated. And when such people aggressively insist on these rights, the U.S. authorities feel free to react as they choose. Where we have evidence at all, it appears that the American attacks on Cambodia were governed by such assumptions, though it is possible that in some cases it was believed (apparently falsely) that Vietnamese military targets were being attacked.

A European resident of Phnom Penh described to a re-porter a visit, before the recent coup, to Svay Rieng, a town in the Parrot's Beak area, five kilometers from the closest border point:

> During lunch, an American plane came over and looped the loop over the governor's house. The plane kept diving at a Cambodian flag which was flying in the front garden. A policeman took out his pistol and fired a few shots at the plane. I suppose if he had hit it, the Ameri-cans would have come in and napalmed the whole town.[10]

An exaggeration or a joke? One can hardly say so, given what evidence we have regarding American military actions. Very likely something of the sort accounted for many, per-haps most, of the attacks on Cambodia.

The first attested case of a Viet Cong installation within Cambodia was in November 1967, when American journalists claimed to have found a Viet Cong campsite four miles within Cambodian territory. Since that time, Viet Cong and North Vietnamese Army forces took refuge in eastern Cambodia after intensive bombardment and American ground sweeps in South Vietnam, using these territories much as the United States makes use of Thailand, Vietnam, the Philippines, Taiwan, Japan, Okinawa, Guam, Hawaii, and the oceans of Asia and the Pacific. (The analogy is, of course, inexact, since the Vietnamese obviously do not dispose of anything like the resources that the United States employs for its war against the people of Vietnam, Laos, and now Cambodia.)

I need not comment on the hypocrisy of the reference to

"sanctuaries" by the American government and its propagandists and apologists. An appropriate remark, in this connection, was made by Prince Sihanouk after the coup:

> The cynicism of the United States executive reached its peak when he demanded that the resistance forces of our three peoples [i.e., of Vietnam, Laos, and Cambodia] evacuate their own countries in response to the withdrawal of a part of the United States forces, and especially when our resistance has become "foreign intervention" on our own soil. Where then should our liberation armies go? To the United States?[11]

Before Cambodia was fully drawn into the Indochina war, Prince Sihanouk managed to maintain neutrality by a delicate balancing act and thus save it from the terror that ravaged Vietnam and Laos. The contrast between Cambodia and its immediate neighbors prior to the coup was chillingly described by T. D. Allman some months ago:

> . . . in a commercial plane, I flew over Svay Rieng province. From the air the frontier is now clearly defined: beyond the parrot's beak peninsula of neat Cambodian rice fields and villages the land is pitted by literally hundreds of thousands of bomb and shell craters. In some cases the years of day-and-night bombing have changed the contours of the land and little streams form into lakes as they fill up mile after square mile of craters. Above this desolation and along and just across the Cambodian frontier, the American helicopters and planes whirr continually, firing their guns and cannon, dropping their bombs.[12]

It is safe to predict that the frontier will no longer be so clearly defined.

It was, as I have noted, the coup of March 18 that destabilized the Cambodian situation. It created an entirely new situation within Cambodia, and may also prove to have affected significantly the long-term relations among the peoples of Indochina.

The immediate background for the Cambodian coup of March 18 is described as follows by T. D. Allman:

The underlying cause for Sihanouk's fall probably lay in the fact that although he revolutionised Cambodia's foreign policy, and his own relations with the peasants and workers, he left the traditional Khmer elite free to occupy office and eventually use their traditional power against him.[13]

The report notes that "the common people continued to revere Sihanouk," but a "tiny minority . . . brought Sihanouk down." However,

The new rulers, as they busy themselves taking back in power and financial opportunities what Sihanouk took away from them, doubtlessly will have a much harder time retaining the loyalty of the countryside—where all real Asian revolutions begin and are won. By biting off the hand which fed them, the tiny group of aristocrats, army officers and businessmen which toppled Sihanouk may have insured its own doom.[14]

The coup, as Allman writes in an article included in this book, was not only short-sighted in that it upset the delicate balance that Sihanouk had maintained, but was also selfish. The main complaint of the tiny elite that staged the coup was that Sihanouk "had deprived the aristocracy, the bourgeoisie and the army of their traditional slice of the financial action and of their accustomed place in the sun. It was an upper-class coup, not a revolution."[15] This fact must be appreciated. It goes a long way toward explaining the American invasion of Cambodia.

The March 18 coup was the culmination of a carefully prepared series of actions taken over the past several years that slowly eroded the position of the Cambodian left—tenuous at best—within the government. In the elections of 1966, Sihanouk departed from his usual practice of endorsing candidates. Under the conditions of Cambodian society, the result was a general victory for the most corrupt and the wealthiest candidates, those who could freely distribute bribes, patronage, and promises. The only exceptions were three left-wing delegates—Hu Nim, Hu Yuon, and Khieu Samphan—who won easily. At the time, Sihanouk was warned by the leftist minister Chau Seng that a right-wing coup led by Lon

Nol might be in preparation, but he apparently felt that he could keep the right under control, relying on the loyalty and support of the people. Step by step, he succumbed to right-wing pressures that were directed as much against his economic reforms as against his personal power, with its extensive and unique popular base among the peasantry and the small urban proletariat. By the end of 1969, much of Sihanouk's "Khmer socialism" had been dismantled, and the few left-wing members of the government had been removed. To a large extent, these developments must be seen as an internal struggle for power among the Cambodian elite.

While this shift to the right was taking place within the government, the radical left took on a more activist policy in the cities, with demonstrations and popular agitation; and rebel groups were formed in rural areas. The intensification of the Vietnam war, with the spillover into Cambodia, also served to increase polarization within Cambodia, which was held in check by Sihanouk's personal popular strength.

On March 4, General Lon Nol, then President of the Council of Ministers and Minister of Defense, also took on the post of Minister of Information, thereby gaining control of the press, radio, and television. A few days later the army organized anti-Vietnamese demonstrations in Svay Rieng province, and staged a demonstration in Phnom Penh, where soldiers in civilian dress sacked the Provisional Revolutionary Government of South Vietnam and Democratic Republic of [North] Vietnam embassies. Sihanouk, who was then visiting Paris, noted the rising threat to his rule, and commented:

> If I do not obtain satisfaction that the Communists will respect Cambodia's neutrality, then I will resign. A showdown between the extreme right wing and myself is most probable.

He went on to speak of the possibility of a coup d'etat, led perhaps by General Lon Nol. He observed that many army officers are naturally right-wing and "are nostalgic about American aid, which would enable them to lead an easy life. . . . The Americans are inside the castle walls—that is, inside our homes." He expressed certainty that right-wing leaders in the government were in contact with the United

States, "whether through the embassy, the CIA or any such like organization, I do not know."[16]

On March 18, the coup took place, led by General Lon Nol and Sirik Matak. A tiny Cambodian elite, hoping to win for itself a larger share of control in the economy and political life and resentful of Sihanouk's personal authority and prestige, plunged the country into civil war and set the stage for the American invasion that now threatens to turn Cambodia into another Laos or Vietnam.

The role of outside governments in the March 18 coup can only be guessed, and will probably never be known in any detail. Most observers take for granted that the Americans played a part. Jean Chesneaux, the respected French scholar, states that "the taking of power by the Lon Nol group is the result of a long series of attempts by the Cambodian right, supported by the United States."[17] The actions of the Khmer Serei provide evidence for this view. Several months before the coup, members of the Khmer Serei began crossing into Cambodia and "rallying" with their arms and equipment to the Cambodian army. In retrospect it appears that the Khmer Serei may have been a "Trojan horse" infiltrated into the Cambodian forces, perhaps by the CIA, to stiffen the right-wing elements that were readying the anti-Sihanouk coup.[18]

When immediately after the coup, pro-Sihanouk demonstrations broke out, eighty to one hundred Cambodians, all unarmed, were shot down. ("Significantly," noted Allman, "no Vietnamese was killed.") Jean-Claude Pomonti of *Le Monde* reported:

> Repression of pro-Sihanouk demonstrations among the peasants toward the end of March in the wake of the coup could only have served to swell the small bands of insurgents generally referred to, rightly or wrongly, as "Red Khmers." Many peasants, fearful of arrest after the demonstrations, took to the jungle rather than return to their homes. And today the Red Khmers are in a position to exploit the discontent in the country areas where the army opened fire on the peasants. The conditions for an active rebellion have been fulfilled one by one.[19]

Pomonti continued:

Information coming in from the provinces early last week seems to confirm that Khmer peasants in Viet Cong areas are now armed and trained. The nucleus of a "liberation army" is very probably being constituted, and the Phnom Penh government could find itself in a more precarious position before long, particularly if it fails to reassert its authority in the areas abandoned for more than two weeks by the central government.[20]

He quoted a diplomat who said:

It did not surprise me in the least to hear announcements of liberated zones being established . . . or of a "liberation army" being formed. It would not surprise me either if the Viet Cong say they are pulling out of certain zones and that from now on dealings should be with the "new Khmer authorities." Then they might well announce the return of Prince Sihanouk to one of these zones—armed with a powerful radio transmitter.[21]

Within days after the coup, elite troops of the Saigon army, with American air and logistic support, entered Cambodian territory for extensive attacks on Viet Cong positions. American advisers accompanied these troops and also took part in planning meetings with military officers of the Army of the Republic of Vietnam and Cambodian armies. Air strikes and large-scale attacks continued through late March and early April. The Viet Cong response was predictable. Viet Cong and North Vietnamese Army troops simply moved away from the sparsely inhabited border regions and deeper into Cambodia and, for the first time, began to take an active part in creating a Cambodian guerrilla army. They also, for the first time, conducted military operations against Cambodian troops. Shortly before the full American-ARVN invasion began in late April, the situation was described by T. D. Allman:

Under Sihanouk, areas of Viet Cong control were measured in kilometres—even metres—from the border. Now they are measured in districts or whole provinces. . . . In Takeo, Kampot and Kandal province, south of

Phnom Penh, villages have been taken over by mixed bands of armed Cambodians and Vietnamese calling themselves "Sihanouk's Army."[22]

Le Monde commented editorially that "the 'Red Khmer' movement is led by able men, and now that it has some support in the countryside, it can no longer be dismissed—as Washington tends to do—as a mere appendage of the North Vietnamese Communist Party." The new government announced by Sihanouk from Peking includes the three Khmer Rouge leaders mentioned earlier, who, as delegates to the Cambodian parliament, had been reelected with "overwhelming majorities" in the last (1966) elections and who "can hardly be considered 'Vietnamese agents.' "[23] They were generally regarded as the only delegates elected who represented a constituency other than the feudal and wealthy sectors in Cambodian society, and they appear to have had a reputation for honesty and integrity that is rare among Cambodian politicians.

Among those who have joined Sihanouk in China are Huot Sambath, Cambodian delegate to the United Nations, Penn Nouth, one of his long-term associates and advisers, and Chau Seng, formerly Minister of Education, Minister of National Economy, and editor of the leading left-wing journal, one of the outstanding personalities and political figures of Cambodia until his exile to Paris in 1967 during the early stages of preparation for the takeover by the right.

Speculating a year before the coup about the prospects of the Cambodian rebels for success, Michael Leifer wrote that these prospects "will depend (discounting external factors) not only on the exploitation of genuine grievances but also on an ability to identify with the nationalist cause for which Prince Sihanouk has been the most ardent and passionate advocate. This would seem unlikely."[24] Before March 18, this was a reasonable assessment. Now, however, Sihanouk, the "most ardent and passionate advocate" of the national cause, the person whom one American expert described as being "a significant expression of the Cambodian people's will,"[25] has identified himself with the rebels. It is doubtful that the right-wing Lon Nol government, with its narrow urban base, can counter this popular force or win it over.

The March 18 coup reflected a split within the Cambodian

elite, the exact nature of which is not entirely clear. However, two things do seem clear. First, the best-known members of the Cambodian left are now aligned with Sihanouk. Second, the Cambodian left is now in a position to mobilize the peasantry, capitalizing on Sihanouk's personal prestige and with the backing of the Vietnamese resistance forces; while the Lon Nol government, isolated from the peasantry, will increasingly be driven into an alliance with the extreme right-wing forces in Indochina, the Saigon authorities, and the Americans.

The bankruptcy of the elite that managed the coup is reflected clearly by its resort to terror against the Vietnamese minority, reported in ample detail in the press. Reports of Cambodian military operations fortify this impression of weakness and ineptitude. We know what to expect when we read of the commanding officer who sent Cambodian civilians, ethnically Vietnamese, who were described as "volunteers," to be mowed down by a cross-fire, in a well-publicized story.[26]

It is interesting to observe the Viet Cong strategy in the same incident. According to a detailed report by Allman[27] the Viet Cong captured the village of Saang, killed eight soldiers, and then "distributed arms and ammunition to the villagers in the name of the 'Sihanouk' Army." Three Cambodian spies reported that "the Viet Cong were backed by local Khmer and Cham villagers, who had joined the Communist forces." Jean-Claude Pomonti reported after the American invasion that the aim of the war

> ... is no longer to push [the Viet Cong] out of Cambodia but to prevent their gaining enough local support and power to sooner or later threaten General Lon Nol's government. On one side, an embryonic Khmer Communist Party, backed by active and vital support from the Viet Cong, has temporarily allied with Prince Sihanouk to organize a liberation army. On the other, a large segment of the upper class has called for foreign aid in order to build up its authority throughout the country.[28]

Pomonti's report has a familiar ring to it.

The Viet Cong strategy of establishing freed zones in

which the Red Khmers can build up their own armies explains why initially the Communists "carefully refrained from moving against towns they could probably capture without firing a shot."[29] They appear fully confident that without the commitment of major forces they can help create a peasant-based guerrilla force loyal to Sihanouk that will restore him to power, this time in a firm alliance with the Cambodian left and a peasant-based popular movement. Reports from the field support this judgment. No doubt the Americans agree as well. This was surely one major reason for the invasion of Cambodia during the last week of April.

There were, no doubt, other reasons. Nixon implied in his April 30 speech announcing the invasion that the alternatives were escalation or defeat. That seems a not unreasonable assessment. The invasion may indicate that "Vietnamization" is so fragile that even reduction of American forces to a quarter of a million men was regarded as unfeasible in Washington—that it was believed that to secure this immense army of occupation much wider areas of Indochina had to be turned into free fire zones, empty and desolate.

However, it is hardly clear that there were "reasons," in any serious sense, for the escalation, any more than one can hope to construct a sensible and reliable explanation for the thinking, such as it was, that led to the unprovoked bombardment of North Vietnam in 1965. Shortly after the anti-Sihanouk coup in 1958, the Saigon government diplomatic representative in Phnom Penh (later a minister under Diem), who appears to have been implicated in that coup, told a reporter: "You must understand that we in Saigon are desperate men. We are a government of desperadoes."[30] An accurate description that applies with equal force to those who design American policy. These men have enormous power at their command and can do very much as they wish, with few restrictions. As the invasion of Cambodia once more reveals, the Constitution, which remains, if anyone cares, "the supreme law of the land,"[31] and unorganized public opinion serve as no serious constraint, and international law and our "solemn treaty obligations"—to the UN Charter, for example—have long faded from consciousness. Reference to them has become "moralistic," or "naive," as it no doubt is.

More seriously, the victims have absolutely no way of striking back at the United States, the source of aggression, and it is unlikely that their allies will risk the fury of American nuclear attack by threatening the United States with retaliation. Therefore, the Americans can "experiment" with one technique of destruction after another—"population control methods" and other police state tactics, assassination teams to destroy the enemy "infrastructure," defoliation, forced evacuation, concentration of the population in camps and urban slums, bombardment on a scale unknown in human history,[32] invasion of other countries, and any other ideas that happen to occur to them. The disparity of force between the American government and its victims is so enormous that American planners can pretty much do as they wish, without fear of serious retaliation. In such a situation, it is quite pointless to try to explain the actions of these frightened and limited men on rational grounds. They have the force at their command and can use it with impunity. Further explanations are in a sense superfluous.

President Nixon wishes us to believe that after the right-wing coup in Cambodia, the Viet Cong and North Vietnamese became a more serious military threat to South Vietnam. This is as convincing as his fantasies that North Vietnam can surround the South with its awesome military might. He also alluded ominously to the sanctuaries in Svay Rieng province (Parrot's Beak), "as close to Saigon as Baltimore is to Washington," and spoke of the rapid NVA buildup in Cambodia in April. As to the latter, military sources in Saigon report that they knew of no Communist buildup in Cambodia.[33] What of the prior situation in the densely populated flat riceland of Svay Rieng province? The province was visited by T. D. Allman in early 1970, before the coup.[34] Four things, he wrote, seemed evident as a result of his investigation. I quote:

1. The Viet Cong use Cambodian territory much less than the Americans in Saigon claim.

2. US aircraft violate Cambodian air space and bomb and strafe Cambodian territory in violation of the US guidelines, frequently with no cause at all, and much more often than the US admits.

3. In fairness to all sides, it is obvious that the Americans, South Vietnamese, Viet Cong and North Viet-

namese are all making some degree of effort to keep the
war out of Cambodia.

4. The Cambodian effort to hold ground against all
comers belies any reports that they have an "agreement"
with the communists—or for that matter with the
Americans.

Allman described this dangerous "sanctuary" as "an absolutely flat country—rice paddies, villages, occasionally a small
grove of trees . . . scanning the open horizon, broken only by
Cambodian villages and mango groves, there seemed no place
the Viet Cong could hide, let alone establish a permanent
sanctuary." Allman spent a day in the border district of
Chantrea. The evening before, American planes had bombed
and strafed a village "2300 metres inside Cambodia and
clearly visible across a rice field," killing two farmers and
destroying a hectare of paddy. The district officer stated:

There are no Viet Cong in Chantrea district. They never
enter our territory more than 500 metres, even at night.
Mostly they are passing. There are no camps here. No
sanctuaries.
During 1969 [the district officer added], in this one district of Svay Rieng province, nine Cambodians were
killed by American bombs or guns; 20 Cambodians
were wounded; 100 hectares of rice paddy were damaged; and more than 100 farm animals were killed; no
Viet Cong were killed by Americans, and no Cambodians
were killed by Viet Cong.[35]

As they spoke, a policeman entered to report bombing and
strafing 200 meters inside Cambodia: "Incidentally, there is
no one there [the policeman reported]. No Viet Cong, no
Cambodian. But one rice field and a grove of mango trees are
being destroyed."

From these accounts, it is not difficult to predict the character of the invasion of Svay Rieng province. It leads to the
destruction of villages and the displacement of population,
but probably little else. Reports indicate that this is exactly
what has been achieved. James Sterba has reported that "few
people were to be seen in the Parrot's Beak . . . but animals
were everywhere," water buffalo and herds of cattle near

abandoned houses.³⁶ The ARVN soldiers as usual were stealing chickens. "Dozens of houses were burned by South Vietnamese troops in the Parrot's Beak. Their charred frames dotted the landscape."

American troops were unable to match the ARVN accomplishments, since the Fishhook area that they invaded is more thinly settled. But at least they tried:

> . . . troops of the US 11th Armored Cavalry Regiment burned down at least five villages, each with 30 to 40 houses. Officers said they were told to burn the villages because they could be of use to North Vietnamese and Viet Cong troops. The Americans met no resistance. Villagers fled.³⁷

Peter Arnett is quoted as reporting that American troops entering Snoul were ordered to "blow the town away."³⁸

The *Observer* (London), May 3, cites

> . . . reports that seem to carry a grimmer significance. Apart from the Viet Cong casualties, the Americans have announced that scores of "persons" have been detained by the allied forces. They have been led out of the area under guard, blindfolded with their hands tied behind their backs, suspected of being North Vietnamese soldiers. The area is inhabited by many civilians, both Vietnamese and Cambodians, families of rubber plantation workers and woodcutters.
>
> This lends a fearful emphasis to the remarks of American officers on the spot that American observation and gunship helicopters have been given clearance "to fire on anything that moves" in an area extending about three miles north and west of the ground operations.

And so we proceeded to save the people of Cambodia from Vietnamese aggression, just as we have been saving the Laotians and the Vietnamese themselves.

The amazing, unanticipated popular revulsion against the American invasion of Cambodia indicates that it will be very difficult for the government to make use of American or Allied ground troops to ensure its control of those who remain refractory. The Pentagon will, therefore, have to learn to rely more effectively on the technology of destruction. Chances are that a ring of fire and devastation will surround the outposts of the "free world" in South Vietnam, protecting the American army of a quarter of a million men and its permanent bases from attack. If eastern Cambodia must be sacrificed to this end, neither General Thieu nor his employers can be expected to shed many tears.

As in Laos and Vietnam, the United States was intervening—whatever its immediate reasons—to support reactionary, even feudalistic, elements, and to suppress an emerging peasant-based movement of national independence. There is some evidence that the CIA had a finger, and perhaps a hand, in the March 18 coup. In any event, when Sihanouk refused to retire to France like a well-behaved Bao Dai, and as the Viet Cong strategy of arming the peasants and encouraging the formation of a pro-Sihanouk Cambodian liberation army became evident, direct American intervention became essential. And the Khmer liberation forces, as they continue to expand, are linking up with the NLF (now the Provisional Revolutionary Government of South Vietnam), the Pathet Lao, and the North Vietnamese in a general Indochina war against the right-wing elements backed by the United States.

It is widely admitted that the revolutionary groups we confront in Laos and Vietnam—and soon, very likely, in Cambodia—are the only indigenous forces that have any immediate prospect of mobilizing mass support in Indochina. For example, a recently published RAND Corporation study concedes that apart from the Neo Lao Hak Sat (the political party of the revolutionary movement in Laos), there is no "broadly based political organization" in Laos, a country run by an "extremely small elite,"[39] to be more precise, hardly more than a facade for the Americans. The same has become true of Vietnam.

By its insistence on imposing right-wing governments with virtually no popular support on the people of Indochina, the United States may ultimately succeed in bringing about a Pacific or even a global war. Though this may not appear likely at the moment, it is easy to imagine a sequence of events that would lead to this consequence. In any event, the future for the people of Southeast Asia is dim. The United States is using its incomparable technological resources and its internationally based military forces to occupy and destroy vast territories, to uproot and demoralize the population, and to disrupt social life in the areas it cannot physically control. So long as the American people tolerate these atrocities, the people of Southeast Asia can look forward only to continued misery. The American policy of conquest in Indochina has continued, without fundamental change in goals, for twenty years.[40] And the grim game may be far from ended.

In the United States, so long as the war continues, it may be impossible to reduce inflation and unemployment to "tolerable" limits without imposing the kinds of controls that are unacceptable to the business community. If so, American workers may refuse to continue to sacrifice their jobs and livelihood in the cause of American domination of Southeast Asia. Perhaps much wider circles will be drawn into the movement against the war. There is no doubt that many, many people are confused and troubled, and they might be brought to join those great numbers who actively oppose the war. There is resistance in the military and continuing resistance to military conscription. According to a recent report, "The Oakland induction center, which processes draftees for all of Northern California and a portion of Nevada, says more than half of the young men ordered to report fail to show up—and 11 percent of those who do show up refuse to serve."[41]

To pursue the war, the government will have to subdue dissent and protest, which is sure to take more militant forms as the war expands and its character becomes continually more clear. It may have to make a choice between abandoning this war, with long-term and unforeseeable consequences for American imperial policy, and jettisoning what remains of the structure of American democracy. The choice might arise fairly soon. I would hesitate to predict the outcome.

PART TWO

PRELUDE TO CRISIS

4

The Khmer Empire, French Rule, and the Path to Independence

by Roger M. Smith

The kingdom of Cambodia is what remains today of the once powerful Khmer empire, which at its height in the twelfth and thirteenth centuries extended throughout a large part of that area of Southeast Asia now occupied by Cambodia, Laos, Thailand, and Vietnam. . . .

During the first millennium A.D., Khmer culture was subjected to an almost continuous inflow of Indian ideas and practices relating to royalty, law, and religious mythology. Perhaps the most influential of these among the Khmer kings were notions on the organization of the state and the religious justification of kingly rule. As they were assimilated and modified, they reached their apogee in the politico-religious concept of the devaraja, or god-king, which was adopted by Jayavarman II.

According to the concept of the devaraja, the state was a manifestation of the universe and its capital was the earthly symbol of the city of heaven.[1] As the cult was practiced in the Khmer empire, a divine king served as the intermediary between the gods, especially those controlling water and the fertility of the soil, and the social order. Among members of the monarchy and the aristocracy, the devaraja cult centered on the worship of a royal linga, which embodied the king's sacred personality as transmitted to him by the gods through the medium of Brahman priests. The prosperity of the empire was believed to be closely linked with the worship of the linga, and thus the great temples, which were the glory of the empire, were built by each king as sanctuaries for it.

For the peasants, the court was a distant structure with which they could scarcely identify.[2] If the world of the mon-

Roger M. Smith is a member of the Ford Foundation, currently in Thailand. He is the author of *Cambodia's Foreign Policy* and other publications on Cambodia and Laos.

archy and the aristocracy had any meaning for the people, it
was probably in its role as the ultimate source of authority
and as the preserver of peace and order. The kings justified
their ability to perform these tasks through the prestige of
unbroken dynastic rule and the claim that the political order
was an extension and application of the cosmic order. But in
terms that were probably more meaningful to the people,
authority was justified by the effective management of the
extensive hydraulic system,[3] which distributed and conserved
water for agriculture, and the maintenance of a standing army
to defend the peace of the country. Unfortunately massive
temple-building programs and expansionist wars, which necessitated the organization of *corvées* and the imposition of
heavy taxes upon the peasantry, soon became the major pre-
occupation of the rulers.[4] With the consequent neglect of the
hydraulic system and the diversion of manpower from agriculture to construction programs and military campaigns, the
economic strength of the nation declined. About the mid-
twelfth century, an exploited peasantry began to express its
discontent in a prolonged series of revolts.

Under the reign of Suryavarman II (1112–ca.1150), the
empire's domain was extended by a series of successful wars
against the kingdom of Champa, which controlled the area
now known as South Vietnam, against the Annamese, and
against peoples living as far westward as the region between
the Salween and Irrawaddy rivers in Burma. Suryavarman II
has gone down in history also as the builder of Angkor Wat,
which is not only the largest religious building in the world
but also the greatest single work of architecture in Southeast
Asia. . . .

In the early thirteenth century, Khmer power began to
wane. At least four factors contributed to the eventual disappearance of the empire. First among these was the rebellion
of the people against the demands of the kings for forced
labor and military campaigns. Second, as an increasingly
heavy labor and military burden was placed upon the people,
the hydraulic system was neglected, and thus the empire's
economic strength was weakened. Third, the arrival of a new
religious doctrine helped to turn the tide against the old regime: Theravada Buddhism, which was introduced into the
empire at the end of the twelfth century, preached the salvation of the individual through his own efforts. Thus there

was more to recommend it to the people than the established Hindu metaphysics which fostered an aristocracy whose opulence was based upon the virtual slavery of the masses. Fourth, these changes took place at about the same time as the growth of power and influence of the Thai peoples who, in the twelfth and thirteenth centuries, began to replace Khmer authority in the Menam (Chao Phraya) Basin and along the upper Mekong River. It was in the face of these events that the way was laid open to the sack of Angkor by the Thais in 1432 and the subsequent collapse of the empire. Cambodia then entered upon a troubled and unhappy epoch from which it was not to emerge until the French intervention in the mid-nineteenth century.

FRENCH COLONIALISM

During the 400 years following the fall of the Khmer empire, Cambodia was beset from within by a long series of dynastic rivalries and subjected from without to encroachments by Siam [Thailand] and Annam [Vietnam]. Only by adroit diplomatic maneuvering was Cambodia able to maintain its independence, but at a cost of rendering vassalage to both Siam and Annam and of sacrificing provinces along its northern frontier and in Cochinchina.[5] When, in the mid-nineteenth century, France embarked upon its program of colonial expansion in Asia, King Ang Duong was striving to rehabilitate Cambodia, which had only recently emerged from nearly a decade of Annamese colonial rule and a devastating but inconclusive Siam-Annam war fought on its soil. Fearing that upon his death these neighbors would seek to partition Cambodia between them, Ang Duong appealed to Napoleon III for assistance.[6] His effort, however, was foiled by Siam, which threatened reprisals if negotiations were entered into with Napoleon's ambassador. During 1857–1859, France intervened in Annam to protect French Jesuit missionaries and to establish a commercial foothold on the Indochina peninsula and in the process released Cambodia from Annamese pressures; Ang Duong made another attempt to establish relations with France, but he died before an accord could be concluded.

His efforts bore fruit posthumously in 1863 when, following the consolidation of its position in Cochinchina, France of-

fered Ang Duong's son, Norodom, its protection against
external attacks and internal strife. This was an attractive
offer on both counts, for Norodom's brother, Sivotha, coveted
the throne for himself and was preparing to renew the revolutionary activity which had provoked the re-entry of Siamese
soldiers into Cambodia in 1861–1862, and it would enable
Norodom to remove Cambodia from under Siamese tutelage.
In return, Norodom had only to permit Frenchmen to settle
in Cambodia, to grant them rights to exploit the land, to
bring in goods free of duty, and to allow the establishment
of separate courts for foreigners. Norodom accepted the
French offer. . . . He was, in fact, crowned by the new
French *résident* in 1864. But it was not until 1867 that France
succeeded in persuading Siam to renounce its suzerainty over
Cambodia. In return, France, acting on Cambodia's behalf,
abandoned claims to Battambang and Siem Reap; King Norodom protested this action in vain, for the French at the time
considered it a good bargain.[7]

The French protectorate was not uncontested within Cambodia. Revolts, led by a self-proclaimed prince named Pukoumbo, broke out in 1866–1867, and Prince Sivotha
remained a constant threat to Norodom until the late 1870s.
Franco-Cambodian troops, some of which were under the
command of another of the king's brothers, Prince Sisowath,
were able to quell the rebellions. Following Pukoumbo's
defeat in 1867, France attempted to introduce much-needed
reform in the poorly organized and corrupt Cambodian administration. These attempts further alienated Norodom, who
continued to rue the loss of the northern provinces. The
French were able to overcome the king's opposition to their
modifications only by threatening in 1877 to withdraw and
leave Norodom to the mercy of Sivotha, who was then em-
barking upon still another rebellion. But after Sivotha's defeat,
France became preoccupied with events in Tonkin, and the
reforms fell into disuse. Norodom began to resume full
control over Cambodia. When, in 1884, he refused to participate in a customs union with Cochinchina and Annam, the
Governor-General of Cochinchina, Charles Thomson, reas-
serted France's dominance. On June 17, 1884, Thomson
arrived in Phnom Penh from Saigon with a contingent of
French troops and several gunboats. With these placed in
strategic positions around the royal palace, Thomson coerced

Norodom into signing the convention which made Cambodia a *de facto* colony of France.[8]

France's primary interest in Cambodia was defensive. Once it had gained control over the rich coastal area of the peninsula, which is today Vietnam, it needed to control Cambodia in order to prevent Siam, and possibly England also, from challenging its new acquisition. Its principal activity in Cambodia, therefore, was directed toward the maintenance of law and order; only secondarily was it interested in the development of natural or human resources.

The administration of colonial Cambodia was directed by a skeleton hierarchy of French *résidents* and small staffs, which were placed in key positions throughout the country.[9] A centralized and highly bureaucratic Cambodian administration was maintained in existence by the French,[10] but its top officials were merely figureheads. To the French, the Cambodians in general appeared to be incapable of serving in administrative capacities. They were relegated to minor government positions which were under strict supervision by the *résidents;* at the more important operating levels of government, and especially in the police, the French preferred to utilize Hanoi- and Saigon-trained Vietnamese, in whose competence they expressed more faith.

The French did little to train Cambodians to fill positions of responsibility and trust. . . . It did not suit the French purpose to have an educated elite which might demand government reform or, worse, independence. Thus by 1939 only four students (in a population estimated at slightly over 3 million) had been graduated from a senior high school established in 1935. Others in search of higher education were usually sent to high schools in Hanoi or Saigon. Only a very few, sons of royal and aristocratic families, managed to go to French universities. Education was left primarily to Buddhist *wat* and community-supported schools. . . .

The institution of the monarchy was supported and encouraged in the eyes of the people, and as a result it continues today to be a key factor in the country's stability and unity. But at that time, the French were exploiting the loyalty which the Crown commanded from the people, for as long as the people owed allegiance to the king and he was controlled by the French, then France could govern with a minimum expenditure of money and effort. As far as the people were concerned, the king exercised his traditional powers of lawmaking, directed Cambodian administration, supervised the Buddhist hierarchy, and was responsible for their well-being. They were not aware that all of his acts were subject to the approval of the *Résident Supérieur,* whose role was facilitated by his control of the Cambodian Council of Ministers and by the fact that the provincial representatives of the king were employees of the *résidents.*

Further control over the monarchy was obtained by manipulating succession to the throne. Under ordinary circumstances, the king would designate his own successor, or, failing in that, a new king would be chosen by the King's High Council. But when Norodom died in 1904, the French forced the passing over of his sons in order to reward the loyalty of his brother, Sisowath, who had helped the French to put down several rebellions. Sisowath was succeeded by his son, Monivong, in 1927. When the latter died in 1941, France was faced with a difficult decision, for Monivong's son, Monireth, appeared to be too independent and independence-minded at a time when France was beset with defeat in Europe and Japanese encroachments upon Indochina. Thus it was that Norodom Sihanouk, a great-grandson of King Norodom, then attending high school in Saigon, was elevated to the throne.[11] He was thought to be weak and accommodating, but in this appraisal the French were later to discover that they had been badly mistaken.

In its administration of the Indochinese Union, France revealed that the eastern states, that is, Cochinchina, Annam, and Tonkin, were more important to it than Cambodia. Much of the revenue from Cambodia was channeled to support public services in Cochinchina. Customs and monetary offices did not exist. All foreign trade was transshipped at Saigon and financed and controlled from there. The extensive road and rail network built by the French in Cambodia was designed to bring the protectorate closer to Cochinchina, especially in order to facilitate the shipment of rice, rubber, and other agricultural goods to Saigon.

THE PATH TO INDEPENDENCE

On the eve of the Second World War, France had been in complete control of Cambodia for fifty-seven years. During this period, it had preserved the monarchy as a symbol of Cambodian unity, but the power of the king had been emasculated by French authority. Representative institutions had been created, but their importance was nominal, and the mass of the people remained indifferent to public affairs. Cambodia's identity had been preserved, but its political and economic development was subordinated to French interests in Cochinchina.

Unlike many other colonial areas in Southeast Asia, there were no independence or nationalist movements in Cambodia before the war. . . . The very few educated Cambodians were apparently confident that France was ruling in their interests; in any case, they were quickly absorbed by the colonial administration where, if their talents and energies were not given free rein, they were at least assured of a comfortable existence. For this reason, attempts by Son Ngoc Thanh, who founded the first Cambodian-language newspaper, *Nagaravatta* in 1937, to arouse the semi-educated class to demand more autonomy under French rule fell upon deaf ears.[12] The weakness of the French in the face of Japan's advances in Indochina, however, seriously undermined Cambodian confidence in the colonial regime and set the stage for important political changes in the postwar period.

A significant step toward these changes was taken in March 1945, when the Japanese occupation forces took over the colonial administration, imprisoned French officials, and induced King Norodom Sihanouk to declare Cambodia's independence. With Cambodia now apparently under their own control, political interest was at last aroused among the small group of Cambodians who had been in the French administration or close to the king. Two sharply divergent views on the course which Cambodia should follow developed among these men. One group, which controlled the government organized in late March 1945, favored the return of France and a slow evolution toward independence. Its members, including King Sihanouk and his uncle, Prince Monireth, believed Cambodia to be ill-prepared to cope with the numerous economic and political problems created by the war and looked to France for assistance. Among the second group, which received its major direction from Son Ngoc Thanh, nationalistic sentiments ran so high that the hard facts of the political and economic situation were barely recognized.

Political independence from France and the vision of a new republic were their panaceas for all problems.

A major problem facing Cambodia during the postwar period was the dearth of trained leaders who could assume responsibility for the direction of their country. When the French were suddenly eliminated in 1945, the reaction of the Cambodians was to fall back upon and to strengthen the one institution which they knew best and which the French had preserved—the monarchy. One of the government's first acts was to re-create the absolute monarchy and to assign to it all the powers of the French *Résident Supérieur*.[13] The only limitation imposed upon the monarch directed him to share his initiative in lawmaking and administration with a Council of Ministers.

In May 1945, upon his return from exile in Japan, Son Ngoc Thanh was appointed by the Japanese to the post of Foreign Minister, in which capacity his chief official function was to assure liaison between the new government and the Japanese command. Unofficially, he supported the organization of the Green Shirts, or Cambodian Volunteers, a successor to a French-run youth group which had received paramilitary training during the war.[14] On the eve of Japan's capitulation to the Allies, Son's group staged a *coup d'état* and arrested all of the pro-French ministers.[15] King Sihanouk, who had been acting as his own Premier, now resigned from the cabinet, and Son installed himself in that position. The policies which he adopted were designed to consolidate the government's control of the country and to prevent the reestablishment of French rule. . . .

Following the Japanese surrender and the assumption of the reins of government by Son and his supporters, Phnom Penh became the scene of frequent conflicts which involved especially Cambodians and the local Vietnamese. In this tense atmosphere, King Sihanouk expressed the desire to abdicate in favor of Princh Monireth. Another uncle, Prince Norodom Montana, however, persuaded Sihanouk to remain on the throne. Surprisingly, Son Ngoc Thanh also urged Sihanouk to retain the crown. Monireth, who had been passed over for the throne in 1941, then took steps to subvert Son's position: he was able to persuade one of Son's lieutenant's Khim Tit, to go to the British occupation forces in Saigon and urge the immediate occupation of Cambodia and Son's arrest as a traitor. British and French officers, escorted by Indian troops, flew to Phnom Penh and on October 16 arrested Son on the grounds that his activities threatened the security of Allied forces and were detrimental to Cambodian interests. Son was subsequently tried for treason in Saigon by the French, but because he enjoyed widespread popularity within the government and among the people and because the issue was a controversial one, it was decided to send him into exile in France rather than to have him executed.

French administrators returned to Cambodia in late 1945, but the protectorate was not re-established. Having now to contend with an awakened political consciousness—especially in the person of Prince Sisowath Youtévong, a cousin of the king who had returned from France in time to assume the leadership of the agitators for independence—the French proposed a period of dyarchy leading to eventual independence. This idea was accepted. . . .

On January 7, 1946, a *modus vivendi* was signed by which Cambodia became an "autonomous state within the French Union. . . ."[16] In fact, France continued to rule Cambodia more or less as it had before the war. A Cambodian army was created, but France remained responsible for public order. Cambodia's foreign relations were controlled by the French government. Public services, including the treasury, secondary and higher education, customs, mines, railways, immigration, some judicial matters, and certain public works, were transferred to the newly established Indochinese Federation. In spite of these restrictions, the *modus vivendi* allowed Cambodians to assume responsibility for some local administrative matters, which they had not previously enjoyed. The period of tutelage, however, was left vague. France succeeded in maintaining its control until 1953, for its only opposition was the Democrat Party, which was riven by petty jealousies and the desire of its members to improve their financial positions, a desire that the French were not above trying to satisfy. As a result, the initial efforts made by a minority of Cambodians to win significant concessions from the French failed.

During this period, King Sihanouk maintained that only through patient negotiation could any progress be made toward independence—that, given Cambodia's weaknesses, it was the only reasonable course to follow.[17] It was in this mood that eight years of negotiations were begun.

Other Cambodians were convinced that only force of arms would win independence. Following Son Ngoc Thanh's arrest, many of his followers fled to Thai-held Cambodian territory in the north, where they formed themselves into armed bands called Khmer Issarak, or Free Cambodians. Some went to Bangkok, where they gained the support of Thai Prime Minister Pridi Phanomyong, whose government was interested in preventing France from retaking Battambang and Siem Reap. A government in exile was formed by the Khmer Issarak, but its armed forces never seriously threatened the French. Many of its leaders surrendered soon after the French had re-established themselves. The subsequent return of Battambang and Siem Reap to Cambodia by the terms of the Washington Conference of 1946[18] was followed by a considerable diminution of the Thai interest in the Khmer Issarak.

Still another group opposed the French in Cambodia—the Viet Minh. Coming from South Vietnam and basing themselves among Vietnamese living in south and southeast Cambodia, Viet Minh guerrilla forces soon established liaison with certain Khmer Issarak elements. The Viet Minh portrayed themselves as "liberators" of Indochina from French rule and tried to entice the Cambodian rebels into cooperation with them with material aid and guidance. In this they were never wholly successful, for by late 1946 the Khmer Issarak had already begun to splinter, with each faction maintaining its own private army and controlling its own territory. Some elements did accept Viet Minh aid, but only for short periods of time, and then turned against the Viet Minh and actively fought them. The lack of receptivity among the Khmer Issarak to Viet Minh overtures was in large part due to the antipathy and distrust with which Cambodians have traditionally regarded the Vietnamese.

In 1950–1954, the Viet Minh set up a "resistance" government in southern Cambodia with the cooperation of a handful of Cambodians who served as front men. Little is known about the political orientation of these men, but evidence is lacking that they belonged to the Khmer Issarak movement.[19]

In the meantime, the clash between the conservative views held by the king, Prince Monireth, and other members of the royalty who wished to maintain the full power of the monarchy and those being promoted by the group of young elite which looked forward to the creation of a parliamentary democracy necessitated an immediate compromise. . . . [This] small group of intellectuals—a new phenomenon in Cambodia —foresaw a democratic government in which they could utilize their talents, and they clamored for the abolition of French colonial rule. [But] Sihanouk, although he owed his crown to the French and was sufficiently foresightful to anticipate the economic and political chaos which would result from the abrupt dismissal of the French, was also shrewd enough to appreciate the momentum with which the new nationalism was spreading and to ride on its crest lest he find himself excluded from the helm of the emergent regime.

Once he accepted the inevitability of independence, he pursued it in earnest, but with reason rather than fervor guiding his actions. Negotiation rather than armed revolt was the method he adopted, for only in this way could he get the French army off Cambodian soil and preserve the French amity upon which he believed he would have to rely for assistance in the economic development of the newly independent nation. . . .

[In] mid-1952 . . . the king began to take matters into his own hands. . . . Faced with increasing opposition, he dissolved the Assembly and declared martial law in January 1953.[20] Then, leaving the country's affairs in the hands of trusted advisers, Sihanouk set out for France on the first phase of what has since been called in Cambodia the "Crusade for Independence."[21]

In France, Sihanouk tried to convince President Vincent Auriol that the use of the Cambodian army by the French to combat Viet Minh forces gave the Issaraks, Democrats, and others reason to believe that he, the king, was the principal obstacle to independence. But France was preoccupied with what it considered to be more important problems in Vietnam. Auriol referred Sihanouk's letters to the government, invited him to Paris for lunch, and issued a communiqué which merely underscored France's unwillingness to hand over Cambodia's future to Cambodians. Thus snubbed, Sihanouk returned to Cambodia. En route, via Ottawa, New York, and Tokyo, he met with newspaper reporters to whom he complained that French policy was depriving the Cambodian government of popular support and was slowly convincing the people that only the Viet Minh was fighting for national independence in Indochina.[22] He arrived in Phnom

Penh in June 1953 but remained there only long enough to relate his experiences to the people. Immediately thereafter, he dramatized his position by departing for voluntary exile to Bangkok, and later to Battambang, vowing not to return to his palace until Cambodia was free.

The king succeeded in embarrassing the French.[23] On July 3, seeking to recoup their position, they offered "to complete the sovereignty and independence" of Cambodia but on the basis of further negotiations. Sihanouk replied by demanding nothing less than complete and unconditional authority in all fields. Eventually the French yielded on all points at issue. Upon the turnover of military control, Sihanouk, satisfied that his crusade had succeeded, returned to Phnom Penh in triumph on November 8, 1953, as the liberator of Cambodia from French rule.[24]

The victory was, however, only half the battle for independence. There remained the problem of the Viet Minh. Their increased activity in southern Cambodia and their invasion of the northeastern province of Stung Treng in April–May 1954 revealed clearly that they were foreign invaders and not fighters for Cambodian independence as they had been representing themselves. The problem was taken up at the Geneva Conference on Indochina, May–July 1954,[25] among the representatives of Cambodia, Laos, the Republic of Vietnam, the Democratic Republic of Vietnam (DRV), the Soviet Union, the Chinese People's Republic, the United States, France, and Great Britain.

Following the initial French statement of its position, that the situation in Vietnam was a matter of civil war and the one in Cambodia and Laos a matter of Viet Minh invasions, the DRV delegate, Pham Van Dong, posed what was to become one of two major issues of the talks: should the resistance government set up by the Viet Minh-supported Cambodian Communists be regarded as the undertaking of local elements or should it be viewed as the work of foreign forces? To settle this issue, he strongly urged representation at the conference for the Cambodian Communists. He was, however, opposed by the Cambodian delegates, Nong Kimny, Tep Phan, and Sam Sary, as well as by the United States, France, and Great Britain. The Cambodians argued that their country's independence had already been obtained from France and that the so-called Free Khmer government had been established only at the time of the Viet Minh invasion in April.[26] Vyacheslav Molotov and Chou En-lai, however, added the Soviet Union's and China's support to the DRV proposal, but both suggested that the matter be settled in private discussions. The question was not disposed of until late in June, when Chou En-lai made concessions that substantially met the Cambodian position.[27] He recognized the legitimacy of the Sihanouk government and acknowledged that it alone had been instrumental in achieving Cambodia's independence.

The second major issue grew out of the DRV demand that a cease-fire be made contingent upon the acceptance by the conference of Viet Minh terms for a political settlement.[28] Chou En-lai again supported his Vietnamese colleague, arguing specifically for the neutralization of Cambodia, that is, the prohibition of adequate armed forces and of the receipt of foreign military assistance. Again with the support of the United States and Britain, Cambodia refused to accept the DRV proposal, arguing that although it did not intend to authorize the establishment of foreign military bases on its territory or to use its armed forces for aggressive purposes, it would not countenance any restrictions on its right to act in accordance with the United Nations Charter or to solicit military aid in the interests of its own defense.[29] The Communists' position, like the first one, was dropped in mid-June. On June 16, after discussions with Anthony Eden on the future of Cambodia, Chou proposed that all foreign troops be withdrawn from the Indochina peninsula and that there should be military talks between the two sides in each case. He agreed that Cambodia should receive arms up to the level required for defense but stipulated that it should not become a base for the United States. It was not openly admitted that the Viet Minh had in fact invaded Cambodia, but there was little doubt that they were meant to be included among the "foreign troops" which Chou was prepared to see withdrawn.

Following a short recess, June 20–July 12, the foreign ministers quickly reached agreement on the composition and functions of the International Commissions for Supervision and Control, which were to oversee the implementation of the Geneva decisions. Before this was accomplished, a series of restricted meetings were held between the British, Russian, and Chinese delegates at which assurances on the status of Cambodia and Laos were traded. Chou En-lai's main concern

was the five-power talks, then being held in Washington, on
the advisability of establishing a defense system in Southeast
Asia. Chou told Eden that he could persuade the Viet Minh
to withdraw from Cambodia and Laos, and that China would
recognize their governments, provided there were no American
bases in their territories.[30] He was concerned that the United
States would attempt to mold Southeast Asia into an anti-
Communist alliance. Cambodia, Laos, and Vietnam must remain independent, he insisted. Eden assured Chou that they
would. From this point, the conference moved rapidly toward
successful conclusion.

5

The Politics of Sihanouk

by Roger M. Smith

In the brief period since 1953, Cambodia has evolved from a parliamentary democracy to a benevolent authoritarianism in which Prince Sihanouk has come to dominate the executive, legislative, and judicial branches of government. Control of Cambodian politics by Sihanouk has been made possible by the unsurpassed loyalty which he commands from the masses and by his remarkable adaptability in the face of continuing change. Although he abdicated from the throne in 1955 on his own initiative, he has never been able to erase in his mind his responsibilities as a monarch, and he continues to feel that he alone must bear the burden of his country's development. In his powerful position, he has employed a liberal interpretation of his own definition of a "good constitutional sovereign":

> He would deceive himself if he believes it to be sufficient for him to adopt a passive attitude with regard to the Government and the Parliament, to be docile and to sign all papers presented to him automatically. It is necessary for him to play his role of arbiter, councilor, and guide to the fullest extent, without [becoming] authoritarian. In brief, he should give proof of much tact, care, vigilance, and patience in the exercise of his constitutional and state functions. (Norodom Sihanouk: *Realités Cambodgienne*, October 23, 1959.)

Norodom Sihanouk is a dedicated man who more than anything else hopes to see his country, after centuries of oblivion, take its place as an equal among modern nations. He has definite ideas about how this feat can be achieved, and at times he can be ruthless in eliminating those who attempt to deprive him of his kingship. At the same time, his genuinely paternal concern for the peasants has won him their indestructible loyalty. More than any other ruler in

Cambodian history, Sihanouk has fostered intimacy with the peasantry, making frequent visits to the remotest villages and there abandoning his regal façade and lecturing in the vernacular on his hopes for them and their country and on their foibles. To the people he is still the king, and they respond to his admonishments and praise by addressing him as "Papa" and disclosing to him their problems and grievances against local officials. . . .

Once a constitution was adopted, which, partly owing to Sihanouk's conciliatory acts, was more liberal in its provisions than had been intended by the monarchists who sat on the Commission d'Etudes Franco-Khmères, and independence attained as a result of his own efforts, Sihanouk was able to forestall the campaigns of those who sought to undermine him. Furthermore, because he had used legal means to win his objectives from the French, he found himself still the head of the country and of its military and police forces. Those who had opposed him now found it in their interests to serve him or, if this was not practicable, to quit the country.

Meanwhile, the various political parties, which had been organized on the basis of specific issues—independence and the type of government which should be provided by the constitution—rather than on ideologies, lost their *raison d'être* and were demoralized by the petty bickering which ensued. When personal grievances of party members followed them into the National Assembly and interfered with the effective functioning of the state, Sihanouk attributed the difficulties to the multiparty system. Impatient to get on with the reconstruction of his country, he sought to effect an uncoerced dissolution of parties by founding the Sangkum Reastr Niyum, a national "movement" with objectives so broad that other political groups could easily be absorbed by it. Because of the overwhelming electoral victories of the Sangkum and the disunity which characterized the existing parties, it was not long before most of their members had defected to the Sangkum. Soon membership in the Sangkum came to be identified with patriotism and active leadership. . . .

Although the Sangkum has not succeeded in suppressing factionalism, as evidenced by the persistent conflicts between the all-Sangkum National Assembly and the all-Sangkum cabinet, existence of this movement promotes among the people an appearance of unity within the country's leadership. It is noteworthy that the tension which has often built up between the Assembly and the government has been the result of concern not over the extraordinarily wide political latitude which Sihanouk enjoys but rather over who will compose his entourage and thus share in the prestige and rewards of power. . . .

As part of the campaign of the prince and the Sangkum to cultivate an *esprit de corps* among the people, they have revived several timeworn symbols by injecting them with new significance. Among these is *monarchy,* which has come to represent the continuity of Cambodian history and culture and the present regime's wise political conservatism. As this symbol has become personalized in Prince Sihanouk himself, it no longer arouses an image of a remote power indifferent to the needs of the people but one of a benevolent paternalistic authority upon whose judgment rests their welfare and the nation's destiny. Another symbol which has been kept alive in the public consciousness is *Buddhism,* which further ties the people with their historic past and which, by providing them with a common philosophy, acts as a cohesive agent. Among the Buddhist values which Prince Sihanouk extols are brotherhood of man, self-help, and self-sacrifice for the good of the group.

A concept that is new to the masses is *nation.* Long accustomed to village life which received little direction from the capital, the Cambodian peasant finds this notion difficult to comprehend. Further, the view that the aristocracy and other elite, on the one hand, and the masses, on the other, are irreconcilable groups having different interests and objectives has had to be overcome. The prince has tried to make both groups equally active participants in the socioeconomic development of the country by recruiting from both the labor force required for the construction of schools, roads, and bridges and for other public services. At the same time, he has urged the elite to exercise moderation in their ostentations and has tried to inculcate in the peasantry the idea of their equality under the Buddhist religion and before the law. He has also tried to extend the people's thinking beyond their villages by keeping them informed of national problems.

Neutrality in foreign affairs is another concept with which the people have become indoctrinated. To attest to the wisdom of neutrality, Sihanouk has frequently pointed to the losses Cambodia suffered as a result of past entanglements with other nations, particularly with Thailand and Vietnam. The people have also been warned that involvement in the Cold War may lead to preoccupations which will detract from the internal development of their nation.

The fact that these various catchwords have been introduced into their working vocabulary does not mean that the people are more politically sophisticated than in the past. They quickly respond to queries designed to assess their political knowledge by bandying these labels about, not, generally, because they comprehend the full significance of them but because the prince supports them.

A major threat to the country's domestic peace lies in the growing number of politically ambitious youth who are impatient to occupy decision-making positions in the government. In pursuit of their objectives, they have inevitably clashed with the "old guard," who feel they have earned their voice in the government by virtue of their participation in the independence struggle.

The youth for the most part are products of French colleges and universities, and they believe that their superior education entitles them to important political roles. They get only as far as the National Assembly, they complain, where their voices are ignored, and they are barred from responsible political positions. Although they express discontent in the National Assembly, where they enjoy parliamentary immunity, and in anonymous letters addressed to the prince and the old guard, they have generally failed to take advantage of their right to initiate legislation. Some have explained that, unlike legislators in other parliamentary regimes, they lack the funds and personnel to conduct the investigations necessary to draft legislation and thus they must resign themselves to debating the issues of the day and enacting measures introduced by the government or by National Congress resolution. It was a lack of resourcefulness on the part of Cambodian legislators generally and their obstruction of the government's programs which led Sihanouk to the creation of the National Congress.

A man standing out as an exception among those frequently designated "les jeunes intellectuels" is Chau Seng [currently Minister of Special Missions in Sihanouk's government-in-exile]. . . . Upon his return from France in 1957, he undertook on his own initiative a study of the public school curriculum and published a book which contained his recommendations. In 1958, he was elected to the National Assembly and thereupon was appointed Secretary of State for Education, a position he held in three successive cabinets. . . While still a deputy in the National Assembly, he became editor of *La Dépêche du Cambodge,* a privately owned French-language newspaper. . . . He was re-elected a deputy from Phnom Penh in 1962 and appointed Secretary of State for Agriculture in the Norodom Kantol government which was formed in October 1962. Chau Seng's case is of interest because it reveals that Sihanouk and the old guard do recognize new talent and are quick to utilize and reward it whenever possible.

With a new crop of "young intellectuals" returning from French universities every year, all impatient to hold government offices, the problem of absorbing them has become increasingly difficult. Sihanouk has explained in several speeches that the government cannot accommodate all of them immediately and has urged them to act constructively in the National Assembly instead of behaving petulantly and to enter other areas where their talents would benefit the people. He has especially tried to encourage them to return to their provinces where good teachers and other public servants are urgently needed.

The unrest among "les jeunes" in the National Assembly came to a peak in the spring of 1962; some of them went so far as to accuse Sihanouk of leading the country into the Southeast Asia Treaty Organization and others criticized Son Sann's fiscal policies as being detrimental to Cambodia's economy in their ultraconservatism. Sihanouk's rebuttal was that in the 1962 elections they would have to make their own way without hanging on to his coattails, that is, without running on the Sangkum ticket. Interestingly enough, when candidacies were filed with the Sangkum in the early spring, those of the rebel deputies were among the first to be approved, probably because the prince felt that the National Assembly serves as an outlet for their discontent and because he can keep a closer watch on them there. As has been mentioned earlier, Sihanouk also assigned some of them significant positions in the new government; his motives, it appears, were to provide them with an opportunity to put their abilities to a realistic test and to forestall the formation of an effective opposition to his rule.

6

Portraits of the Prince

by Han Suyin and Robert Shaplen

A Patriot by Han Suyin

. . . Prince Sihanouk has often disconcerted the West, and will do so again. No amount of name calling can alter a fact which certain powers, unconsciously contemptuous of small nations, underestimate: the Prince is first and foremost a patriot, dedicated to Cambodia and to the Khmer people.

In this sense, Sihanouk the patriot is a phenomenon. It is rare that a man born of royal blood and endowed with a French education should have transcended the barriers of his own kingly, feudal upbringing and his acquired "Western orientation," and achieved such insight into the forces that transform emergent nations. Kings reign, but Sihanouk is above all the well-beloved leader, father, brother, cherished ideal inspiration and animator of his people. Given all the opportunities for doing the wrong things, he has avoided the pitfalls of a complex and dangerous situation; nor has he followed the example of so many other Asian leaders who have found repression easier than reform. For 11 years he has maintained his country in an almost miraculous state of peace and stability and achieved social reforms that others might envy.

This is not to say that the Prince does not have his faults, or to claim that Cambodia is a paradisaical State. Sihanouk is essentially a very human person, with great talents, enormous intelligence, an indefatigable brain and abounding energy. He may be mercurial; in a Western statesman that would be praised as "enormous vitality," and Sihanouk is well endowed with both nervous and physical stamina. He becomes overly irritated by the inanities certain foreign correspondents inflict upon him, reacts to them perhaps too promptly, but

Han Suyin is a well-known essayist, novelist, and political commentator. Her most widely read work is probably *A Many Splendored Thing*.

that is a fault on the right side. He has a keen sense of Cambodian dignity and national pride. "It is Cambodia they insult, through me." That is why he springs to his pen and lashes back. Where his own people are concerned, he has an almost angelic patience, good temper and humility with the small, the humble, the poor. And however angry, he never loses his head, nor does his so-called irrational behaviour appear irrational to his subjects; to them it is righteous anger on their behalf; and since it is in their name he speaks, their honour he defends, they give him unbounded approval. . . .

For a time the French . . . mistakenly judged him convenient for political manipulation, but Sihanouk, in a remarkable speech apologising to his people "for not realising that their desire for independence was overwhelming," disconcerted the French and was returned by an overwhelming plebiscite (925,812 against 1,834) on the basis of complete independence for Cambodia in February 1955. He abdicated in March 1955, saying he could not "head a small privileged aristocratic class to exploit his own people." As a monarch, he was a prisoner of tradition; by leaving the throne, he would democratise and liberalise the regime. This is what he has largely succeeded in doing. It is this "going to the people" which is the secret of Sihanouk's enduring success. That the West, which forever talks of "social democracy" as opposed to Communism, yet seems dead set against a successful experiment in "reformism," is what intensely irritates Sihanouk.

He is beginning to say that by and large *no* Western power (except possibly France) has learnt from history; that the talk of "promoting prosperity in underdeveloped countries" is mere eyewash, that the West is *not* prepared to recognise or acknowledge the achievements of countries like Cambodia, *primarily because these achievements are truly nationalistic,* in the sense that they are not camouflage for a continued stranglehold of foreign vested interests in another guise.

In 1955 Sihanouk attended the first Afro-Asian conference in Bandung. This deepened his understanding of the international political scene. Cambodian neutrality was then clearly defined by Sihanouk, and one of his aims was to have this neutrality guaranteed and acknowledged by all the great powers. But until today America and Britain have either refused or ignored this demand.

When the Prince says: "All I do is for Cambodia," he is

speaking the truth, and unless his detractors understand this unswerving dedication, they will not be able to assess his character, or his motives. Analysts who base their assessment of politicians in South East Asia on self-interest are at sea when they come to Sihanouk. With him, self-interest comes last, for he has identified to such an extent with the welfare of his people that when he says: "I am quite happy to die for my country" he is really laying bare his heart. And in this he is living up to what he feels is his duty as a Khmer King. . . .

Sihanouk's concept of happiness for his people is peace, security, a modest prosperity, the abolition of feudalism and some form of socialism based on Buddhist concepts. He does not see his country as an expanding nation, nurtures no dreams of empire. He wants Cambodia a small and contented Switzerland safe within her own frontiers, safe to work out her problems. Not a wide ambition, but extraordinarily difficult, since, to this day, this reasonable aim has not been able to obtain a guarantee from the most powerful nation in the world, the U.S. The fact that Cambodia was once described as a "geographical expression" by a certain American states- man, that all through 1962, 1963 and 1964 attacks (physical infringements of Cambodia's frontiers) have taken place from Thailand and South Vietnam, both considered by Sihanouk as hereditary enemies of Cambodia and American satellites, led to his rejection of American aid two years ago and the break in diplomatic relations this year [1965].

Sihanouk says: "I do not aspire to play a great interna- tional role . . . all I want is the peace and integrity of my country." But history is putting him in a position where, unless he makes his voice well heard on international affairs, he feels Cambodia will be in danger.

"We are small, and therefore we've got to shout very loud in order to be heard," he says. And hence, on the interna- tional scale, Cambodia makes her voice heard. It might repay great powers to listen.

For such an inoffensive little country, ready to be every- one's friend, the amount of venom expended by the Western press is truly astonishing. That is because of Sihanouk's friendship with China. Yet this friendship, if only for geo- graphic reasons, is very understandable. China has treated Cambodia and her Prince with great respect and admirable understanding; Sihanouk's welcomes in Peking have been magnificent; the Chinese have been scrupulously at pains not to interfere with internal matters in Cambodia. "Better a good bourgeois, than a bad Communist," Chen Yi once said. But in the American press, Sihanouk is represented as a puppet of Peking, although anyone studying his career knows that he can never be anyone's puppet. Sihanouk is completely at ease with the Chinese leaders: he admires what they have done in China, but makes it clear that he has his own ideas what to do in Cambodia. When he does not like something in the Chinese, he says so openly, which means that he says it over the radio to several millions of Khmers. Sihanouk keeps nothing to himself. I remember him pulling letters from foreign statesmen out of his pocket, reading and translating them to his delighted Khmer audiences, evoking roars of laughter. "My people have the right to know everything."

"Anything you tell him, he'll go to the radio the next day and tell it to the world," groaned a diplomat. The best way to know what Sihanouk really thinks is to turn on the radio . . . and learn Khmer.

"I have never had the slightest illusion on the fate that awaits me at the hands of the Communists, as well as that which is reserved for my Government, after having removed from our region the influence, and especially the presence, of the 'free world,' and the US in particular. I concede again that after the disappearance of the US from our region and the victory of the Communist camp, I myself and the People's Socialist Community that I have created would inevitably disappear from the scene. I know the Chinese well enough to understand that they cannot be 'bought' and that it is perfectly useless to bend before them, or to play their game occasionally in the hope of extracting some ulterior advantage. If I acted thus, I would be despised, and rightly so, by the Chinese people, who would not alter their plans one iota so far as my country is concerned.

"But there is one thing that you Americans seem incapable of understanding. And that is that Cambodia has broken off with the US not because it is a 'pawn of Peking,' as you write, but for reasons of dignity and national honour that we have indicated." (Letter to *The New York Times,* May 16, 1965.)

Sihanouk has made it clear that he does not wish a destruction of American influence in South East Asia. Because, he says, forthrightly, this will mean that Cambodia will have to go Communist, and that he, Sihanouk, will have to disappear.

The best way to maintain American influence in South East Asia is, he says, for the US to give up her doomed adventure in South Vietnam and to withdraw her troops. Only by withdrawing her military force and bases in Indochina can whatever honour, prestige, presence or influence America still retains in Asia be maintained. For in this era of rising nationalism, he argues, the maintenance, against a people's will, of bases and foreign soldiers in uniform on their territory is to invite hatred and resistance, in fact the very opposite to what is desired. Sihanouk says that every bomb dropped by the Americans in Vietnam creates more Communists than all the propaganda from Peking.

Cambodia Is Sihanouk by Robert Shaplen

In recent years the visitor making the half-hour plane trip from Saigon to the Cambodian capital of Phnom Penh has invariably experienced the sensation of having momentarily escaped the turbulence of the Southeast Asian hurricane for its calm eye. The differences between the two cities became manifest the moment the plane set down at Phnom Penh's Pochentong airport, where it was likely to be the only one on the field, in contrast to the scores of fighters, bombers, transports, and helicopters on the ground or overhead at Tan Son Nhut, in Saigon. The ride into town was swift and smooth, along clean, broad avenues and streets relatively free of traffic and of the cloying smell of exhaust fumes. The stucco houses and villas of residential Phnom Penh, painted serene pastel colors, stood far apart amid lush, well-tended lawns and imparted an air of comfortable and unhurried living. The food and wines in the French restaurants were still good, and the Vietnamese-run dance halls and cafés, although their operators had begun to acquire some of Saigon's money-grabbing habits, retained much of the old French atmosphere of *joie de vivre*.

Such manifestations of contentment, however, could not

Robert Shaplen is an American journalist who reports for *The New Yorker* from Southeast Asia. Among his publications is *Time Out of Hand*, which deals with contemporary Southeast Asia.

conceal that the storm was close by, and to watch Prince Norodom Sihanouk, the Chief of State, perform his extraordinary feat of navigating above it was an often breath-taking experience. Sihanouk, the former King who stepped down from the throne in 1955, at the age of thirty-three, to take over the controls of his flimsy state, continued, for the most part, to meet with astonishing *élan* and vitality the challenge of staying politically aloft. He not only forecast the political weather, in all its variability, but frequently played the exciting role of daredevil barnstormer and test pilot, and, while the crowd gasped and sometimes criticized his swift and sudden maneuvers, he repeatedly proved his ability to entertain but more importantly to survive as the leader of a people and a country he has both personified and dominated.

Sihanouk always liked to refer to his Khmer people as his "children," and they, for their part, cherished and revered him, but in a wider sense the relationship went far beyond that of parent and offspring, to that of a Superman-style hero and his audience. In a more historical and sophisticated sense, he looked upon himself as an Asian knight-errant engaged in a sacred mission to save his nation from the Infidels and the barbarians, which included, in varying degree, both the Communists and the Americans and their allies. Although the situations and the circumstances kept changing, there was a certain consistency to the story line—the predicament of the beleaguered hero-prince surrounded by enemies seeking to devour or destroy him; his compulsion to preserve Cambodia's sovereignty at whatever cost, including his own life; his repeated narrow escapes and re-emergence, girded in fresh moral armor, to do battle yet again with the wicked forces of the world who would not leave him alone. For all his protestations, it is doubtful that Sihanouk ever wanted to be left alone—neglect would probably have caused him to languish sadly—but as he moved from crisis to crisis, some imposed upon him and others created by himself, his assurance and bravado increasingly failed to hide the uneasy desperation beneath the suave exterior. With the passing of the years, anger and frustration on more than one occasion prompted him to succumb to near-hysterical outbursts, followed by periods of dejection and depression. There was never much doubt that Sihanouk, as a self-driven and dedicated man, was sincerely striving to remain neutral and independent while the countries surrounding him in Southeast Asia were at war, but the more I observed him during several visits to Cambodia between 1965 and 1968, the more he seemed to me a tragic and lonely figure out of the past, and at the same time something of a medieval flagellant. In his rear-guard campaign to hold on to what was left of the ancient and remarkable Khmer empire and heritage, he sometimes drew so much attention to his own vulnerability as to increase rather than diminish it. One could readily sympathize with his predicament of feeling himself surrounded by the Vietnamese on one side and the Thais on the other.

7

Dissension in the Kingdom
by William Rosoff

Recent events in Cambodia have been all too sudden for many of us, but the forces involved in the present situation were not suddenly born out of the crisis of Sihanouk's overthrow. General Lon Nol is not a Cambodian Popodopolous, but has been the "second man" in Cambodian politics for at least the past decade; the Khmer Rouge (Cambodian Communist insurgents) have quite suddenly gained in numbers, but have been around an equally long time; and if the American presence in Cambodia has not before been as visible or dramatic, its mere proximity has played a key role in recent Cambodian history. In retrospect, we should not be so much surprised that the coup took place at all, but that it did not take place sooner.

Sihanouk had managed to keep his country out of the war that raged around it not only by his foreign policy of neutrality—by balancing off one government against another—but also by his internal policy—by manipulating and neutralizing the political and social forces within Cambodia itself. And his overall success had rested on his relative ability to isolate and keep distinct internal and external pressures. However great internal instability may have at times become, and however much the American war in Laos and Vietnam may have flowed over into Cambodian territory, the two struggles were never allowed to become the same conflict. This fact was the key to Sihanouk's very carefully constructed neutrality—not simply the rather vague notion of "nonalignment." With the accession to power of Lon Nol this "neutralization" of external and internal forces has, of course, been shattered: Cambodia has become simply another front in the Indochina war. But over the past few years before the coup, it was becoming increasingly difficult for Sihanouk him-

William Rosoff is a graduate student in Modern South Asian History at the University of California, Berkeley.

self to continue isolating these various internal and external factors. Just as American-South Vietnamese "hot pursuit" operations and Vietcong-North Vietnamese military supply activities seem to have encroached more and more onto Cambodian territory, so the internal conflicts of the country seem to have pointed increasingly to external forces for their resolution. And as external and internal forces became increasingly intertwined, as Cambodian conflicts became international conflicts, Sihanouk himself seems to have become less and less the controller and manipulator of events.

Cambodia has not been free of its own internal problems. And as in external affairs, Sihanouk has had to move back and forth between left and right simply to keep the state together. One of his difficulties, however, was that although he may have been moderately favorable to China and at least sympathetic with the Vietnamese Communists, he was quite avowedly anti-Communist when it came to affairs inside Cambodia. The Prince considered himself above all a nationalist, and in his own view, communism and nationalism were totally incompatible (at least in Cambodia); and if he backed the Vietnamese revolutionaries, he backed them rather as nationalists than as Communists.[1] Cambodia, already independent, was, however, another matter, and Communist insurgents within it were seen simply as just one more imperialist force.[2] "The Asian communists and their Khmer lackeys . . . claim they are trying to liberate us from the Americans," Sihanouk stated last September. "However, we who are independent do not need to be liberated."[3]

Through the early and mid-sixties, Sihanouk did not appear to feel threatened by either indigenous or external Communist forces, but, in fact, seemed much more concerned with the threat from the American-supported Khmer Serei based in Thailand and South Vietnam.[4] On several occasions he complained that the CIA was planning to overthrow his government through its support of such right-wing groups as the Khmer Serei. At the end of 1963, the chief-of-state refused to accept further United States economic and military aid and a little over a year later broke off all diplomatic ties with Washington, claiming that the Americans were trying to interfere in Cambodian internal affairs and to dictate its policy. Sihanouk's fears, especially of the CIA, continued up until the coup (when they may have perhaps been vindicated). But toward the end of the decade he was becoming increasingly concerned as well with the Communist threat.

At the beginning of April 1967, there was a peasant uprising in Battambang province, in the western part of the country. Battambang, as the only province with a relatively high degree of tenancy, had been for some time the source of small-scale peasant uprisings and revolts. The 1967 revolt was perhaps the largest of such uprisings, but it certainly posed no serious threat to the government at Phnom Penh and was, in fact, put down fairly quickly by the Royal army. What was significant about the revolt, however, was Sihanouk's reaction to it. Previously the Prince had attributed all the trouble in the area to the activities of the Khmer Serei, but now, for the first time, he attributed this internal revolt to outside Communist leadership, specifically Hanoi.[5] According to Sihanouk, Viet Minh cadres, who had gone underground at the time of the Geneva Agreements, were now resurfacing and, at the instructions of Hanoi, were fomenting unrest in the countryside.[6] Yet all the evidence we have would seem to indicate that Hanoi was not, in the spring of 1967, interested in making things difficult for Sihanouk; that it was not interested or even capable of inciting peasant rebellion in Cambodia, least of all in the western sections, away from the areas of military strategic significance.[7] According to *Le Monde*, the government had quite clearly played up the extent of outside influence in the Khmer Rouge uprising at Battambang; but if such influence existed at all, it was in the areas near the Vietnamese border, where, significantly, there had been no disturbances.[8]

It is difficult to determine with the information available the reasons behind this apparent shift in attitude. But it is perhaps of some significance that at the time of the uprisings in April 1967, Sihanouk had just recently returned from a vacation in France. The day-to-day activities of the government had been left in the hands of Lon Nol, who at the time was both premier and chief of the army. Some months earlier, in 1966, Lon Nol had been named as head of a conservative-dominated government, which by April 1967 had already removed many leftists from positions of influence. (Just after the formation of the government Lon Nol had threatened to resign when Sihanouk, worried by the conservative nature of the new cabinet, had formed a left-oriented "counter-government"—Sihanouk backed down.) The government was, if not in policy as much as temperament, decidedly pro-American. Lon Nol, of course, had close ties with Cambodian military leaders, who, according to one report at the time, "doubtless remember fondly the heyday of U.S. military assistance when they lived extremely well."[9] And Sihanouk had even claimed that the CIA had been trying to gain influence within the Staff Corps.[10] Lon Nol, along with others in the cabinet, seems also to have had close ties with the business community, which had been suffering from the termination of U.S. aid and was looking forward to renewed cooperation with Washington and the opportunities for investment and assistance that such cooperation implied.[11]

Even before the April revolt in Battambang the conservatives in the government had evidently been voicing growing concern over ties between indigenous insurgents and Vietnamese Communist forces. In March, there were, it is true, a number of demonstrations within the capital, carried out by left-wing students and intellectuals; but the specific demand of the demonstrators was simply the removal from Pailin district in Battambang of the army units that Lon Nol had earlier stationed there. As far as one can tell, it was not Vietnamese Communist activity that was increasing at the time but Cambodian reaction to the activities of the army. The Vietnamese, it seems, were present in government rhetoric only. It is impossible to trace any causal link between Lon Nol's position as premier and the presumed increase in Vietnamese Communist activity among the local Cambodian rebels. But as we shall see, this was not the last time that such a "coincidence" occurred. And even when he was not serving as premier, Lon Nol seems to have been the man most often to voice the government's concern with the Vietnamese threat of internal subversion.[12]

In May 1967, Sihanouk forced the Lon Nol government to resign; and replacing many of the conservatives with left-wing and moderate ministers, took personal control of the new government. By including a number of ministers favorable to China and North Vietnam in his new cabinet, the Prince successfully disarmed the left-wing opposition in the capital. By June the rebellion in the countryside had also come to an end. By the fall of 1967, however, the situation was once again becoming tense. The "exportation" of the

Chinese Cultural Revolution into Cambodia and the resultant pro-Communist agitation infuriated Sihanouk and almost led to a break in relations with Peking. Throughout the summer, Sihanouk had complained of the subversive activity of "Sino-Khmer Communist elements" in the Khmer-Chinese Friendship Association. On September 1, all such associations were banned. And when a telegram sent by Peking in support of the dissolved Khmer-Chinese Friendship Association was published in the left-wing *Nouvelle-Dépêche,* Sihanouk was so angered by what he considered to be external involvement in Cambodia's internal affairs that he threatened to break off diplomatic relations with China. The Chinese, however, valuing Cambodia's neutrality and not wanting to undermine Sihanouk's position, quickly apologized. Relations with Peking were once again normalized, but a little while later, several left-wing ministers were dismissed from the cabinet and disappeared from the capital, presumably to lead the rebellion in the countryside. Sihanouk's "swing to the right" had supposedly begun.

In November 1967, Jackie Kennedy paid her "unofficial" visit to Cambodia. And in January 1968, Chester Bowles was sent to Phnom Penh to discuss with Sihanouk ways of bolstering up the International Control Commission. Nothing very concrete seems to have come out of these discussions. The Cambodian left, however, charged that Sihanouk was seeking a rapprochement with the United States. Sihanouk denied the charge, but did appear quite willing to reopen diplomatic channels with Washington that had been cut in 1965.

Whether there was a direct link between these diplomatic maneuvers and the internal activities of the Cambodian left is difficult to determine. But early in January, Sihanouk revealed a new "Khmer-Viet Minh rebellion" in Battambang. During the next several months, guerrilla activity spread to other provinces, and Sihanouk renewed his charges that these rebels were receiving aid from outside sources. At the same time, however, the Prince seems to have been careful not to antagonize Peking or Hanoi, and quite deliberately did not charge Vietnamese forces with direct intervention.[13] These new outbreaks were apparently little more than a series of local skirmishes and, according to government reports, were rather quickly subdued.

But in May 1968, a far more serious armed rebellion broke

out in the "Three Frontiers" area in the mountainous northeast. The rebellion began when most of the 60,000 Khmer Loeu (hill tribesmen) deserted their villages and fled into the jungle to escape the resettlement program being carried out by the Cambodian army. Although often confused with the Khmer Rouge insurgency, the Khmer Loeu rebellion was not, it seems, connected with the activities of the lowland Khmer Rouge forces that were taking place predominantly in the western and southern sections of the country, but existed quite independently of the more "politically" inspired Communists. The causes of the rebellion were rooted not in political ideology but in the ancient antipathy between hill and lowland groups and the recent attempts of the government to "Cambodianize" these previously independent tribesmen.[14] Early in 1968, the government had begun sending army units into Rattanakiri province in an attempt to gain control over the area, which had hitherto been independent in all but name. The army's aim, apparently, was to resettle the hill tribesmen into new villages and towns, where they could be used to work the expanding rubber plantations, as part of an overall program to develop the northeastern area and integrate it into the Cambodian economy. Roads and schools were built, police were established, and various development projects were begun, all under the direction of the army. To the resistance of the tribesmen the government reacted with more troops. Sihanouk blamed the Vietnamese Communists with having incited the rebellion and grew increasingly vocal in his denunciation of Vietnamese infiltration. There were, apparently, a small number of Vietnamese soldiers—no more than fifty—active in the northeast border areas, arming the Khmer Loeu and urging them to resist the army, but they were simply taking advantage of an already explosive situation.[15] Once again, it seems to have been the actions of the Cambodian army rather than of Vietnamese agitators that sparked internal rebellion.[16]

By the fall of 1968, Sihanouk was taking a much more active stance against Vietnamese Communist intrusion into Cambodian territory. Refusing to recognize any longer the distinction between the Khmer Loeu activity in the isolated northeast and the activities of local Khmer Rouge forces in the more central areas, he more and more attributed *all* disturbances (not merely the hill tribes' rebellion) to the infiltration of Vietnamese guerrillas. And more and more he voiced his fear of Hanoi as the real threat to Cambodian neutrality.

Throughout 1969 there seems to have been increasing activity on the part of local Khmer guerrilla forces and an increasing number of confrontations between Communist and Royal army units. It is extremely difficult, however, to judge the meaning of such activity. At the beginning of the year, Sihanouk himself claimed that the Khmer Rouge were only a handful of dissidents, perhaps no more than 1,500 in all.[17] By the fall, the figure may have been 3,000.[18] These small numbers of local Communists did not, Sihanouk believed, pose a serious threat.[19] But the Prince was coming more and more to fear Vietnamese guerrillas, who, he claimed, were becoming increasingly aggressive and were actively trying to lead the population to rebellion. More and more Sihanouk voiced his concern over the *external* Communist threat, and for the first time he began to speak openly of the extent of Vietcong infiltration and the necessity to stop it. What for years the Americans had contended, and for years Sihanouk had denied, he now openly admitted. With increasing bitterness the chief-of-state spoke of Hanoi and their "Khmer Rouge henchmen."[20]

In retrospect, however, the situation seems not to have been quite as simple as Sihanouk's statements would have us believe. It is impossible to determine precisely just how much influence Hanoi actually had in the activities of the Cambodian Communists, or how close were the ties between Vietnamese infiltrators and local Khmer Rouge units. It is quite clear, however, that Sihanouk, incapable of believing that the Cambodians might have any cause of their own, overemphasized the Vietnamese role and underestimated the extent of Khmer Rouge independence and the importance of local factors as a source of discontent. The Communists in Cambodia did not form a uniform and coordinated movement. On the contrary, there appear to have been, in addition to the special case of the Khmer Loeu rebellion discussed above, two distinct types of base areas for guerrilla activities, representing essentially two different types of movements: 1) in Prey Veng and Svay Rieng provinces, in the eastern part of the country, a small number of Khmer Rouge were organized and strongly supported by Vietnamese units that were using the areas not necessarily as sanctuaries but as supply and infiltration routes; 2) other base areas were spread out over southern and western Cambodia and were particularly concentrated in a hundred-mile area stretching from Kampong Chang (west of Phnom Penh) south to Takeo and Kampot. In these latter areas the Khmer Rouge forces were acting quite independently of Vietnamese direction and constituted an entirely indigenous group.[21]

Cambodia was not without its sources of peasant discontent, whatever Sihanouk may have claimed. Although not nearly as impoverished as most other countries in Asia, and spared the problems of landlessness or absentee landlordism (except in Battambang, as we have already noted), the Cambodian economy had for several years prior to 1969 been stagnating; and the bad harvest of the last year may have been just enough to create at least pockets of peasant discontent. Yet with all this, the Khmer Rouge remained a very small group. The vast majority of peasants continued to look upon Sihanouk as a modern-day god-king. Clearly these Khmer Rouge units posed no serious threat to the chief-of-state.[22] As to the Cambodian insurgents in the Vietnamese border areas, they in some ways posed even less of a threat than did the more independent groups in the central regions. Throughout the fall of last year [1969] increased attention was focused in the western press on the growing amount of Vietnamese infiltration into Cambodia. Yet one should perhaps ask whether such concern was caused more by official claims of a Vietnamese threat than by any significant shift in Communist policy; whether increased Cambodian army casualties were due more to the increasingly aggressive policy of the Cambodian military than to an increase in Communist armed attacks. According to T.D. Allman of the *Far Eastern Economic Review*, the Vietnamese in the eastern provinces, throughout 1969 and the first months of this year [1970], were making a determined effort to stay away from Cambodian troops.[23] Vietnamese support of the local Khmer Rouge was not, it seems, intended to create local insurgency, but merely to safeguard their own supply routes, which were often located in remote areas over which the Cambodian government had always had rather tenuous control. Whatever their long-range objectives, the Vietnamese were not, in the short run at least, interested in subverting the Sihanouk government, but on the contrary, seem to have found his neutral policy very convenient.[24]

It is difficult to determine the reasons both behind this "over-dramatization"[25] of the Communist threat and Sihanouk's apparent shift to an increasingly aggressive policy toward Vietnamese infiltrators, whose presence in Cambodian territory had hitherto been denied or ignored. It appears, however, that the Prince's new attitude may have been at least partially forced upon him by growing pressures from the Cambodian right—pressures which were in part the result of steadily deteriorating economic conditions.

Over the past several years the Cambodian economy has become subject to increasing strains. Cambodia has been extraordinarily dependent on manufactured imports, both for day-to-day consumption and in the form of capital goods for industrial development. The exports exchanged for these goods have been rubber and rice. But the surplus of these commodities has never been enough to meet the country's foreign exchange needs. Until 1963 these needs had been met largely by U.S. economic and military assistance. When in 1963 Sihanouk terminated the aid agreements with the United States in his efforts to remain free of political pressure from Washington, the flow of dollars stopped, and since 1964 there has been a growing balance of payments deficit. Although France, China, and Russia, as well as a number of other countries, both Communist and non-Communist, have provided economic assistance, it has not been sufficient to enable meaningful economic growth to take place. Development was also hindered by the problems of adjusting to nationalization programs, inadequate planning and technical personnel, a continuing downward trend in the world rubber price, and bad harvests. The country became more dependent than previously on rice exports to bring in foreign exchange. Further, more and more rice was being diverted from export markets into the Cambodian-Vietnamese black market where payment was mostly in Cambodian *riels,* not in foreign currency.[26] Even as early as 1967 the situation had become so serious that in the fall of that year Sihanouk sought a rapprochement with such groups as the World Bank, the International Monetary Fund (IMF), and the Asian Development Bank (ADB), which he had earlier opposed on the grounds of their having attached political strings to their economic assistance. (And it is perhaps significant that it was precisely at this time that Sihanouk's so-called swing to the right occurred.) But these institutions, controlled at least indirectly by the United States, were not eager to lend money to a country which had nationalized its foreign trade and banking facilities and whose leader pursued policies of which they often did not approve. Nor was capital forthcoming from private investors, who did not view Cambodia, with its "Buddhist Socialism," as a particularly safe place for their funds.

Economic necessity, not the fear of the Vietnamese Communists, seems to have been the prime reason for the resumption of diplomatic relations with Washington.[27] With a growing budget deficit and increasing numbers of university-trained men without adequate employment opportunities, Sihanouk seems to have been forced to turn to the Americans for help, if only because they controlled the capital resources on which he believed economic development depended. But significantly, Sihanouk would not give up his *politically* neutral position. A few days after diplomatic relations with Washington were restored in June [1969], Sihanouk and representatives of the NLF signed an agreement against U.S. aggression; and shortly after that, the Provisional Revolutionary Government (PRG) was given diplomatic recognition as the legal government of South Vietnam. Whatever the economic pressures, the Prince was willing to go only so far in his dealings with Washington.

By the end of July 1969, the economic crisis, made more acute by the expectation of a bad harvest and substantial reductions in rubber production due to U.S. defoliation, had become so serious that Sihanouk even spoke of resigning.[28] He made known his frustration at his own failure to motivate the government to move on the economic condition and announced the organization of a new government. A few days later, Sihanouk revealed a budget deficit of $20 million and indicated that the government was even willing to reconsider accepting direct aid from Washington. Cambodian membership in the Asian Development Bank was reactivated and the government applied for membership in the International Monetary Fund, which Sihanouk had previously opposed as being U.S. controlled and too politically oriented. Finally, on August 14, General Lon Nol, openly pro-American and an outspoken anti-Communist, was named head of a new "government of national salvation." Lon Nol and the second man in the government, Prince Sirik Natak, were given wide authority to revitalize the stagnating economy. The General, no doubt remembering the difficulties of his last premiership, accepted office only on the condition that he be given full authority over his government; and Sihanouk, under increasing pressure to somehow procure foreign capital, gave in.

Contrary to expectations, neither American economic aid nor ADB nor World Bank assistance immediately followed the resumption of U.S. diplomatic relations. Washington, it seems, was putting pressure on Phnom Penh to denationalize the economy as a prerequisite for receiving aid.[29] After the formation of the new government in August, however, Sirik Matak, who had long been the leading advocate of accepting U.S. aid to solve economic problems and had from the start been opposed to Sihanouk's nationalization program,[30] immediately began formulating plans to denationalize, ending the government monopoly on foreign trade and paving the way for foreign investment. The new government, particularly Sirik Matak, also began to strengthen its hold over the bureaucracy and its independence of the chief-of-state. Departmental reports were no longer submitted first to Sihanouk, but were ordered to be given directly to the cabinet, which Lon Nol and Sirik Matak controlled. Finally, in December, with Lon Nol away in Europe, Sirik Matak dissolved state control over banking and foreign trade and set forth proposals for general governmental disengagement from various economic enterprises. Four ministers loyal to Sihanouk, protesting the rapid rate of economic liberalization, were immediately forced to resign; and a few days later, Sirik Matak weakened the chief-of-state's position still further by shutting down the Phnom Penh casino over Sihanouk's personal opposition. Subsequently, the chief-of-state left for Europe.

By the time of his departure in January, Sihanouk had become increasingly isolated from both left and right. Lon Nol, who, as we have seen, was the man most "active in cracking down on the Khmer Rouge,"[31] had been putting increased pressure on the left, which only led to growing hostility and militancy; on the right, continued economic stagnation and lack of employment were creating unrest among students and professionals as well as businessmen.

"When at the beginning of January Sihanouk left on his long foreign journey," *Le Monde* reported, "his influence on public affairs had already been greatly reduced."[32]

In February, Lon Nol returned from France and, no longer under any restraint from the chief-of-state, began putting increased pressure on the Vietnamese Communists in Cambodia. (One of the most significant of these anti-Communist moves, *The New York Times* reported, was—anticipating things to come—cooperation between Cambodian and South Vietnamese armed forces in fighting the Vietcong along the border areas.)

One month later, anti-Vietnamese demonstrations "broke out" in Phnom Penh and several provincial towns. It is clear that these demonstrations were not a spontaneous outpouring of anti-Vietnamese feeling among the Cambodian population as a whole. On the contrary, they appear to have been carefully planned and organized by the government itself. According to Tristan Sarong in *Le Monde,* plans to attack the North Vietnamese and PRG embassies, by organizing "cyclos" (pedicab drivers) and "street people" directed by plainclothes police, had been carefully drawn up ahead of time.[33] A campaign of anti-Vietnamese propaganda was set in motion. Again the government deliberately tried to place on the Vietnamese the responsibility for the growing Khmer Rouge movement. The newspapers in the capital now spoke openly of the "rebel lackeys of the Vietnamese."[34]

In the border areas where there were Vietnamese infiltrators, the local population profited substantially from the sale of goods and contraband to these soldiers and were hardly about to demonstrate against those from whom they drew their livelihood. Demonstrations had to be organized elsewhere; and certain incidents involving Vietnamese armed attacks appear to have been deliberately provoked by Cambodian officials.[35]

During the first week in March, the North Vietnamese and PRG embassies were attacked by "mobs," and anti-Vietnamese demonstrations occurred in a number of provincial towns. On March 18, Lon Nol took over complete control in order to end the disturbances which he himself had organized. The coup itself was quick and bloodless.

At the time of the coup, a Cambodian officer indicated that one reason for Sihanouk's overthrow had been his anti-

American stance.[36] And about a week later, Cheng Heng, President of the National Assembly and chief-of-state of the new regime, claimed that it had been Sihanouk's failure to keep the Vietnamese out of Cambodian territory that had led to his ouster.[37] The openly pro-American, anti-Communist policy of the new regime dissolved Sihanouk's carefully constructed dichotomy between domestic and foreign policy. Internal and external Cambodian policy became, perhaps for the first time, "consistent," at least in ideology. But as external and internal policy become more clearly tied together, so the external and internal opposition forces to that policy become more closely united. Where once, because of Sihanouk's policy of neutrality, Khmer Rouge and Vietnamese Communist forces operated for the most part in separate areas and with different objectives, they were now more and more drawing together. As long as Sihanouk was in power, he had tried, to one degree or another, to keep separate the national and international policies. Thus he was sympathetic to communism abroad, but harsh in its repression at home. To the extent that he was successful, the Cambodian Communists had been denied the only issue from which they could hope to gather broad-based support—nationalist opposition to foreign imperialism. The massacre of Vietnamese civilians in the name of anticommunism marked at least a symbolic end to Sihanouk's unique political synthesis. By viewing internal problems simply as external ones, the new government misrepresented its own situation, but far worse for the Cambodian people, it transformed an internal conflict into an international one.

The coup of March 18 marked a final stage in the rather drawn-out process of Cambodian deneutralization. The economic benefits for which much of this process was initiated may, if the present regime lasts long enough, be forthcoming. Months before the coup, when the "liberalization" of the economy and the concomitant diplomatic shifts toward Washington were only in their early stages, one Cambodian official described, with what in retrospect must be seen as prophetic irony, what such benefits *would* have meant *if* Cambodia had followed a more pro-American policy:

> We could have had the billions of American dollars you see spent in Saigon, the skyscrapers and traffic jams of

Bangkok and the low-cost imported luxuries of Vientiane
if we had wished. But we also would have had, like
those countries, our cities filled with unemployed youths,
a communist insurrection all around us, galloping inflation and an enormous trade deficit. We have preferred
to forego these.[38]

Preferences, it seems, have changed.

PART THREE

THE COUP, THE INVASION, AND BEYOND

8

Anatomy of a Coup

by T. D. Allman

The move to take advantage of Sihanouk's absence from the country was in many ways a short-sighted and selfish one. Short-sighted because Sihanouk's removal from office endangered the delicate balance that Cambodia has kept between war and peace, the communists and the anti-communists; selfish because the anti-Sihanouk forces' main complaint— when all the charges are boiled down—was that the prince, during almost three decades of one-man rule, had deprived the aristocracy, the bourgeoisie and the army of their traditional slice of the financial action and of their accustomed place in the sun. It was an upper-class coup, not a revolution.

Norodom Sihanouk ruled Cambodia's seven million people for the better part of three decades—from 1941, when as an 18-year-old schoolboy he was proclaimed king, until March 18, 1970, when from a foreign land he saw power slip away from him into the hands of men with whom he had often clashed but with whom he entrusted power during his absence from the country.

Sihanouk's downfall was, in one sense, the result of the unique style he used to rule his nation. Although supreme, he preferred to leave administrative power vested in a parliament and cabinet, and the symbols of monarchy in the hands of his aging mother. From his rather anomalous position as chief of state, he guided Cambodian government and foreign policy for almost 10 years. But the post, tailored to Sihanouk's desire to maintain royal authority as well as the prerogatives of a popular politician, in the end deprived him of both the inviolability of his royal status and the benefits of the enormous following he retained among the common people.

As an uncrowned king, the parliament could risk the con-

T. D. Allman is an American journalist who has covered Cambodia and Laos for *Far Eastern Economic Review*, the respected Hong Kong weekly.

stitutionally dubious act of voting him out of office. As a politician, he made the fatal mistake of assuming that popularity could be a substitute for direct control of the apparatus of power. When the final crunch came, the attenuated prestige of the crown, embodied by his mother, Queen Kossomak, was insufficient to save him. By choosing to rule indirectly through a premier and cabinet, Sihanouk also allowed the army and the bureaucracy to fall under his enemies' control.

That Sihanouk's enemies were so numerous is evident in retrospect, but it was virtually unthinkable in practice until a warm, lazy Phnom Penh afternoon when the president of the National Assembly, Cheng Heng, read over the national radio a brief announcement that "the National Assembly and the Council of the Kingdom, meeting in joint session, have withdrawn, on the 18th of March 1970 at 1300 hours, conforming to the Constitution, in a unanimous vote, their confidence from Prince Norodom Sihanouk in his position as Chief of State."

The announcement pledged to continue Sihanouk's policies —though in foreign policy and economics they already had been significantly altered—and ended with an appeal for calm and order.

The assembly's action was probably unconstitutional but, if nothing else, it refuted the charge that Sihanouk was an absolute dictator. The parliamentary vote, in fact, did little more than confirm a "coup de chef d'etat" which already had taken place. Sihanouk, following a policy of trying to win over his opponents rather than destroy them, had left the army and the government honeycombed with officials up to the highest rank who were willing to turn the knife if the opportunity arose.

It is still not clear whether the two men most responsible for Sihanouk's ouster—General Lon Nol, premier and defence minister, and Prince Sisowath Sirik Matak, the deputy premier and cabinet strongman—had all along planned to oust Sihanouk.

Most probably they did not aim to go so far until just before the parliamentary vote. However, both men for months had been trying to manœuvre Sihanouk into the position of a figurehead chief of state, rather than the active one he insisted on being until the end.

Ironically, both men achieved high office at Sihanouk's

behest. Last summer he made them the principal figures in a "government of salvation" charged with energising Cambodia's stagnant economy.

From the beginning, Sirik Matak showed himself eager to encroach on what Sihanouk for decades had considered his personal prerogatives. Often serving as acting premier, Sirik Matak attempted to take control of foreign affairs into his own hands by ordering Cambodian embassies to report directly to the cabinet, not to the prince.

Sihanouk publicly reprimanded Sirik Matak, but did not fire him. Sirik Matak then pushed on with a series of important economic reforms—devaluing the riel, rejoining international financial institutions, liberalising trade and banking —which not only dismantled Sihanouk's "Khmer Socialism" but threatened the position of many of the prince's closest followers.

In December the new economic policies, called "disengagement" here, won the approval of a national congress composed of provincial representatives meeting in Phnom Penh. It was a victory for Sirik Matak and a setback for the pro-Sihanouk faction in the cabinet. Four of Sihanouk's followers resigned from the cabinet—one of them on charges of corruption.

Soon after Sirik Matak's victory on economic policy, Sihanouk left here for his first vacation in three years. Unhappy and a little petulant, Sihanouk apparently never dreamed that the same officials who had dared to defy him on economic policy less than three months later would also presume to depose him.

His absence, however, gave Sirik Matak and Lon Nol the chance to exploit anti-Vietnamese feeling in Cambodia in an attempt to discredit the prince's policy of seeking an accommodation rather than war with Cambodia's most powerful neighbour. On March 8, as the prince prepared to leave France for Moscow and the Soviet Union, the army organised anti-Vietnamese demonstrations in Svay Rieng province. Three days later, Phnom Penh students, soldiers and some 200 Buddhist monks were ordered to gather at the Independence Monument. In a peaceful and amiable mood, they followed government organisers to the Provisional Revolutionary Government embassy less than a mile away. While the marchers were encouraged to shout anti-Vietnamese slogans, a team of

45 trained soldiers in civilian dress entered the embassy and sacked it. The demonstrators—numbering about 10,000—were hardly hostile to the sacking in a country where anti-Vietnamese feeling runs deep. But the demonstration was hardly spontaneous. Few of the students and civil servants would have shown up had they not been ordered, and they undoubtedly had no idea that the ultimate result of their demonstration would be the ousting of Sihanouk.

The scene was repeated a little later at the North Vietnamese embassy; and then the demonstrators dispersed peacefully. Significantly, no Vietnamese—more than 100,000 of them live in Phnom Penh—was molested that day although the government radio was claiming that the demonstrations amounted to an upheaval of popular anger at Sihanouk's policy of having good relations with the communists.

Cruder violence did follow, however: a Vietnamese Roman Catholic church and several houses and restaurants were destroyed a few days later. But these actions, according to well-informed Cambodian sources, were the work of pro-Sihanouk agents who by that time were seeking to discredit the government and the popularity of its anti-Vietnamese demonstrations.

The sacking of the two embassies, as planned, gave the cabinet the pretext to express their frustration at years of living under Sihanouk and having to accept obediently the superficially pro-Vietnamese policies that had managed to save Cambodia from involvement in the Vietnam War. The same afternoon, the National Assembly passed a unanimous resolution explicitly encouraging the disorders. The next morning, the cabinet, in a move apparently planned well in advance, cabled Sihanouk in Paris, in effect presenting him with a fait accompli of radical change in foreign and military policy. The cable claimed that the demonstrations represented the "legitimate indignation" of the population and announced that the 25,000-man strong Royal Cambodian Army would be augmented by 10,000 recruits. The same day, the cabinet's pro forma note of apology to the Vietnamese communists for the sacking of their embassies was couched in the form of an ultimatum. Although the note, signed by Lon Nol, expressed the government's "sincere regrets" for demonstrations which the government itself had organised, it ended by ordering the Vietnamese to withdraw all their troops from Cambodian territory "at the latest by dawn of Sunday, March 15, 1970."

This was Friday—appropriately enough for Cambodia, Friday, March 13—and it was at this point, according to sources here, that things began to become unstuck.

Up to that time, the government's ploy had worked well. The Vietnamese had been humiliated; the National Assembly had been rallied to an anti-Vietnamese fever pitch; the Cambodian people were inclined to rally behind anything that was anti-Vietnamese. In Paris, on the eve of his departure for Moscow, Sihanouk found himself wedged. By presenting him with a fait accompli at home, his own government had challenged Sihanouk to come up with something dramatic in Peking and Moscow—such as a timetable for the withdrawal of communist troops from Cambodia—or hand over to them the initiative in Cambodian policymaking they had so long coveted.

But Sihanouk, characteristically, refused to be manoeuvred. He immediately sent a cable to his mother, imperiously dismissing the demonstrations as the work of "personalities attaching more importance to their personal interests . . . than to the future of the country and the people. They have profited from my absence to realise their designs. I therefore am going to return to the country to speak to the nation and army and ask them to make a choice. If they choose to follow these personalities in the path that will make Cambodia a second Laos then they will permit me to resign."

Sihanouk's analysis, virtually alone among the proliferating hypotheses of the moment, was proved by events to be substantially correct, though most observers at the time assumed he was very clearly manufacturing a crisis to better his own bargaining position in Peking and Moscow. However, nobody, least of all Sihanouk, imagined that his threat to resign was no longer as effective as in the past.

Sihanouk's first angry but well-argued cable, if nothing else, showed the premier and Sirik Matak that their dream of hemming Sihanouk in to fit their own policies was impossible as long as he remained the sure victor in a face-to-face contest for popular support. Nonetheless, following the announcement that Sihanouk would return here on March 18—the very day he ultimately would be deposed—the government prepared to receive him. Cambodian flags were raised along the Avenue de l'URSS which leads into town from the airport. Everyone assumed that Lon Nol and Sirik Matak would be punished appropriately for their insubordination. In the meantime, both sides were gathering their forces.

Ranged against Sihanouk were Lon Nol and the army, Sirik Matak and most of the cabinet, and the National Assembly. With Sihanouk were the police, the secretaries of state for ground defence and national security, and most of the provincial governors. In between, but undoubtedly leaning toward Sihanouk, was the rest of the population with the exception of the intellectuals and businessmen.

There followed a disguised but increasingly sharp propaganda contest between Sihanouk and the cabinet. Sihanouk had called the demonstrations "extremism contrary to the higher interests and good reputation of our country" and ordered them stopped. They continued, organised by the army and exaggerated in the government press, as official statements lauded them.

The communists in the meantime were taking a conciliatory tack lest they give the government a pretext for further embarrassing Sihanouk. Vietnamese diplomats met at the Palace of the Government with Cambodian officials on March 16, but the talks foundered on priorities. The Vietnamese asked for compensation for damages—a normal diplomatic procedure—and said they could not negotiate substantial changes in Vietnamese-Cambodian relations until they were able to re-establish communications with Hanoi. The Cambodians demanded an immediate and total withdrawal of all communist troops from the country. The talks ended politely but inconclusively.

About the same time, Sihanouk was saying that the events in Phnom Penh amounted to a right-wing coup. But after cabling the queen to curb the government, he made a serious error. In the interests of protocol, he delayed his return to Phnom Penh until March 24 in order to be able to spend an equal amount of time in Peking and Moscow.

The prince was playing it too cool. He had given the cabinet and National Assembly time to embolden themselves even more. Perhaps even more fatally, Sihanouk's delay forced his loyalists to desperate action which apparently gave parliament the final pretext to depose the last of the pro-Sihanouk officials and, ultimately, Sihanouk himself.

According to highly placed sources, the crucial day was

Monday, March 16, the same day the Cambodian and North Vietnamese officials conferred. That afternoon Queen Kossomak, at Sihanouk's behest, summoned the premier and Sirik Matak to the royal palace. She ordered them to end the demonstrations and return to Sihanouk's policies. The same day, she dispatched a letter to Cheng Heng telling him that if the National Assembly did not back down from its anti-Vietnamese stand she would dissolve it.

The only concession the cabinet and parliament offered the queen was a proposal to send a delegation to Paris to negotiate with Sihanouk. The offer was rejected. The same night, the pro-Sihanouk police—acting under orders from Colonel Oum Mannorine, secretary of state for ground forces and Sihanouk's relation through marriage—mounted an abortive coup. They tried to arrest Lon Nol, to deprive the anti-Sihanouk faction of both the army and the prime ministership, but failed. The head of the army signal corps—a vital position—may also have been killed that night although his death, still unexplained here, was not revealed until several days later.

The army retained the upper hand. The next morning, the National Assembly met to force Mannorine's resignation, ostensibly on charges of financial corruption. The only other pro-Sihanouk official with any power to halt the accelerating course of events was Colonel Sosthen Fernandez, secretary of state for national security. He managed to cling to office until the next morning.

With the pro-Sihanouk forces already outflanked, the queen that afternoon addressed the nation through radio. An aging, sickly woman and long nothing more than a figurehead, she had made a valiant effort to save her son's position in the final days. But her last speech came too late. Unable to reverse or stop the wave of anti-Vietnamese demonstrations without giving Sihanouk's opponents even more propaganda fuel, she rather implausibly argued that the demonstrations were an indication of support for the throne, for herself and for the chief of state. Hours later, armoured cars surrounded the post office and radio station and took up positions near the National Assembly and on the main boulevards. Orders were issued to close all airports.

Even if Sihanouk by this time had finally decided to return immediately and take the situation in hand, it would have been too late. The army had cut Cambodia off from the rest of the world.

The next morning—Wednesday, March 18—the assembly met to formalise the end of an era in Cambodian history. After deposing Fernandez, it voted Sihanouk out.

In the next few days, the rest of the pro-Sihanouk members of government—the foreign affairs minister, the police chief, the governor of Phnom Penh and the leaders of Sihanouk's Royal Khmer Socialist Youth—would also be purged. Even Queen Kossomak's photo was ordered removed from public sight, paving the way for the termination of one of the oldest monarchies in the world and the proclamation of a republic.

Almost surrealistically, Sihanouk had been pushed from his pedestal, and probably not in the manner anyone had fully anticipated. But faced with the choice of throwing in their hand so late in the game, or taking a step that in Cambodia amounted almost to an act of lese majeste, the cabinet and National Assembly apparently decided that things had gone so far so quickly that they risked less by deposing Sihanouk than by permitting him to return.

9

The Protagonists:
Norodom Sihanouk and Lon Nol

Sihanouk and Lon Nol revealed their respective goals and programs in the following manifestos to the Cambodian people. Both appeals were addressed to the same national audience. Sihanouk's proclamation was released to the press in Peking on March 23, 1970. Lon Nol's declaration was delivered by radio from Phnom Penh on May 11, 1970.

Message to Compatriots by Norodom Sihanouk

I pay my highest respects to Her Majesty the Queen, and extend my respectful regards to the Buddhist clergy and my dear compatriots.

I convey to you my most sincere, constant and affectionate feelings.

The handful of reactionary bourgeois elements and princes, who were able to climb to the highest positions thanks to the Sangkum Reastr Niyum and its President and consequently seize all kinds of privileges, have not only expressed their "gratitude" by "deposing" me illegally but moreover have slung mud at me, vilified me with monstrous slanders and base accusations including the accusation of my betrayal of the motherland "to serve foreign interests."

But my grief at these slanders and accusations is not so acute as my grief at the present very unfortunate fate of our country which is being wantonly ravaged by the group of traitors and renegades who have unbridledly imposed on the nation a dictatorship (after having violated and thrown overboard the Constitution of the Kingdom) and is leading our country straight to anarchism and war provoked by U.S. imperialism. Our country of Khmer had been known in the world as an oasis of peace and stability (for many years up to the eve of the crisis created by men of the March 1970 coup d'etat).

At present the liberty, democracy, relative prosperity, unity and national union which our people enjoyed not long ago have all been destroyed, reduced to nothing.

Our soldiers have been ordered to give up defending the frontiers and the country's territory to set themselves against their own compatriots and ruthlessly repress all those who dare to show even the slightest verbal opposition to the new fascist power which serves U.S. imperialism.

This is not an accusation made by me but an obvious fact seen by all clear-sighted observers in the world.

The Lon Nol–Sisowath Sirik Matak–Cheng Heng clique declared that I was a "traitor" and that I had "sold out" my country to foreign countries, because I wanted to make our nation avoid, on the one hand, losing its good reputation of wisdom and maturity and, on the other, running into great danger in the future by provoking recklessly and with undue hostility socialist Viet Nam which the U.S.A., the richest and biggest military power of the world, failed to bring to its knees.

My devotion and loyalty to the nation have become a crime of high treason owing to the "good will" of my enemies.

However, their "condemnation" does not disturb me much since they themselves are genuine renegades who have insatiable greed for power, wealth and fame, and are mere cowards who only dare to attack Sihanouk in his absence and stab him in the back.

Therefore this despicable clique will not be able to affect me or make me fall back from my unshakable determination to defend the supreme and long-term interests of my motherland and her liberty.

The millions of Khmers at home and the thousands of Khmers abroad will certainly very soon uphold the banner of revolt against the reactionary Lon Nol–Sirik Matak–Cheng Heng clique and its masters—the U.S. imperialists. The patriotic Khmers will overthrow these traitors and drive their accomplices and their U.S. masters out of our country. After victory, our patriots will build up a new Kampuchea whose power will remain forever in the hands of the progressive, industrious and pure working people, who will ensure that our motherland will have a bright future with social justice, equality and fraternity among all Khmers.*

The treason, cowardice, slanders and the despicable attacks by the reactionaries have opened my eyes and made me painfully aware of my unpardonable naivety and my misjudgement which made me believe that a free, democratic, peaceful, prosperous and happy country could be built with the help of such notorious personages, the corrupt bourgeois elements and princes, fascists, reactionaries as those making up the present "government" and "parliament" of Phnom Penh.

The "heavy blow" they dealt me and are still dealing me serves as a painful but very useful lesson to me, a lesson I will never forget all my life.

In view of this misjudgement, I should resign the function as Head of State after our people's certain victory over their enemies, reactionary oppressors and their masters—the U.S. imperialists. And on that very occasion I will give our progressive youth and working people the possibility of fully assuming the responsibility of national construction and defence with the co-operation of the entire nation.

In the present circumstances my task has not yet been fulfilled, because I will never allow the treacherous reactionaries, with the backing of the power of U.S. dollars and at bayonet point, to go on wantonly trampling underfoot the ideals, laws and basic principles of the state with impunity.

And it is in this spirit that I solemnly declare as follows:

1) In my capacity as legal Head of State of Cambodia, a supreme position given me by the Khmer people unanimously, I irrevocably dissolve the Lon Nol government and the two chambers of parliament who have betrayed their constitutional oaths and the Constitution of the Kingdom.

2) I call on all my compatriots and all the foreigners residing in Cambodia not to recognize and carry out the decrees *(prakas, kret)*, laws *(kram)*, orders, messages, circulars, judgements, all kinds of decisions, and verdicts—"works" which the Lon Nol–Sirik Matak–Cheng Heng clique and their

---

* *Editor's note:* "Kampuchea" is the romanized spelling for the name of the country in the native tongue. "Cambodge" is the French derivation, and from the French name comes the English, "Cambodia."

accomplices or servants have produced or are going to produce.

3) A new National Union Government will be established. A Provisional Consultative Assembly will also be established (for assisting the government), whose members will be qualified representatives from all circles of the Khmer society (monks, peasants and farmers, workers and other labourers, merchants, industrialists, armymen, policemen, provincial guard, youth and intellectuals, functionaries, women, etc. . .).

4) A National Liberation Army will be formed.

5) All Khmer people at home and abroad (the clergy and laymen, armymen and civilians, men and women)— who cherish the ideals of independence, democracy, neutrality, progress, socialism, Buddhism and nationalism, and stand for territorial integrity of the country within her existing frontiers, anti-imperialism and anti-neo-colonialism—will unite, to form a united front under the official name "the National United Front of Kampuchea" (Abbreviation: "FUNK").

The essential tasks of the FUNK consist in:

1) Liberate our motherland from the dictatorship and oppression by the reactionary and pro-imperialist Lon Nol–Sirik Matak–Cheng Heng clique.

2) Struggle against the U.S. imperialists who have invaded our Indo-China and are oppressing its peoples and breeding injustice, war and all kinds of calamities, hostility and disunity, troubles, crises and misery among our three peoples— the Khmers, Vietnamese and Laotians; and this struggle will be waged side by side with the socialist, progressive, anti-imperialist countries or peoples, far and near, with their complete support.

3) Rebuild our country and make her advance as rapidly as possible along the road of progress following our victory over our enemies. This task of reconstruction is to be accomplished by all of us, the Khmers, in comradeship, solidarity and perfect unity as in times of hard fight.

I am longing very much for my beloved motherland which is and will always remain the sole purpose of my life.

I also miss very much my poor mother, our Buddhist clergy and our beloved people.

If I am not to die in the struggle our patriotic and progressive people and ourselves are going to wage together, I will surely salute and embrace them when we win inevitable victory over the imperialists and their lackeys.

In the course of this struggle I call on all those of my children (compatriots), military and civilian, who can no longer endure the unjust oppression by the traitors and who have the courage and patriotic spirit needed for liberating the motherland, to engage in guerrilla warfare in the jungle against our enemies.

If you are armed and have already mastered military skills, I will provide you at opportune moments with munitions and new arms. If you do not yet have arms but wish to acquire military skills, I will take necessary measures to send you to the military school of the National United Front of our Kampuchea, which is being established way out from your barracks and villages and this is for the purpose that the enemy will not be able to reach or locate it.

Those of my children (compatriots) who live in and around Europe and wish to serve the motherland and the people by joining the Liberation Army or the National United Front of Kampuchea, please come to call on me in Moscow or Peking.

Long live Cambodia!

N. Sihanouk, March 23, 1970

Message to Buddhist Believers by Lon Nol

[Text] I address this appeal to my fellow countrymen who are Buddhist believers. It is believed that our religion will last 5,000 years. We are now at 2,500, right in the middle of the Buddhist era. It is also believed that the Buddhist religion will prosper during the next 500 years. According to an oracle, the current war in Cambodia is a religious war. Our religion is Buddhism. We have our bonzes [monks], our prayers, our disciplines, and our belief that good will be rewarded and ill will be punished. The communists do not believe in religion because they do not believe in the existence of Buddha. When they want to realize a plan of theirs, they do not hesitate to kill to attain their objective, with little concern for justice and morality.

For the present, our Vietnamese brothers will have to return to South Vietnam. But Vietnamese women who are married to Cambodians and possess official marriage certificates are Khmer nationals. They will be considered pure Khmers, but if they collaborate with the Viet Cong, they will be arrested and punished, as other Khmer nationals will if they act as accomplices of the enemy. They will be punished according to our laws. If they want to give up their Khmer nationality and return to Vietnam, they will be allowed to do so. Houses abandoned by the departing Vietnamese will be taken care of by their neighbors in cooperation with our authorities. We must not do anything that contradicts Buddhism. The property in each house [abandoned by the Vietnamese] will be registered by a national committee.

I wish to inform my fellow countrymen who are Buddhist believers that an oracle has predicted that everybody will enjoy equal rights. Everybody will be happy and good when this religious war ends. But while the war is still going on you must respect your religion and pray. Those who follow this advice will be spared all misfortune and will be rewarded with security and prosperity. The oracle who predicted a religious war in the middle of this Buddhist era said that gold and silver palaces will be erected in the middle of the four branches of the Mekong, and that there will be killing in the middle of the four branches of the Mekong. This means the enemy of Buddha will kill the religious people. Then the bad king will flee, and a comet will appear.

When the war ends, everybody will enjoy equal rights, and Cambodia will become a Khmer republic. Democratic power will be put in the hands of the people. The leader of the country will no longer be called king, but the president of the republic, who will be chosen every 5 years by the people. And anybody can stand as a candidate for this post. This choice will be made peacefully through electoral procedures, and not by means of war to gain power among us. Everybody will be equal because there will be no kings. Everybody will enjoy equal rights because our children and the children of others will have the right to stand as candidates in a presidential election.

I would like now to inform you of an affair and ask you

to judge for yourselves. Sihanouk was legally deposed by our National Assembly at the moment he was en route to Peking as an honored guest of China. But Peking did not break the diplomatic relations with Phnom Penh immediately; it waited a long time to let its representatives see me and ask if our government would continue aiding North Vietnam as it had done in the past. China said it would consider the Sihanouk affair with the Khmer authorities an internal affair of Cambodia, forget about Sihanouk, and continue to respect our authority provided: 1) we continued to permit the supply of arms and medicine from China to North Vietnamese and Viet Cong troops—as we had done in the past—so they could continue the war against South Vietnam; 2) we continued to allow North Vietnamese and Viet Cong troops to rest in Khmer territory; and 3) we continued to use our propaganda to support its friends.

After trying to contact me several times up through 5 May 1970—one month and 20 days after Sihanouk was deposed as chief of state—China decided it would not gain satisfaction. It then simultaneously proclaimed the rupture of diplomatic relations with Cambodia and the formal recognition of Sihanouk.

These facts show: 1) That the current war in our country is not a war between Sihanouk and the Cambodian people. China only wants Cambodia to aid the Vietnamese [communists] and does not care much about Sihanouk.

When the Khmer people refused to abandon their Buddhist morality and to aid the Viet Cong aggressors, the war broke out in accordance with plans mapped out by the Chinese and North Vietnamese communists. China does not love Sihanouk; it is using him as a tool to help the Viet Cong wage the war in our country with a view to transforming it into a communist base of war in Southeast Asia.

2) The current war is a religious war. It is said that our Buddhist religion will last for another 2,500 years. When this war ends, the people of the Cambodian republic will enjoy equal rights and prosperity. That is what the oracle said. The same oracle also said that other religions must help Cambodia—a Buddhist country—struggle against the enemy of Buddha.

To make it easy to understand, according to Buddhist religion, there must be a war—a war against the Vietnamese communists who consider religion their enemy. The Khmer people—who practice the Buddhist religion—must avoid all bloodshed among themselves. We must maintain our solidarity. In this religious war against the Vietnamese communists—who are the enemies of Buddha—there are many Buddhists who will have to come to help us. Our country will win final victory on the battlefield, as predicted by the oracle. Therefore we Buddhist believers must rise up together to struggle against the enemy who is committing the war of aggression in our country.

10

The Regime of Lon Nol

by Jonathan S. Grant

The coup d'etat which removed Prince Norodom Sihanouk from power ushered in a new and uncertain era in Cambodia's history. The days of quiet and inconspicuous coexistence with the superpowers quickly disappeared, and the once peaceful nation of the Khmers became a ravaged battlefield, a focus of world attention and hostilities, and the fulcrum on which the balance of powers wavered. With all hopes of neutrality extinguished, the question of Cambodia's future became inextricably interwoven with the fate of Vietnam and, indeed, of all Indochina.

During the first month and a half of the new regime, from the March 18 coup to the April 30 sanctuary invasion, Cambodians lived in a twilight zone. The normal patterns of life continued with apparent regularity, interrupted only by tales of war, promises of prosperity, and the occasional passing of soldiers. Only the "political" arrests of ethnic Vietnamese and the scattered civilian massacres revealed the jarring edge of the government's dreams of prosperity. In Phnom Penh people bustled between shops displaying the customary Vietnamese and Cambodian advertisements, only partially aware of the government's looming problems. From official pronouncements came word of skirmishes in the countryside, but the realities of modern war in Indochina were yet to be understood. Only after the massive sanctuary invasion did the real dimensions of Cambodia's plight become evident to its citizens. Thousands of South Vietnamese troops poured into the major cities, often looting as they came, and the incredible fire power of American air support began to carve its relentless path across the countryside.

The coup unleashed a chain of events which were largely

Jonathan S. Grant is a graduate student in Modern East Asian History and a Fellow of the Center for Chinese Studies at the University of California, Berkeley.

engineered by the new government and its army. This tenuous control, however, both symbolically and effectively was
lost when the Americans and South Vietnamese unilaterally
invaded without the prior consent of the Cambodian government.[1] In response to the sanctuary invasion, the Vietnamese Communists withdrew from their confined positions
along the border. Moving further into Cambodia, they joined
with the small indigenous Cambodian Communist movement
to rapidly organize and mobilize the peasantry. Thus a latent
civil war quickly matured between Lon Nol's government in
Phnom Penh and Prince Sihanouk's rural-based National
United Front of Cambodia. However, this Cambodian conflict soon became subsidiary to the struggle between the National United Front and the South Vietnamese and Americans.
By the June 30 withdrawal of American ground forces, the
Cambodian government controlled only the larger towns and
at best half of the countryside.

The weeks preceding the invasion marked a period of
political turmoil in which the new government attempted to
solidify its support. Through promises of economic prosperity,
its leaders wooed the traditional elite and the urban community. They predicted that the denationalization of the
economic structure and the encouragement of private enterprise would provide increased incomes and job opportunities
for all Cambodians. They proceeded to end government mon-
opolies in most manufacturing industries and to allow bank
interest rates to increase.[2] The economy also would be in-
vigorated by the introduction of foreign investment capital.
Toward the implementation of this goal the government received in early April approval of a $1.6 billion loan for
hydroelectric and other development from the Asia Development Bank, representing primarily Japanese and American
capital.[3] In addition to seeking support through economic
programs, the administration attempted to instill a new spirit
of national purpose and identity by promising to repulse the
Vietnamese Communists from the border regions. Thus the
government attempted to justify an increase in expenditure
for the military in the newly enlarged budget. These economic
and military programs were complementary, for by asserting
its "active" neutrality through an anti-Communist campaign,
Cambodia would most certainly attract American support.

Domestically, the new government gained backing primarily from the army, the urban businessmen, and wage earners, the professional groups such as teachers and bureaucrats, and the students who were largely scions of the middle class. Because the coup was conservative in nature, it was generally accepted by the ruling elite. The initial programs of the government fundamentally accepted the existing political structure, while acidly criticizing Prince Sihanouk's often authoritarian and independent actions while in power. Although a republic was founded on April 10, the political configuration was essentially unaltered. Denationalization of the economy did not mean a redistribution of economic power away from the traditional elite, but rather a transfer of that power from state bureaucratic control to free enterprise management. With the exception of some minor purges, the personnel remained the same. Although Lon Nol and Matak did not succeed in changing the pro-Sihanouk allegiance of the peasantry, they managed to rally support where it was most available and to harshly repress opposition when it arose.

Although Prince Sihanouk in exile claimed that three battalions of the Royal Cambodian Army defected from the new government,[4] the support of the army was almost completely behind the new regime. Only fifteen officers were removed from their commands after the coup. The army possessed not only a professional loyalty to its commanding general, Lon Nol, but a desire to benefit from the U.S. military aid which would surely result from a pro-American policy. The army staff remembered fondly the bountiful days of American aid before 1963 when Sihanouk terminated the military assistance program. By 1970 the equipment of the Cambodian army was obsolete by the standards of contemporary war in Indochina. From a professional military perspective, if Cambodia's army was to obtain a position of strength relative to that of South Vietnam, Laos, and Thailand, a dramatic improvement in military equipment was necessary. Furthermore, Sihanouk's neutralist policy placed the army in an untenable position by instructing it to resist American air strikes on Cambodian territory through which Vietnamese Communists were permitted to pass. This predicament is illustrated by an incident in November 1969, when the loss of an American fighter-bomber was attributed to Cambodian antiaircraft fire. The Americans retaliated with a heavy aerial attack that killed twenty-seven Cambodians. In explaining the coup d'etat a military spokesman referred to this incident as an example of the reasons for opposing Sihanouk's policy.[5]

To ensure the support of the urban commercial and wage-earning groups, the new government translated the future benefits of increased investment and gradual industrial development into promises of imminent prosperity. Reports in the press indicate that these promises were taken at face value and readily believed. At Sihanoukville's luxurious Hotel Independence a desk clerk commented, "This is a state-run hotel. So we will all be getting raises soon. Lon Nol has promised it." A restaurant manager in Kep who was told that his food was so good he should move his business to Singapore replied, "Oh no, no need to do that now. With the new government Kep is soon going to become a major resort. We will have plenty of customers and money." For the poorer urban workers, the prospects of a burgeoning, well-financed army stirred excitement. A pedicab driver stated, "Before, this was the only job I could get. Now at least I can go into the army. They will give me a uniform and a gun and a few thousand riels a month. I can send the money to my family."[6] Thus the government's vision of prosperity for managers and workers and of enlarged opportunities through free enterprise appealed to the personal hopes of one segment of the Cambodian people.

The new government was also able to rally a large following among the students. Dissatisfied with the prospect of low-paying jobs and the inability of the stagnating economy to fulfill their aspirations, the students were easily organized behind the government cause. This is evidenced by the numerous reports of their participation in pro-government demonstrations. Large groups of students participated indirectly in the sacking of the North Vietnamese and Viet Cong embassies. They organized a march in front of the National Assembly carrying signs hostile to the NLF and demanding the departure of Vietcong forces from Cambodia, and they posted anti-Sihanouk posters around the city.[7] The strength of student support was further indicated by the government's reliance on them to explain to the populace the meaning of Sihanouk's fall and the aspirations of the new regime. At the end of March classes for the 100,000 high school and 30,000 to 40,000 university students in Phnom Penh were suspended to facilitate their political activities and in order to hastily organize students and faculty into an unpaid home guard. This mobilization had all the features of a festival, with ebullient students in unmatching fatigues drill-training without guns or other equipment.[8] By the middle of April hundreds of students could be seen in the streets of Phnom Penh with suitcases and bags setting out to join the army.[9]

In contrast to this show of support, however, there was widespread opposition in the rural areas. Sihanouk had often gone into the fields to talk with farmers and occasionally had taken a turn at the plow. Some of the peasantry still viewed him as the traditional god-king, a legitimacy not readily destroyed by a mere coup. Pro-Sihanouk demonstrations sprouted throughout the countryside. In Kompong Cham province, workers on a 17,000-acre rubber plantation went out on strike, carrying pictures of Sihanouk and shouting slogans demanding his return.[10] Cambodians living near the Vietnamese border in Svay Rieng province launched a series of daily demonstrations. In Siem Riep near the famous ruins of Angkor Wat, pro-Sihanouk and anti-American protests by the local farmers were widespread. Where once American tourists had been welcome, they now had to fear for their lives.[11] From all over the country busloads of pro-Sihanouk demonstrators tried to reach the capital, Phnom Penh, to make their voices heard.

In many instances the government's response to gestures of opposition was harsh. On March 26, for example, several thousand demonstrators arrived at the outskirts of the capital in buses and trucks carrying pictures of the prince and singing patriotic songs. Although most of them dispersed, at least 30 were killed when soldiers opened fire. In another instance, peasant youths marched from the countryside to Kompong Cham, where they shouted demands for the return of Sihanouk and sacked a government building, destroying documents and files. In response the Cambodian army was ordered to open fire, and the government reported 27 killed and 62 wounded. The following day in the southern province of Takeo about 3,000 demonstrators spread through the town, stopping cars to paint "Long live Sihanouk" on the doors and to distribute portraits of the prince. Again the army opened fire and again civilians were killed. At Koki, 20 kilometers west of Phnom Penh, additional protests in favor of the prince oc-

curred; the army encircled the village, evacuated the populace, and killed 10.[12]

It is significant to note that student support of the new
government was not affected by these massacres. In Kompong
Cham the protesting peasants failed to enlist the support of
university students.[13] As one professor in the capital observed,
"The students are not against this [the shooting of peasants]
because they know that the Vietcong are behind it."[14]
Whether or not the government reports claiming the demonstrations were organized by the Vietcong are true, it is clear
that considerable antigovernment dissent existed among the
peasantry. Because the government was concurrently attacking the ethnic Vietnamese minority in Cambodia on the dubious claim that they were Communist collaborators, the government had logical propaganda reasons for insisting that the
peasant demonstrations were simply manipulations of the
people by the Vietcong.

Although the new government found a receptive audience
among businessmen, salaried workers, and students, it lacked
a basis for appeal to the peasantry. Lon Nol and Matak were
confronted with the formidable task of displacing Sihanouk's
reputation as a nationalist leader and acquiring that image
for themselves. In an attempt to achieve a broad expression
of national purpose which would outdo Sihanouk and simultaneously transcend urban and rural differences, the administration began a campaign to persecute the ethnic Vietnamese
minority that lived in Cambodia. It hoped to inflame the
traditional animosities which existed between the Khmers and
the Vietnamese and create a new nationalism based on anti-
Vietnamese sentiment. By insinuating that all of Cambodia's
Vietnamese were Communists or Communist sympathizers,
the Lon Nol regime hoped to wed this deeply rooted hostility
to the government's anti-Communist campaign. The government pursued this task ruthlessly until the massive intrusion
of South Vietnamese troops during the sanctuary invasion.

Animosity between the Khmers and the Vietnamese has its
origins in century-old conflicts. When French Indochina was
formally subdivided into Laos, Cambodia, and Vietnam in
1954, some 400,000 Vietnamese found their homes to be
within the boundaries of the independent Cambodian nation.
Because of the feelings of animosity between these two peoples, the Vietnamese lived clustered together in urban neigh-

borhoods and villages. As a major commercial class in Cambodia, they benefited from the growing illegal rice trade with the Vietcong. However, this does not mean they were pro-Communist. Because they were petty merchants, rich peasants, skilled laborers, and clerks, and thus members of the bourgeois class, they were largely opposed to Communism.[15] Furthermore, about 10 percent of these Vietnamese were Roman Catholics, among whom even less sympathy for communism existed. The Khmer people, nevertheless, resented not only the different cultural pattern of the Vietnamese, but also the monopoly over the commercial sector of society which they shared with the Chinese minority. The ethnic Vietnamese had long been viewed as aggressive and often exploitative in their relations with the Cambodians.

Since the days of French rule, Prince Sihanouk, in the pursuit of domestic tranquility, had practiced a policy of accommodation toward the Vietnamese living within his country, and managed to keep traditional resentments submerged. In contrast, the Lon Nol government proceeded to whip up this latent hatred in order to rally popular support for the regime and for its anti-Communist campaign. Following the ouster of Prince Sihanouk, "Vietcong" became a catchword applied indiscriminately to all the 400,000 Vietnamese in Cambodia. Signs appeared in the streets announcing, "We must kill all Vietnamese in Cambodia."[16] In addition, the government circulated inflammatory tracts denouncing the "traditional enemy," and encouraged students to perform dramas depicting Cambodians beating Vietnamese.[17] As the regime increased its "selective arrests" of Vietnamese civilians both in Phnom Penh and the countryside, detention camps grew and massacres occurred.

By slandering and persecuting the Vietnamese minority as Communists or Communist sympathizers, the government hoped to create a tangible reference for the rather distant and unknown military campaign against the Vietnamese Communists on the border. Most Cambodians had never seen a Vietcong soldier; and because of Sihanouk's sympathy for the Communists in Vietnam, the Cambodian populace had no strong predisposition toward their new enemy. Therefore, the government had to act to identify ethnic hostilities with the enemy. The ruthless manner by which the government executed this campaign is informative of the character of its rule and deserves a brief examination.

Shortly after the coup, Cambodian police rounded up approximately 30,000 Vietnamese and after a rough screening, about 7,000 were kept in jail, where some were summarily executed to intimidate the others.[18] On April 10, eighty-nine Vietnamese were killed in the village of Prasaut by the Cambodian army. The wounded were given no medical aid, and those who did not bleed to death were held as Vietcong suspects or as relatives of suspects.[19] In another instance, 800 Vietnamese men, most of them Catholics who worked as building-trade laborers in Phnom Penh, had been taken from their village of Chrui Changwar. They were herded onto boats, shot, and dumped into the river.[20] In the town of Takeo, American journalists who chanced upon the scene of a massacre and who hoped their presence would protect the remaining villagers were told by the Cambodian troops that all ethnic Vietnamese were being assumed to be Vietcong.[21]

The news of these massacres aroused widespread disfavor among most diplomats and foreigners. In response to international criticism, the Cambodian government hastily instructed its soldiers not to speak to newsmen and to keep reporters away from detention centers, at gunpoint if necessary.[22] The official excuses repeatedly claimed that the Vietnamese were caught in crossfire or were murdered by the Vietcong, and the government insisted that it was not engaged in an anti-Vietnamese campaign. But on April 27 the Lon Nol regime admitted that more than 3,500 noncombatants, many of them Vietnamese civilians, had been killed during the past month.[23]

In addition to these mass executions, the government developed detention centers for the internment of "political prisoners." Under the guise of repatriation to South Vietnam, Lon Nol began to round up the over 100,000 ethnic Vietnamese who lived in Phnom Penh and nearby towns and place them in detention camps, which suffered from severe overcrowding and insufficient food. The government proceeded to seize Vietnamese houses and distribute them to Cambodians.[24] Any Vietnamese who chose to remain in Cambodia would be assumed to be a Communist sympathizer and shot.[25]

This repressive government scheme had striking parallels to the situation in Indonesia after Suharto's military coup deposed President Sukarno. In Indonesia the army declared that the commercially powerful Chinese minority was Communist and massacred many, thereby unleashing deep-seated popular hostilities and channeling them into support for the new regime. It is perhaps significant that in late 1969 a group of Cambodian army officers reportedly went to Indonesia to study this process in depth.[26] Although the antiminority scheme evidently elicited active participation by some Indonesian civilians, the effect of the anti-Vietnamese campaign on the attitudes of the Cambodian people is difficult to assess. There were no reported instances of Cambodian civilians attacking ethnic Vietnamese, and there were no indications of such hostility. Nevertheless, in the cities anti-Vietnamese emotions were probably aroused. By making the Khmers suspicious of any Vietnamese as a probable collaborator, the government may well have sensitized the urban populace to the presence of a Vietnamese menace without involving them in the anti-Communist warfare itself. Anti-Vietnamese sentiment perhaps contributed to the polarization of many Cambodians behind the government's nationalistic and xenophobic war. The persecutions have probably served to transfer a traditional hostility to a Communist Vietnamese enemy. Although the importance of this factor in the rise of nationalism among the urban populace must remain a matter of speculation, enthusiasm for the fight against the Vietnamese Communists grew, especially among the students in Phnom Penh. Thus the Royal Cambodian Army could count on new recruits, but they in turn simply exacerbated the fundamental problem of inadequate equipment and training. The military, indeed, was hopelessly unprepared for the task it had set for itself.

At the outset of Lon Nol's campaign to force the Vietnamese Communists out of Cambodia many observers perceived it as a honeymoon with disaster. Militarily the 35,000-man Cambodian army had no realistic chance of defeating the alleged 40,000 North Vietnamese and Vietcong troops in northeastern and eastern Cambodia. Although Wilfred Burchett claimed that before the coup large numbers of Special Forces-trained and -equipped mercenaries from the right-wing Cambodian Khmer Serei had been quietly incorporated into the Royal Cambodian Army, the army's overall combat weakness was transparently evident.[27] Military training still followed French instruction manuals designed for World War II, not for counterinsurgency in Indochina. Ammunition, guns, uniforms, and logistics equipment were all inadequate. The tiny Cambodian air force did not even possess napalm, let alone modern rockets, antipersonnel bombs, or defoliants. But it was anticipated that such would soon be acquired from the United States.

Regardless of the government's rhetoric of complete victory, the program followed by Lon Nol suggested a much more modest and realistic objective. After the government organized the sacking of the Vietcong and North Vietnamese embassies, Lon Nol concentrated on a diplomatic effort to dislodge the Vietnamese Communist troops. Soon thereafter, government spokesmen began speaking of a reactivation of the International Control Commission of the United Nations as a means of resolving the conflict.[28] Had a settlement supervised by the United Nations been accomplished, Lon Nol might well have succeeded in eliciting American military and economic aid, while largely avoiding the human and economic destruction wrought by an extended war.

Shortly before the coup, the new government pledged to use political, diplomatic, and international pressure to confront the Vietnamese Communists. Yet, conspicuously, no mention was made of a military effort.[29] On March 13 Lon Nol gave the Communists an ultimatum to evacuate Cambodia within 48 hours. Actual negotiations did not begin until three days later, and by March 18 they had reached an impasse. The Cambodian government claimed that the North Vietnamese were unwilling to discuss the issue of withdrawal and instead requested property compensation for their damaged embassy.[30] The Cambodian government then attempted to apply limited force by attacking North Vietnamese troops who had failed to meet the March 16 withdrawal deadline.[31] The fighting, however, was largely a symbolic gesture, and General Lon Nol never launched a major attack on the Vietnamese forces. Nevertheless, Lon Nol's combination of diplomatic and military pressure was not without success, for reports soon indicated that some Communist units were withdrawing from Cambodia into South Vietnam.[32]

During the negotiations, however, Cambodia abandoned its neutrality and embarked on a series of joint operations with the South Vietnamese army. The South Vietnamese were eager to form such an alliance, and Lon Nol probably thought the South Vietnamese would contribute to the fighting without reducing his power. On the day of the coup, South Vietnamese artillery fire was coordinated to aid Cambodian troops in another minor battle with Vietnamese Communists near the border. The day after the coup, five meetings between Cambodian and South Vietnamese officers took place to coordinate attacks on the Vietcong. An American military advisor attended at least one meeting. ARVN air strikes quickly followed. On March 27–28 three battalions of South Vietnamese Rangers swept more than two miles into Cambodia to join Cambodian troops in an attack on a Vietcong hideout. Ninety-four Vietcong were killed and three captured.[33] At least five other similar incursions, some including American advisors, preceded the massive April 30 sanctuary invasion.[34] These joint operations were due largely to South Vietnamese initiative and occurred primarily in the Parrot's Beak area, where there were only transient units of Vietcong. To the Communists, however, the Cambodian–Saigon military entente provocatively demonstrated the growing pro-American stance of the Lon Nol government.

Fighting continued throughout the first six weeks of the new government's rule, although largely confined to the eastern border province of Svay Rieng. Even though the Communists were stronger in this area, they did not move beyond the informal deadlock line at Prasaut, some six miles from the South Vietnam border.[35] A military source in Phnom Penh refuted the exaggerated claims that the Communists were launching a massive assault from the northeast sanctuaries: "If you had a map with red pins in it representing communist troops and their positions, nothing much would be changed since the ouster of Sihanouk."[36] Nevertheless, isolated attacks by the Vietcong and pro-Sihanouk soldiers occurred sporadically in the south, the northeast, and occasionally near the capital. By the second week in April the Cambodian government was proclaiming that Vietcong columns were marching on Phnom Penh. These claims proved erroneous and a careful examination of the battle accounts reveals only small bands of Vietcong harassing military outposts. The most celebrated instance occurred at the town of Saang, where some 150 enemy soldiers occupied the town for three days before retreating into the night.[37] The government portrayed this incident as a major threat to the capital in an apparent attempt to elicit military aid from the United States. In this task the government was partially successful, for two days later President Nixon agreed to send small arms to the beleaguered nation.[38] Had the Communists decided to attack in full force, all observers in Cambodia agreed that they could easily have overrun most of the country. However, the Communists were guided by their major concern with the war in Vietnam and refrained from a major diversion of man power and energy into Cambodia. By mid-April the fighting had leveled off, leaving the Communists in control of their northeast sanctuary and the border areas through which they had previously operated.[39]

Although the new government had reached a partial stabilization of the military situation, the destruction of war had a strong impact on the countryside. The heavy-handed tactics of the Cambodian army were a long-standing grievance in some areas of the country, and had been a major source of contention during the 1967 rebellion in Battambang province. During the April anti-Communist skirmishing this was drastically intensified, and led to the embitterment of many peasants. For example, artillery and air attacks were used extensively during the three-day counterattack at Saang, inflicting considerable damage. After the Vietcong withdrew, the Cambodian army entered the town and proceeded to loot and burn the shops.[40] In another incident Cambodian MIGs bombed villages in Svay Rieng province in an attempt to eradicate the Vietcong. A group of subsequently homeless peasants began to march toward the provincial capital to protest the destruction, but were stopped by Cambodian army units who fired on them with 75 millimeter recoilless rifles, killing many. The fighting led to the disruption of economic life, and the extensive black market trade which had developed in the border areas also became a casualty of the war. Peasant dissatisfaction multiplied, although the number of people affected was relatively small until the sanctuary invasion.

By the end of April, the new Cambodian government had made a strenuous effort to heighten nationalist sentiment, to suppress dissent among the peasantry, and to rally support among the ruling elite and the urban Cambodian populace. In the military arena the Royal Cambodian Army had demonstrated the obvious: that it was hopelessly ill equipped and lacked the fighting initiative which develops from thorough training and drilled courage. Although the Cambodian troops were clearly unable to resist a full-scale offensive by Vietcong, North Vietnamese, and Khmer Rouge forces, the Vietnamese Communists had chosen to avoid a major confrontation and the diversion of resources that would result. Reports of impending attacks on Phnom Penh turned out to be false, for the skirmishes near the capital were primarily a demonstration that the Communists could successfully harass almost at will. By mid-April, although the Cambodian government's position was far from secure, there were some grounds for hope that a settlement could be made under the auspices of the International Control Commission. It was anticipated that the upcoming Djakarta conference of pro-American Asian nations would help implement such a stabilization.

Two weeks before the Djakarta conference convened, the situation in Cambodia was drastically changed when the United States and South Vietnam embarked on the sanctuary invasion. A major effect was that the North Vietnamese and Vietcong troops were forced to withdraw deeper into Cambodia, where they rapidly began to mobilize the Cambodian peasantry for a war of national liberation. Another effect was to deny the Cambodian government its principal nationalistic theme—opposition to the Vietnamese. Before the invasion the only Vietnamese in Cambodia were its ethnic minority and the Vietnamese Communists, and around this situation Lon Nol had succeeded in arousing some patriotic support. But with the arrival of heavily concentrated South Vietnamese troops on Cambodian soil, this rallying focus was undermined.

Although the April 30 invasion was intended solely to attack and destroy the enemy sanctuaries, the South Vietnamese quickly seized the opportunity to move beyond the border sanctuary area and to advance to the urban centers of the country. Their participation in the defense of the capital was not critical, for the United States had flown mercenaries into Phnom Penh from South Vietnam. The gunboat flotilla which sailed over one hundred miles into Cambodia served the triple purpose of securing the Mekong from Com-

munist harassment, transporting the persecuted Vietnamese
back to refugee camps in South Vietnam, and securing for
the ARVN troops a major presence in Cambodia.

The Lon Nol government soon found itself in a very difficult position in relation to the South Vietnamese. Following
the sanctuary invasion the South Vietnamese army steadily
augmented its troop strength in Cambodia to a total of 40,000
soldiers, a force larger than that of the entire Cambodian
army. The anti-Vietnamese campaign, which Lon Nol had
initiated in order to rally support, began to backfire. ARVN
troops who arrived at Prasaut, where there had been a massacre of ethnic Vietnamese, wrote anti-Cambodian slogans
on the charred walls.[41] An American journalist reported that
South Vietnamese troops appeared pleased with the prospect
of being able to kill Khmers.[42] On the other hand, in Phnom
Penh Cambodian hostility erupted and a Vietnamese corporal
from the gunboat flotilla was bludgeoned to death and two
other soldiers and a diplomat were injured.[43] Antagonism
between the two groups became widespread.

The Cambodian government soon fell under pressure from
Saigon to alter its political programs. The regime quickly
halted its persecution of the Vietnamese minority, announcing that any such acts would be severely punished. Other
concessions, such as compensation for the loss of Vietnamese
property, were exacted.[44] Intense negotiations began over the
definition of Cambodia's territorial boundaries, which had
never been recognized by South Vietnam. Even though the
South Vietnamese government claimed two islands which had
long been administered by Cambodia, a confrontation was
avoided through an agreement that any area administered by
either of the two countries would be recognized as territory
belonging to that country.[45] Subsequently, Saigon developed
a plan to relocate the ethnic Vietnamese held in the detention
camps to areas within Cambodia along their mutual border.
These people would live under the "security" provided by
ARVN forces stationed indefinitely in the area, and the
refugees would receive American aid funds to supplement
earnings derived from working for the ARVN units.[46] Although this plan implied a future loss of Cambodian territory,
the program was only partially implemented.

Although the new Cambodian government became rapidly
dependent on the South Vietnamese military presence, the

ARVN troops adversely affected Lon Nol's already limited support. Many Cambodians viewed the troops as an unwelcome occupation force. In addition, the spread of warfare throughout Cambodia engaged the South Vietnamese troops in the inevitable destruction of the Cambodian countryside. South Vietnamese air force planes bombed and strafed a rubber-processing plant at Chup, killing 15 and wounding 80. An hour later the planes returned for another attack, dropping napalm and wounding several persons attempting to aid the previously wounded.[47] The populace was further alienated by the widespread practice of ARVN troops of looting the towns they had liberated. At Kompong Speu, the South Vietnamese troops went so far as to demand watches and rings from the town's inhabitants.[48] Indeed, the conduct of ARVN against the Cambodian citizenry was so offensive that the American military publicly remonstrated with President Thieu.

The destructive impact of the war in Cambodia was also intensified by the intrusion of American troops and air power. American B52 saturation bombing became the customary prelude to all major operations. After one such preparatory aerial raid for an ARVN operation, American advisors found the bodies of 33 civilian victims.[49] At Sre Khtum and Snoul, Communist resistance elicited massive American artillery and aerial attacks which literally destroyed the towns. In Snoul American troops looted cases of liquor, a motor bike, and a tractor.[50] These realities of war could not help but alienate the local populace. At a French rubber plantation 1,600 laborers caught in the path of the American invasion were given arms by the North Vietnamese and fled with them. The plantation manager, a Frenchman, said, "We cannot stay. The Americans have been here and now nobody would ever trust us again."[51] After the destruction of the town of Mimot by American air power, one Cambodian soldier commented, "If one wants to help the communists, one has only to continue [this way]."[52]

Amidst the escalating warfare, the significance of the Royal Cambodian Army steadily decreased, and with it the position and influence of the Cambodian government. The National United Front steadily gained territory, and the Lon Nol government was reduced to requests for military assistance from such previous enemies as Thailand. South Vietnamese troops gained permission to move anywhere in Cambodia at will, and the Cambodian army was bolstered principally through the inclusion of greater numbers of U.S.-trained Khmer mercenaries from South Vietnam. Although the injection of these soldiers expanded the Cambodian forces, they caused disunity in the army, even though they were ethnic Khmers. On one occasion they actually engaged in a gun-battle with regular Cambodian troops in the course of a barroom brawl.[53] By June 11, reports from Phnom Penh indicated that the government had ceded half the country to the Communists. A foreign ambassador in the capital claimed that Lon Nol had admitted publicly that he had no control over the country outside of Phnom Penh.[54]

When the American ground forces withdrew at the end of June, the Lon Nol government held a precariously isolated position. The four northeastern provinces were completely under National United Front control and the government forces were harassed in most of the remainder of the country. Even the security of Phnom Penh was dependent on the continued presence of ARVN troops. American saturation bombing continued at an increased level. Perhaps most tragically for the Lon Nol government, the hopes of economic development were dashed, perhaps beyond repair. Trade was at a standstill, 90 percent of all rubber plantations had ceased to function, tourism to the famous Angkor ruins had halted, and inflation was severe. Pending foreign investments, such as a Japanese loan of 700 million yen, were being reconsidered in the light of Cambodia's instability. With financial prospects falling, support among the urban populace was certain to wane. Indeed, there was some indication that even the elite had become divided in its support for Lon Nol.[55] The illusion of a future Cambodia enjoying the fruits of foreign investment and American aid had been shattered.

Since the coup which overthrew Prince Sihanouk, Cambodia has been drawn into the maelstrom of the Vietnam War. From the beginning, the new government's attempt to weld a base of support led only to greater division. The suppression of the peasantry and the persecution of the Vietnamese minority ultimately fed the discontents which nourish civil war. With the intervention of the allied armies, the Communists gained in both popular support and territorial control. What began as a domestic struggle between Lon Nol and Sihanouk quickly emerged as the latest stage for the struggle between the free world and communism. The Cambodian people had become the unfortunate victims of an escalated war.

11

The National United Front of Cambodia

by Banning Garrett

"Armed struggle, led from the underground, is the only path that will lead our people to victory and will permit its ideals to triumph,"[1] declared Prince Sihanouk after calling for a national united front to liberate Cambodia. Armed struggle is now underway, led by Sihanouk and his former Khmer Rouge antagonists, Hu Nim, Khieu Samphan, and Hou Youn. Their strategy is one of "protracted war," but the U.S. and South Vietnamese invasion, along with Lon Nol's army, has so quickly and thoroughly alienated the rural population that the progress of the "protracted war" has been dramatically advanced.

The Lon Nol coup has also brought together the Indochinese people in a coordinated struggle, much as the Laotians and Viet Minh, and to a minor extent the Cambodians, united in 1951 to struggle against the French. On April 24 and 25 of 1970, leaders from the Pathet Lao, the NLF, North Vietnam, and the National United Front of Cambodia met in China to organize a cooperative effort against the United States and its client governments. They informally agreed to create a joint military command[2] and to hold summit meetings when necessary. However, they also declared that "inspired by the principle that the liberation and defence of each country is the affair of its own people, the different parties undertake to do everything possible to render mutual support in accordance with the desire of the interested party and on the basis of mutual respect."[3] With respect to Cambodia, this statement is very significant, for although the United States claims that Cambodia is solely the "victim" of a North Vietnamese and "Viet Cong" invasion, in fact the Vietnamese are only aiding—training and equipping—the

Banning Garrett is a graduate student in Political Science at Brandeis University and a member of the Pacific Studies Center, Palo Alto, California.

Cambodians to fight for themselves. The North Vietnamese Army could have easily overrun Cambodia militarily after the coup and installed a puppet government. This, however, as the Americans know from their own experience, would have required a large occupying army to fight against the Cambodian population. The reverse, of course, became the case: it is the United States, her allies, and the Lon Nol government who find themselves fighting against the Cambodian population. Thus, for both practical reasons (avoidance of the need for an occupying army) and for ideological reasons (the doctrine of people's war), the North Vietnamese and NLF are prepared to aid, train, and, to a decreasing extent, fight with the Cambodian Liberation Army, but they are also prepared to follow the Summit Conference doctrine that ultimately the liberation of each country is the affair of its own people. Sihanouk himself noted this in a July 3 interview with a French correspondent. The Prince stated:

> It is true that there are Vietnamese in Cambodia. But why should anyone be astonished that the Indochinese unite? In Vietnam, the Americans erased the line of demarcation and they have turned the Vietnam war into an Indochinese war. Henceforth, Indochina must be considered as a single battlefield, and the Indochinese will remain united until final victory.
>
> But the Cambodian resistance exists. I shall not let the Vietnamese liberate my country. I shall liberate it when we are ready to do so. It will be liberated by Cambodians, and Phnom Penh will be taken by Cambodians.[4]

When Sihanouk announced the formation of the National United Front (NUF), he claimed that a National Union Government would be formed which would include "qualified representatives of the Buddhist clergy, the army, the police, the provincial guard, young people, intellectuals, peasants, workers, other laborers, industrialists, shopkeepers, civil servants, women, etc., who belong to all the patriotic, progressive, anti-imperialist leaning groups."[5] In other words, everyone but traitors is encouraged to fight with the NUF—including government officials, army officers, and members of the feudal and business elite. Like the National Liberation Front in South Vietnam, the NUF appeals to members of all classes to join in fighting the United States and the unpopular government it backs.

Released by Sihanouk on May 5, the NUF program, similar to that of the NLF, is an appeal to all classes, though its emphasis is placed on peasants and workers. The program claims that the people are the source of all power and that power is and always will remain in the hands of the "working and progressive people." Furthermore, the Front is committed to building and developing an independent national economy by relying principally on the resources and productive forces of Cambodia. The economic policy guarantees to the peasants property rights to the land they cultivate, institutes an equitable program for land rents, and foresees agrarian reform and the development of mutual aid and cooperatives in the countryside. It encourages the formation of workers' unions, guarantees employment security and just pay, and guarantees social security. The NUF intends to develop industry, communication, and transportation, and to maintain the nationalization of banks and exterior commerce, while encouraging exports and limiting imports to equipment and products necessary for the needs of the national economy. The NUF also wants to ensure that education is free and is extended to the entire community.[6]

The French journalist Jacques Decornoy points out that this program combines "the traditional ideas of the chief of state [Sihanouk] concerning the nature of the regime and its foreign policy, and a catalogue of measures to take which go no further than a prudent reformism."[7] However, the organization and nature of the NUF have set in motion a social revolution which may lead beyond "prudent reformism" and "Sihanouk's traditional ideas," since the leadership and organization of the NUF come from the leftist "Khmer Rouge" ("the Cambodian equivalent of the Vietcong in South Vietnam and the Pathet Lao in Laos"[8]), which is a well-organized and experienced revolutionary movement that has been fighting in Cambodia since 1957. It is unlikely that the Khmer Rouge would be willing to return Sihanouk to power if this meant a return to the same type of government and the same economic and social system which existed before the coup.

The Khmer Rouge leaders hold the essential posts in the NUF government:[9] Hu Nim is Minister of Information and Propaganda; Khieu Samphan, Minister of National Defense;

and Hou Youn, Minister of Interior, Communal Reforms, and Cooperatives. These men were all popular deputies to the National Assembly who fled to join the Khmer Rouge in the spring of 1967. Sihanouk had denounced them publicly for their involvement in the alleged Communist conspiracy which inspired a peasant rebellion in Battambang province in April 1967,[10] and reportedly they were on Sihanouk's "liquidation" list.[11] Many urban intellectuals were arrested at that time, and others went underground and eventually joined the guerrillas.

The peasants had been forced into insurgency by actions of the government, army, and police.[12] Their main complaint was exploitation by the local administration. The peasants were asked to pay "voluntary contributions" for the building of schools and medical centers, and if a center was actually built, those who were treated there were asked to pay exorbitant prices for drugs. They were also asked to pay for receptions whenever Sihanouk visited the area. According to journalist T. J. S. George, "the last straw for the peasants was the local administration's decision to deprive them of land. This was done by [the government bureaucrats] for personal gain. For the peasants, however, it meant complete ruin. At best a typical peasant family would make barely US $15 a month; without land they could make nothing at all."[13] Apparently the April 1967 revolt was brutally repressed by the provincial guard. But "even more than the revolt itself, the repression seemed to have helped the communists. As mass killings of peasants took place in Battambang, hundreds fled into the mountains. There they were joined by some teachers who similarly sought refuge from the government."[14]

The strength of the Khmer Rouge was estimated at between 1,500 and 3,000 armed men prior to the April coup, but though small it had a popular following and operated in fifteen of the nineteen Cambodian provinces.[15] The small guerrilla bands were dependent upon the cooperative support of villagers for food. In one instance during the summer of 1969, a small band of the guerrillas defeated a government patrol unit just fifty miles south of Phnom Penh. No publicity was given to this incident, George reports, both because the guerrillas had struck so close to the capital and because it was evident that the local population had supported the guerrillas. In the eyes of one knowledgeable observer, "it is this local backing which communist guerrillas have been able to win in the countryside that made the movement a major problem for Sihanouk for years. Apparently Sihanouk's much-touted popularity with the peasants was no serious obstruction to the communists."[16]

Decornoy says that since 1967, the Khmer Rouge "have spoken of the 'men party to treason, with Lon Nol at their head,' who have 'conspired with American Imperialism,' and its 'lackeys,' the Thai and South Vietnamese governments and the Khmer Serei (trained and armed by the Americans, and now fighting for General Lon Nol).[17] The Khmer Rouge accused the authorities connected with Lon Nol of continually harassing the peasants and of suppressing popular dissent. Sihanouk, however, was never attacked. The Khmer Rouge invariably referred to General Lon Nol and his friends as "American stooges," "but have never said as much of Prince Sihanouk. They remember that he refused American aid when times were hard, knowing that Washington's generosity would have entailed a proportional reduction of independence."[18] Decornoy comments further that "it is curious to see that for the past three years, the present leaders of Phnom Penh [Lon Nol, and so on] have been presented to the population as future allies of General Ky."

Even more interesting, however, is that the slogans used during the 1967 uprising, as reported by Decornoy, are found word for word today in the declarations of the United Front: "Down with the American Imperialists and their lackeys inside and outside the country!"; "Down with the government and Assembly sold to the Imperialists!"; "Stop all repression!"; "Distribute arms to the people!"; "Lower prices of goods!"; and "Stop abusive taxes!"[19] The struggle of the NUF is dramatically more widespread than the 1967 revolt, but nevertheless is an outgrowth of a revolutionary movement which began several years ago over internal conditions in Cambodia as well as over external forces pushing in on (and now occupying) the country.[20]

The coup and the allied invasion have pushed together former enemies and have vastly intensified the struggle. As George comments, "It is one of the war's ironies that Sihanouk has joined hands with men and forces he once tried to liquidate. . . . The important point is that it is the prince who has joined the leftist movement in Cambodia, not the other way round. And it is the leftist movement, not Sihanouk individually, which will benefit from the marriage of convenience."[21]

A measure of the importance of the Khmer Rouge in the NUF is that Hou Youn, Hu Nim, and Khieu Samphan each now head one of the three military zones in Cambodia, decided upon at a conference in Cambodia on May 7 and 8. Zone One, under Khieu Samphan, comprises the eastern region between the Mekong and South Vietnam. Zone Two, under Hu Nim, includes southwestern provinces bordering on the Gulf of Siam. And Zone Three, under Hou Youn, includes the northwestern regions bordering on Thailand and Laos.[22] These men have declared their tasks to be the following: 1) "to step up armed and political struggle"; 2) "to promote propaganda, training and organizational work to turn the forces of the masses into solid revolutionary organizations, enhance the people's solidarity in fighting in all fields, encourage the people to give mutual assistance, morally and materially"; 3) "to strengthen the building of the armed forces . . . so as to have enough strength to annihilate the enemy, expand the liberated zone and defend the life and property of the people"; 4) "to step up the movement of developing and protecting production, the movement of savings in support of the resistance according to one's abilities and voluntariness"; and 5) "to strengthen the militant solidarity with the . . . Vietnamese and Laotian peoples who are fighting . . . against the common enemy." In another part of the communique, these leaders said, significantly, that their goal was to "unite closely with the people of all strata at home and foreign residents, especially Vietnamese and Chinese residents. Strictly observe discipline concerning our relations with the masses and refrain from any encroachment upon the life and property of the people. Realize the 'army-people one-mindedness,' the army being the fish and the people the water. . . ."[23] These guidelines for a united front in a "people's war" are being practiced, it seems, carefully and effectively by the NUF forces.

The differing modes of operation of the NUF forces and the Cambodian army clearly indicate the effects the two groups are having on the rural population. A typical example of this difference was the attack in mid-April on the town of Saang. T. D. Allman reports that small NLF forces, with "an undetermined amount of support from pro-Sihanouk Cambodians, seized an important place embarrassingly close to the capital—then stood by while the Cambodian army demonstrated its ineffectiveness as a military force and its unerring ability to alienate the local population." The Cambodian army surrounded the town in overwhelming numbers, called in air strikes, fired mortars and automatic weapons into the town, and finally encircled the town with a convenient hole left for the guerrillas to escape. When the offensive finally came, the guerrillas were gone. They had left the town untouched and had allowed the local inhabitants to flee. On the other hand, "Cambodian soldiers, having faced no resistance at all, entered the town, found the shops in the market neatly shut and locked from the outside, and proceeded to loot and burn them. By the time Cambodian troops were finished, about 40% of the town had been razed. . . ." While the government claimed that the NUF had attacked to replenish their supplies, Allman says that at Saang and at Ang Tassom, as at every other halt they make in Cambodia, "communist troops seemed more interested in giving political lectures than in taking anything from the inhabitants. They left rice warehouses untouched and, according to one villager, even 'turned down a chicken I offered them, saying they carried their own food with them.' "[24]

Both the Khmer Serei and the Khmer Krom, the Cambodian mercenaries trained by the CIA, have been at least as intent on looting as the regular Cambodian army. The Americans, too, have not only systematically destroyed many Cambodian towns by bombing and artillery, but have engaged in looting.[25] And the South Vietnamese army is managing to alienate the entire Cambodian population: they have been looting the wreckage of the towns they destroy, and have made themselves at home, flying the South Vietnamese flag over occupied buildings and openly showing their contempt for the Cambodians.[26] A Cambodian general was quoted in June as saying that outside Phnom Penh the government army and administration "almost no longer exist."[27]

In contrast to this, the NUF has been remarkably successful, and support from the peasantry has been gained through effective accommodation to local conditions. Richard Dudman, a captured newsman, wrote that although his NUF guards were atheists, they doffed their hats when passing

village pagodas in deference to the peasant mores.[28] Contrary
to Phnom Penh propaganda, the NUF do not exploit the
peasants for food. The pattern of accommodation had been
long practiced by the Vietcong before the "allied" invasion.
A businessman in the Parrot's Beak commented, "The Vietcong when they pass not far from here do not touch
anything. They never levy taxes. When they want something they buy it. Of course, the businessmen and peasants
sell."[29] Thus, an army officer in Cambodia complained,
"Peasants do not flee when the Vietcong come. They are used
to accommodation. . . ."[30]

For the NUF, cooperation with the peasantry is even easier,
for they share Khmer identity with the Cambodian peasantry.
The NUF organization was sufficiently implanted in Kratie
province by May 10–16 that on those dates the province's
populace was going to the polls to elect committees of the
NUF at all levels.[31] By the middle of June more than half
of the country was in NUF hands.

Paralleling this increasingly effective opposition, support for
Lon Nol within the Cambodian elite has been disintegrating.
Many members of the elite, both of the left and right, had
opposed Sihanouk's inefficient one-man rule. Prior to the
coup, some had joined the Khmer Rouge, some had gone into
exile, and others had remained silent in Phnom Penh. For
these people, "the fall of Sihanouk was an old dream. They
thus saw it as a liberation."[32] Although they were encouraged
to join with the Lon Nol government, many of them waited
and became progressively disillusioned with the new government's anti-Vietnamese campaign, its call for aid from the
American camp, and its approval of the U.S. invasion.
Although they did not like Sihanouk, and particularly his
alignment with the Khmer Rouge, they began announcing
their support for the United Front.[33] Even within Phnom
Penh many members of all classes have turned to the NUF.
By the end of June, even Lon Nol's position as "mayor of
Phnom Penh" seemed to be in doubt.

On the other hand, by late June the NUF controlled nearly
all of Cambodia, with the exception of Phnom Penh and the
immediate areas of the U.S. and South Vietnamese inva-
sionary forces.[34] *Le Monde* reported that "the Americans have
discovered, ironically, in reading documents seized in Khmer
territory, that the organization of the United Front of libera-

tion of Sihanouk is better built than they thought." Furthermore, the report comments, "the work undertaken will be a long task. It consists of building a solid instrument, firmly implanted in the countryside, relying on close cooperation between the Cambodians and the Vietnamese. The 'Khmer Rouge' is called upon to play a determining role within the movement. . . ."[35]

The NUF, organized and led by the Khmer Rouge, backed by the NLF and the North Vietnamese, is fighting a protracted war both to introduce revolutionary change in the countryside and to seize control of the government at Phnom Penh. If and when they do take power, they will have already created their own governmental and economic structures in the countryside. Where the present government is a tool of the feudal and business elite for furthering its own interests, the revolutionary NUF government will likely be based on the popular support of the masses of Cambodians—the peasants—and will more likely serve their needs. In other words, when the NUF topples the Lon Nol government, it will be a revolution, not a coup.

12

Mao's Indochina Tactic

by Jonathan Unger

The anti-Sihanouk coup, the subsequent strife in Cambodia, and America's sanctuary invasions have combined to secure for China a major foreign policy triumph in Southeast Asia. During several short weeks in March and April 1970, she managed to unite the Indochinese national liberation movements around her own strategic concepts. Because of the rivalry between Russia and China, a gain for one can often mean a loss for the other, and as China's influence in Indochina has risen, Russia's has waned. This decline of Russia's moderating influence does not bode well for an early negotiated settlement to the war.

China's and Russia's policies toward Sihanouk as well as their respective actions in the Cambodia crisis have been rooted in the historical interests of the two. China, for example, as far back as the nineteenth century regarded the Western military presence in Southeast Asia as a threat to her southern borders. Since World War II, as America fell heir to the role of the former European colonialist powers, she too has ringed China, but with air bases. Although America's designs are "restricted" to the "containment of China," China regards U.S. foreign policy in Asia as imperialist and belligerent. On at least four occasions—Korea 1950–1951, Taiwan 1958, and Indochina 1965, 1967—China feared that the United States would imminently launch air strikes against her cities.

One of China's major strategic goals has been to protect her southern borders by limiting America's military presence in Southeast Asia. Therefore, China was generally willing to give support to Sihanouk's neutralist policies. Although Sihanouk sporadically suppressed the Communist movement within

---

Jonathan Unger is a graduate student in Modern East Asian History and a Fellow of the Center for Chinese Studies at the University of California, Berkeley.

Cambodia, he did manage to keep Cambodia free from American military influence. In 1967, when Red Guard-inspired youths among Cambodia's 400,000 Chinese raucously demonstrated in Phnom Penh, Sihanouk's intercession with Chou En-lai brought immediate actions from China aimed at curbing the leftist disruptions.

Compared to China, Russia's real interests in Southeast Asia are secondary, and the USSR generally has been disturbed by the volatility of the region. Initially the Vietnam conflict, for example, adversely affected Russia's primary interest, the continued stabilization of the political and military situation in Eastern and Central Europe, although the *continuation* of the Vietnam war, by diverting and sapping America's energies, has ironically proven a boon to the Soviets, even in Europe. Russia welcomed Sihanouk's neutralist stance and his ability to keep Cambodia out of the Vietnam conflict.

Hence, in the 1950s and 1960s the policies of Russia and China usually converged in a willingness to grant economic and military aid to Sihanouk's regime. Sihanouk's goal, with Cambodia's neighbors involved in war, was the delicate one of counterbalancing the antagonists in order to maintain Cambodia's neutrality. His flamboyant act of diplomatic tightrope walking utilized China's and Russia's acceptance of his neutralist status. Thailand and Vietnam, Cambodia's historical enemies, continued to provide the two main threats to Cambodia's security; and Sihanouk believed that Russia could help provide diplomatic pressures against Thai and South Vietnamese incursions, while both Communist giants could provide pressure against overt North Vietnamese and NLF activities in the border-region jungles. At the time of his overthrow, Sihanouk was visiting Russia and China to induce them to pressure Hanoi into reducing its presence in the sanctuaries.

Sihanouk also believed that Cambodia might be able to use China and Russia, particularly the former, in the post-Vietnam war period. If, as Sihanouk believed, the Vietnamese Communists succeeded in uniting Vietnam, the consequent danger to Cambodia's political integrity might be ameliorated by Chinese mediation. During the two years prior to his fall, Sihanouk was leaning toward the United States and away from China in the hope that Cambodia could emerge from the war as a neutral buffer between a Communist Vietnam and a pro-American Thailand. Sihanouk, therefore, called for a post-war retention of America's military presence in Southeast Asia. But in the next breath Sihanouk was claiming that Cambodia's post-war security would also depend upon China's interest in keeping Cambodia separate from Vietnam.

It was this deep-rooted distrust that Cambodia holds for its Vietnamese neighbor that gave China the lever to vault into its current role as middleman in the new alliance of Indochinese revolutionaries formed during the conference of April 24–25. In attaining this role, China is reaping the fruits of an ironic history. It was a millennium of Chinese pushing southward to the borders of Kwangtung and Yunnan provinces which drove the Vietnamese and Thais into the geographical cul-de-sac of Southeast Asia, where persistent conflicts with the indigenous Khmers (Cambodians) have given birth to and nourished a heritage of bitterness and mutual enmity. The slaughter of ethnic Vietnamese by Lon Nol's army is but the latest expression of the hostility and fears that persist.

It was this enmity that provided China with its advantage. The expansion of the Indochina war into Cambodia meant that the leadership on both sides of the fighting had to extend their military alliances, come what may. Hanoi, the NLF, and the Pathet Lao, therefore, needed to coordinate their own strategies with that of Sihanouk. In turn, if Sihanouk wished to paste together a Cambodian Front organization, he needed the Vietnamese Communists to aid in securing and protecting "liberated territories" where his new Front could take root and where Cambodian recruits could be mobilized and trained. Sihanouk found it necessary to reverse his former neutralist stance and to seek an overt alliance with the Asian Communists. But the leaders of the three revolutionary movements of Indochina—Sihanouk in particular—were well aware of the difficulties that the histories of mutual distrust presented to any potential alliance among them. Both the Prince and his Vietnamese suitors required a matchmaker, and they found it expedient and perhaps even necessary to turn northward to China in the shaping of a common military front. The coordinating conference of April 24–25—attended by Prince Souphanavong of the Pathet Lao, Premier Pham Van Dong of North Vietnam, Nguyen Huu Tho, head of the NLF, and Prince Sihanouk—was held inside China, and Chinese Premier Chou En-lai hovered over the final day of the proceedings like a proud mother hen.

China was emerging from the Cambodian crisis as a coordinator of Indochina's leftist forces. Moreover, with Sihanouk settling into a politically symbiotic relationship with his hosts in Peking, China had become patron to an exiled leader sufficiently popular in his own country to initiate a national liberation struggle. And thirdly, China's position on people's war was being vindicated, while the Soviet Union's policy of peaceful coexistence was placing the USSR in an awkward spot: infuriated and embarrassed by Nixon's Cambodia escalation, unable to accept Lon Nol's regime, yet abashedly unwilling to bless Sihanouk's Chinese-oriented Front.

To understand the course that China was charting in her new advantageous position, one must be aware both of China's national interests, like the one of defensive posture on her southern borders, and of the ideological framework within which her foreign policy is set. To put this policy framework in simple terms, Chinese ideology advocates people's wars and national liberation struggles by the peoples of the underdeveloped world. However, most analysts of Chinese foreign policy feel that China's propensity for taking risks is low and that in the making of Chinese foreign policy, questions of Chinese national interest generally outweigh ideological considerations. It is significant that in the Cambodia crisis China's national interests converged with her ideology.

The Maoists claim that people's wars provide the vehicle by which Western capitalism will eventually be defeated. The Chinese idea, expressed most recently in Mao's May 20 Cambodia declaration, his first published manifesto in two years, is that the peoples of the Third World shall inevitably rise against their own elites when those elites collude with the exploitation and militarism of the advanced countries. Mao is optimistic that a high tide of such uprisings is at hand and that the events of Cambodia provide evidence of this; he declared on May 20 that "a new upsurge in the struggle against U.S. imperialism is now emerging throughout the world."

Mao Tse-tung believes that the organized will of the masses can surmount seemingly insuperable odds and that people's wars will eventually defeat the United States and its "running dogs." Referring to Cambodia, Mao declared that "the people of a small country can certainly defeat aggression by a big country, if only they dare to rise in struggle, dare to take up arms and grasp in their own hands the destiny of their country. This is a law of history."

The Chinese presume that the victories of the people's wars shall coincide with an uprising in America, kindled by the defeats in Indochina and elsewhere and by domestic oppression perpetrated by the American government. In his May 20, 1970, address, Mao declared that he was "convinced that the American people who are fighting valiantly will ultimately win victory and that the fascist rule in the United States will inevitably be defeated." The various elements of this schema of world revolution were previously part of the Chinese doctrine; in Mao's address they were brought together to focus upon a particular point of time and a particular incident— America in Cambodia. Mao had concluded that "the Nixon government is beset with troubles internally and externally, with utter chaos at home and extreme isolation abroad . . . U.S. imperialism [is] in the throes of its death-bed struggle."

In the course of this process of people's wars and American self-liberation, China offers the example of her own revolution, sprinkled with modest training and assistance programs for Third World uprisings. Beyond that, she believes, each nation's liberation struggle must be internally initiated and developed. Since the founding of the Chinese Communist regime, Peking has never engaged in expansive, aggressive war against another sovereign nation. Even in the cases of Korea and the Sino-Indian conflict of 1962, China was reacting to what she considered with good reason to be threats to her own security, and when the threats receded she pulled back her forces.[1] In accordance with the Chinese doctrine, even the Chinese military apparatus is almost exclusively defensive. China seeks to avoid America's mistake of forcing herself upon the populace of a foreign nation. Those in America who fear Chinese military aggression are mistaken in their apprehensions.

Peking views Chinese revolutionary history as a model for the people's wars and believes that at least three of the important concepts derived from her own experience of the 1930s and 1940s are being vindicated in Indochina. First, that the politically conscious and organized will of the masses, crystallizing around issues of nationalism and social reform, has more significance in war than possession of preponderant military force. Second, that the leadership, manpower, and programs of a liberation movement must arise indigenously, based on the specific needs and aspirations of the local populace. Third, that the enemy's use of indiscriminate force and his introduction of foreign troops, both of which will result from his alienation from the masses, will further rally the population to the ranks of the national liberation front. When Lon Nol's army overthrew Sihanouk, China believed that Cambodia would soon fulfill each of the three criteria favoring a people's war.

Sihanouk was in Moscow when news arrived of the coup deposing him. Russia's initial reaction to the coup was to retain its noninvolvement, and Sihanouk was sent off to Peking, the next scheduled stop of his trip. The Chinese immediately perceived the possibilities for a people's war and that Cambodia would be bound into the Vietnam situation, and they were quick to throw their support behind Sihanouk. It is even possible that it was they who convinced an initially reluctant Sihanouk to fight from exile to regain the leadership of Cambodia. In the next several weeks the Chinese progressively increased their public (though not official) commitment to Sihanouk's Front. This peaked on May 1, 1970, when Mao shared the place of honor with Sihanouk on the dais at Peking's annual May Day celebration. Personal identification with Mao is the highest public commitment that China can bestow.

However, China's strategy was not so simple. While publicly supporting Sihanouk she also continued to pursue her pre-coup policy toward Cambodia. Following the overthrow of Sihanouk, Peking initially tried to win a pledge of neutrality from Phnom Penh and an agreement to respect the sanctuaries. Remarkably—if we can believe Lon Nol—China persisted in these efforts until May 5, despite the anti-Communist declarations of the Phnom Penh regime, several government-sponsored acts of hooliganism in Cambodia against ethnic Chinese, the unexpected momentum that the Sihanouk-headed Front had achieved, and the American invasion of April 30. It appears that until the last weeks of April or the beginning of May, the Chinese remained ambivalent concerning the prospects of the emerging struggle in Cambodia and accordingly hedged their bets. But by May 5, the date that Sihanouk established his exile government, the pattern of events in Cambodia had become sufficiently propitious and the Lon Nol government had become dependent upon the Allied military might; Peking had accordingly become firmly committed to the eradication of the Lon Nol regime.

From the time of Sihanouk's ouster in March, Peking was also pursuing two pro-revolutionary tacks. She was of course supporting Sihanouk, but she was also undercutting him from the left by attempting to strengthen the hand of the Cambodian marxist Khmer Rouge movement. Hou Youn, Khieu Samphan, and Hu Nim, the three leftist intellectuals at the helm of the Khmer Rouge, were the only members of Sihanouk's new cabinet who remained in Cambodia, and they have taken direct charge of the Front's activities within the country. Sihanouk's prestige, however, probably provided him with sufficient leverage to maintain his supremacy within the Front, even from exile in Peking. Sihanouk is supposed to be a superb radio performer, and Peking's radio outlets, giving him direct access to Cambodia's villages, would have reinforced his control. Thus it is not surprising that an examination of the broadcasts that China beams to Cambodia indicates that at least for the quarter year following the coup Sihanouk was denied use of Peking's airwaves, even though his oratory would have considerably promoted the Front's general efforts. In the maneuvering to come, Peking obviously hopes that the Hou Youn group will prevail.

Sihanouk, for his part, was attempting to hold onto his neutralist stance. On May 9th, a French journalist in Peking asked him whether he is a Communist. Sihanouk replied that he is pink, not red, and adroitly added that he admires both Mao Tse-tung and Charles de Gaulle.[2] Two months later, on July 3, he was yet more explicit, telling a second French journalist:

I have not changed. I have not become a communist, and I do not renounce anything I have written in the past. I had chosen not to be with either the Americans or the communists, because I considered that there were two dangers: American imperialism and Asian communism. It is Lon Nol who obliged me to choose between them."[3]

Sihanouk attempted to offset his dependence upon China by securing Russia's support for his Front, but the Soviet Union rebuffed his overtures. The Front of Kampuchea was too much a vehicle of Chinese-style "protracted war" for Soviet taste. To recognize the Front would be to fall into line behind the Chinese. Hence, the Russians were uncomfortably treading the middle course. The Soviet diplomatic mission stayed in Phnom Penh, but minus its ambassador. And where once the Russians referred to the "Cambodian government," they now referred to the "Phnom Penh authorities."

In May and June 1970, the Soviet leaders berated the Chinese, warned the Indochinese Communists that they courted "defeat and destruction" if they followed China's line, and scolded those on both sides of the Indochina war who were promoting a military rather than a diplomatic solution to the Cambodia crisis. The Russians contended that Sihanouk's Front would not necessarily be the war's victor and that Lon Nol's government is not America's puppet and could be negotiated with privately. The Soviet Union tried to strengthen her position by augmenting her arms shipments to Hanoi. But Hanoi, the NLF, and the Pathet Lao disagreed with and ignored Russia's warnings concerning their and China's strategy in Cambodia.

The Indochinese movements and China believe that America both overextended herself and helped fuel the Cambodian revolutionary movement when she intruded into the Cambodia conflict. The Chinese papers, for example, have likened America's action to "lifting a rock only to drop it on its own feet," and they picture the United States as flailing out in panic against the worldwide revolutionary upsurge that China perceives. Referring to America's Cambodia operation, Mao proclaimed on May 20 that "U.S. imperialism, which looks like a huge monster, is in essence a paper tiger. . . . In the world today, who actually fears whom? . . . It is U.S. imperialism which fears the people of the world. It becomes panic stricken at the mere rustle of leaves in the wind."

But China *does* grow fearful when she perceives America panicking in Indochina—although seemingly much less fearful this time than in the past. China has long considered that America's show of force in Vietnam has been directed at China. Statements by Dean Rusk and others provided adequate reason for her to harbor this suspicion. The Chinese were not unhappy to see the Republicans succeed to the Presidency, for they had believed that the Republicans, as the "party of Wall Street," would be more pragmatic and cautious in an economically and otherwise unjustified war. Nixon's escalation, therefore, was probably unexpected by the Chinese. The four massive air strikes against North Vietnam that coincided with Nixon's invasion of the sanctuaries were particularly worrisome to them. The war's overflow into China would most likely occur by means of escalation in the air war, and further, the Chinese are particularly vulnerable to American air power.

In the first half of 1965 America had come horrifyingly close to war with China. Her bombing raids had been closing in on the Chinese-North Vietnamese border, and China had begun to reduce the nonessential populations of her southern cities. The prospect of an impending collision in 1965 brought to a head serious disagreements among the Chinese leadership. Mao and his defense minister, Lin Piao, wanted a defensive military posture based upon Mao's conception of protracted war. An anti-Mao faction was more willing to consider a firmer Chinese military response in North Vietnam. This anti-Maoist faction's strategy would require a rapprochement with Russia (to protect China's rear), vastly increased expenditures on conventional military hardware, and increased professionalism in the army, all of which would have precipitated trends in China unacceptable to the Chinese left. The debate during the 1965 crisis ended in a victory for the Maoists, and the advent of the Cultural Revolution came shortly thereafter. The leaders who desired rapprochement with Russia were subsequently eliminated, the Sino-Soviet rivalry sharpened, and Chinese involvement with Vietnam and with developments throughout the world subsided.

The most recent American escalation has had an opposite effect to those of 1965. China has used the 1970 crisis to reemerge into world politics after five years of relative inactivity and isolation, and her attention has been shifted away from her northern inner borders, where a year earlier she had been engrossed by a border dispute with the USSR. In giving priority to Southeast Asia in the most recent crisis, China initially attempted to mute her quarrel with Russia. On May 1, Mao paid an unexpected call on the Soviet delegation at Peking's May Day festivities, but the USSR, unwilling to give backing to Sihanouk, soon demonstrated that she would not dampen the Sino-Soviet dispute. However, despite the antagonistic Russian position China probably did not feel very threatened militarily by America's provocations. America, she believes, is already overextended in Southeast Asia. Mao declared on May 20 that "the danger of a new world war still exists. . . . But revolution is the main trend in the world today."

In contrast to the current line, Peking had been moving toward more relaxed relations with the United States during 1969 and the early months of 1970. As the foreign policy extremes of the Cultural Revolution years receded into memory and as the Sino-Soviet dispute dragged on, China edged toward a lessening of Sino-American tensions, particularly in northeastern Asia where, remembering the 1930s, China is anxiously watching Japan's rapid rearmament program. On January 20, following a two-year lapse, China and the United States entered into new talks at Warsaw.

Nixon's expedition into Cambodia reversed the trend of U.S.-Chinese relations. If China were to become more directly involved in Indochina, she could not so readily attempt to divorce her northeast Asian foreign policy from her southeast Asian policy. Moreover, the Chinese took Nixon's Cambodia move as an indication that America was generally going to pursue a belligerent line. Immediately following Nixon's April 30 "Cambodia" address the Chinese press observed that Nixon had in effect argued that America could now attack any nation under the pretext of protecting American troops. The Chinese called this "gangster logic." On May 18 China called off the talks in Warsaw, at least temporarily. America's military interference in Cambodia had helped decide the Chinese upon a foreign policy tack that is more in line with her ideological framework.

China is increasing her material support to the Indochina movements. Under an agreement signed in late May, for example, she will provide North Vietnam with augmented military and economic aid, and Mao personally promised Sihanouk adequate free arms for the Cambodia struggle. Furthermore, Chinese newspapers now refer to China's territory as Indochina's "reliable rear area." Before the Cambodia conflagration, China referred to herself as a "rear shield"; that is, a neutral border upon which North Vietnam could rely. The implication of the change in wording is that China is now an integral, though still militarily inactive, component of the Southeast Asian war.

However, it is highly unlikely that China would directly enter the Indochina conflict. As has been noted, the Chinese are convinced, first, that "national liberation wars" can, and should, do without outside armed help. (In Cambodia, the North Vietnamese have pursued the Chinese strategy, and instead of quickly taking Phnom Penh themselves, have attempted to secure rural areas where the Khmer could safely organize their own National United Front.) Second, the Chinese are convinced that the three national efforts she supports in Indochina are already on the road to success. But if North Vietnam decided that America's escalation should be met head on by a Communist counterescalation, China's troops might prove helpful. By pouring troops into *North* Vietnam, China would enable Hanoi to dispatch her own forces southward.

Throughout the period of de-escalation prior to Cambodia, North Vietnamese troops had been withdrawing from South Vietnam, probably in accordance with Hanoi's apparent willingness to permit Nixon's withdrawal program to proceed on schedule. The recent gains in Saigon's pacification programs, many observers believed, had been due to the voluntary pullback of Hanoi's troops into Laos and the Cambodian sanctuaries. Perhaps the greatest danger in Nixon's decision to escalate into Cambodia and to rebomb the North is that the North Vietnamese may eventually react militarily to Nixon's betrayal of the prior *de facto* arrangement of mutual withdrawal. Since Hanoi's own withdrawal program has been endangered by Nixon's decisions to send allied troops into Cambodia and southeast Laos, Hanoi may begin to move numbers of her troops back into the Vietnam conflict, plus large numbers of fresh troops released from duty in the North by Chinese replacements. Such a military response hopefully has been rendered unlikely by the obvious failure of Nixon's Cambodia thrust and by the U.S. Senate's declaration against a second expedition. But if Mr. Nixon again decides to engage in provocative escalation, he may find himself unexpectedly in a war fiercer and wider than this torn nation's fabric might endure.

13

The Cambodian Operation and International Law

by Richard A. Falk

The development of international law since the end of World War I has exhibited a consistent effort to prohibit recourse to force in international society. The Nuremberg Judgment called aggression against a foreign country "the supreme crime" against mankind. The U.N. Charter is built around the notion that the only occasions on which it is legal to use force are in response to an armed attack and as authorized by an organ of the United Nations. The invasion of Cambodian territory by the armed forces of the United States and South Vietnam therefore raises serious questions of international law. The Cambodian Operation was obviously neither a response to a prior armed attack upon South Vietnam nor was it authorized or ratified by the United Nations.

In announcing the decision to the American public on April 30, President Nixon made no effort to justify the invasion under international law. Such a failure illustrates the extreme unilateralism that has been exhibited by the U.S. government throughout the Vietnam War. This failure lends credence to the contention that the United States is conducting an *imperial* war of repression in Indochina and that it believes it owes explanations for its policy only to the American public, if at all, and even then mainly to provide reassurance about the relevance of a challenged policy to the welfare of American troops.

Perhaps the most remarkable passage in Mr. Nixon's April 30 address is the arrogant assertion that an American invasion of an Asian country is of no international concern:

Richard A. Falk is Professor of International Law at Princeton University. His many publications include *The Vietnam War and International Law* (2 Vol.), and a forthcoming volume on the prospects of human survival, *This Endangered Planet.*

These actions [in Cambodia] are in no way directed to security interests of any nation. Any government that chooses to use these actions as a pretext for harming relations with the United States will be doing so on its own responsibility and on its own initiative and we will draw the appropriate conclusions.

The U.S. government had been on record over and over again in support of the position that when a border-crossing armed attack occurs, it is a matter of grave concern for the entire community of nations and that it is a matter of collective determination whether or not a challenged action is disruptive of world order and its fundamental norms of prohibition. What makes Mr. Nixon's statement so troublesome (and it is nowhere qualified or balanced by other statements) is the refusal to acknowledge the possible relevance of any external source of authority in relation to U.S. claims to use force across an international boundary.

It is true that on May 5 Ambassador Charles Yost reported in a short letter to the President of the Security Council that the United States had acted in "collective self-defense" because of the intensification of North Vietnamese activity in Cambodian base areas. Aggressors normally disguise their action by making claims of legal right. The nature of legal analysis makes it always possible to put together a legal argument in support of any partisan position. The whole idea of legal order rests upon the existence of fair and reliable procedures to determine which of several competing legal arguments best fits the facts and governing legal rules. The purpose of this article is to demonstrate that the American invasion of Cambodia was a violation of international law, given the facts, the law, past practice, public policy, and the weight of expert opinion.

I. THE ADMINISTRATION ARGUMENT

It seems necessary, first, to clarify to the extent possible the scope of the claim being asserted by the United States in relation to Cambodia, although the shifting line of official explanation provides ambiguity. On April 30 President Nixon repeated several times in different formulations that the purpose of the invasion was to destroy North Vietnamese sanctuaries along the Cambodian border and, thereby, to protect American lives. In Mr. Nixon's words, "attacks are being launched this week to clean out major enemy sanctuaries on the Cambodia–Vietnam border." The timing of the attack was justified by reference to two separate circumstances:

(1) ". . . the enemy has in the past two weeks stepped up his guerrilla actions and he is concentrating his main force in these sanctuaries . . . where they are building up to launch massive attacks on our forces and those of South Vietnam."

(2) "North Vietnam in the last two weeks has stripped away all pretense of respecting the sovereignty or the neutrality of Cambodia. Thousands of their soldiers are invading the country from the sanctuaries. They are encircling the capital Pnompenh. . . . If this enemy effort succeeds, Cambodia would become a vast enemy staging area and a springboard for attacks along 600 miles of frontier: a refuge where enemy troops could return from combat without fear of retaliation."

President Nixon seemed to suggest that the invasion was responsive to both of these occurrences, given the parallel American decision to provide the Lon Nol regime with arms assistance and to pay for Thai "volunteers." In essence, then, alleged North Vietnamese actions within Cambodia were given as the sole basis for initiating a military attack across an international boundary. Mr. Nixon seemed to emphasize *future* danger rather than any *immediate* threat to the safety of American lives—"Unless we indulge in wishful thinking, the lives of Americans in Vietnam after our next withdrawal of 150,000 would be gravely threatened." And in the course of a news conference on the evening of May 8, Mr. Nixon made even clearer that the focus of his concern was the rather distant set of circumstances existing after the scheduled withdrawal of 150,000 American soldiers was completed in April 1971.

The invasion claim was limited in mission, scope, and duration. The mission was confined to the destruction of sanctuaries which were supposed to have included, according to Mr. Nixon, "the headquarters for the entire Communist military operation in South Vietnam." The scope of the in-

vasion, at least for American ground forces, was confined to
a 21.7 mile strip of Cambodian territory along the border;
and the invasion, again at least for American troops, was to
be terminated by the end of June 1970. In reporting on the
invasion, Mr. Nixon said on June 3 that "the success of
these operations to date has guaranteed that the June 30th
deadline I have set for withdrawal of all American forces
from Cambodia will be met. . . . This includes all American
air support, logistics, and military advisers and personnel."
The President went on to say that "The only remaining
American activity in Cambodia after July 1 will be air
missions to interdict the movements of enemy troops and
materiel where I find that it is necessary to protect the
lives and security of our men in South Vietnam."

An international law argument can be fashioned in support
of this U.S. claim. In essence, this argument would rely on
the following elements: (1) clear and present danger to
American and South Vietnamese troops arising out of the
expansion of sanctuary activity in Cambodia by North Vietnam and the National Liberation Front; (2) a claim by the
United States to use force in Cambodia that is proportional
and responsive to this danger; (3) a claim that the inability
of the Cambodian government to prevent its neutral territory
from being used as a sanctuary for armed forces engaged in
the Vietnam War amounts to an abrogation, in part, at
least, of Cambodia's neutral status, and justifies belligerent
action of limited self-help; (4) a claim that Cambodia has
been primarily invaded by North Vietnam and is a victim
of North Vietnamese aggression; (5) the absence of any
formal complaint by the Cambodian government concerning
the invasion suggests that there has been no victim of aggression and hence no aggression; and (6) North Vietnam is
guilty of aggression against South Vietnam, and the United
States and South Vietnam are entitled to take whatever steps
are necessary to assure the success of their action in collective
self-defense.

Such an argument based on international law could have
been made in coherent form by the Nixon administration.
By mid-June, no such official effort at legal justification had
been made. The main response to the legal challenges directed
at the decision has been an effort to show that the Cambodian
Operation was a valid exercise of Mr. Nixon's powers as

Commander-in-Chief of the armed forces.[1] Such an assertion is hardly relevant to a discussion of the status of the invasion in international law. Surely, the lives of the North Vietnamese armed forces are deeply endangered by the use of air fields in Thailand, Guam, and Okinawa. The point here is that such an explanation is at best responsive to the line of criticism that has contended that the initiation of the Cambodian invasion by Presidential decision amounted to an act of Executive usurpation in violation of the U.S. Constitution.

II. SOME DIFFICULTIES OF LEGAL ANALYSIS

There are several special factors complicating the analysis of the Cambodian Operation.

(1) *The extent of U.S. responsibility for South Vietnamese actions in excess of the limitations of space, time, and mission imposed by the U.S. government.* The underlying claim of the U.S. government rests on a theory of collective self-defense. From the legal standpoint, the victim of attack, not its external ally, defines the necessities of action in self-defense. Of course, the realities of U.S. control do not change the legal situation, except to give evidence of the non-independence and illegitimacy of the Saigon regime. With respect to the Cambodian Operation, it does not seem legally acceptable to confine U.S. responsibility to the actions of its troops. The undertaking is a joint one, and the American claim is derivative from the alleged South Vietnamese right of self-defense; furthermore, American advisers are operating in conjunction with the Saigon regime at every level of military and political operations. Thieu and Ky have repeatedly stated their Cambodian objectives in broader terms than the United States, and South Vietnamese troops have penetrated Cambodian territory beyond the 21.7 mile limit. In my judgment, the United States, from a legal perspective, is a co-venturer, responsible for the full extent of claim being made by the Saigon regime. Indeed, U.S. Secretary of Defense Melvin Laird confirmed on June 23, 1970, that the armed forces of South Vietnam will have a free rein to act in Cambodia after the June 30 deadline, thereby making explicit U.S. complicity with the wider and vaguer South Vietnamese invasion claim.

When the United Kingdom, France, and Israel initiated the Suez War in 1956 as a joint venture there was no effort to assess relative degrees of legal responsibility for the event. It seems reasonable, then, to resolve this initial complication by measuring U.S. responsibility by the full extent of the South Vietnamese claim and conduct in Cambodia.

(2) *The Cambodian Operation represents only a battlefield decision to protect troops in the field and does not constitute an expansion of the U.S. role in Indochina.* The argument has been made by supporters of the administration's decision that the Cambodian Operation has only tactical significance in relation to the Vietnam War. In this spirit, the strike against the Cambodian sanctuaries is not different in legal character from the decision to attack and capture Hamburger Hill. Such matters of battlefield tactics may be criticized as ill-conceived or ill-executed, but they are not appropriately challenged on legal grounds.

This position is defective in a fundamental respect. If a battlefield tactic involves a separate issue of legality, then it is subject to legal scrutiny; sustained border-crossing by armies is always a separate legal event of first-order magnitude in international affairs. The main effort of modern international law is to moderate warfare, and this effort depends greatly on maintaining respect for boundaries.

(3) *The failure of the United Nations to pass judgment.* The political organs of the U.N. system have been singularly ineffective throughout the long course of the Vietnam War. This ineffectiveness is a result of several factors. First, the United States possesses sufficient political influence within the organization to prevent an adverse judgment against it. Second, the nonmembership of China and North Vietnam in the organization makes these governments opposed to any U.N. role; in their eyes, the United Nations, at least as presently constituted—with Formosa continuing to represent China in the Security Council—is itself an illegitimate actor and is in no position to act on behalf of the world community. Third, the United Nations has been totally ineffective whenever the two superpowers were deeply and directly involved in a political conflict. Fourth, the Lon Nol government has not complained to the United Nations about the invasion of its territory or the destruction of its villages either by U.S. and

South Vietnamese forces or by North Vietnamese and NLF forces.

In these circumstances, it is impossible for the United Nations to play any positive role, even to the extent of interpreting the requirements of its own Charter. The Secretary General, U Thant, has tried to undertake peace initiatives at various points during the long course of the war, but his efforts have been resented by the governments of both sides, particularly by the United States during the Johnson administration.

Although the United Nations has been unable to act as an organization, the Charter continues to provide governing legal standards for a case like this one. The Charter is itself *declaratory* of prior legal standards embodied in the Pact of Paris (Kellogg-Briand Pact, 1928), and provides the most authoritative guidelines for identifying the outer limits of permissible state behavior. And surely the U.S. government has not yet claimed the discretion to act in violation of the Charter. Indeed, the Charter has been ratified with the advice and consent of the Senate, and is, according to the U.S. Constitution, part of "the supreme law of the land."

(4) *The failure of the Cambodian government to condemn the invasion.* The Cambodian Operation has an ambiguous character. The claim to eliminate the sanctuaries was explicitly linked by President Nixon in his April 30 speech with the struggle for political control of Cambodia. The United States, South Vietnam, and North Vietnam have intervened in this struggle in a variety of ways.

The Thieu-Ky regime of South Vietnam, despite Lon Nol's anti-Vietnamese policies, is seeking to maintain Lon Nol in power. Thailand has mobilized forces along the western boundary of Cambodia and announced she was sending ethnic Khmers to Cambodia to fight on behalf of the Lon Nol regime.

It is difficult to accord any serious respect to the Lon Nol regime as a government of Cambodia. This regime does not seem able to represent the interests of its people. Its failure to protest the invasion, pillage, and occupation of its territory bears witness to its own illegitimacy, just as the willingness of the Saigon regime to enter into a friendship pact with a governing group that has pursued a harsh set of anti-Vietnamese policies exhibits its illegitimacy in relation to the Vietnamese people. These regimes are struggling at all costs to maintain power in the face of a highly unfavorable domestic balance of power. In this setting, their invitations to foreign governments to send in armies is of only slight legal consequence.[2] The failure of the Cambodian government to protest the invasion of its territory by foreign forces does not, under these circumstances, amount to a valid legal authorization. Cambodia may be the victim of aggression even if its governing elite does not so regard it, especially if, as is the case, a counter-government exists that has protested the invasion. Unless such a position is taken, outside forces could intervene to place a regime in power and then use its invitation to validate its later plans of domination. There is a need to move beyond a pretense of legitimacy whenever a government demonstrates both its dependence on foreign sources of authority for its own existence and its willingness to jeopardize the independence of its country, the welfare of its people, and the inviolability of its territory on behalf of some foreign power whose support is needed to keep the regime in control.

George McT. Kahin, an outstanding specialist on Asian affairs, pointed out the following defects of the argument that the decision to invade Cambodia did not provoke protest from the Lon Nol regime:

It must be noted that Cambodia renounced the SEATO protocol providing protection for the former Indochina states. In point of fact, Sihanouk formally requested SEATO powers in May 1965 to amend Article IV to *exclude* Cambodia from SEATO's perimeter of intervention. His request was ignored but he was advised that the language of the treaty provided that intervention would not be undertaken without the request and consent of the Cambodian government.[3]

It is clearly evident that, whatever took place *subsequent* to the invasion, there is no evidence or even claim that the Cambodian government requested or authorized the invasion, or participated in any way to define its limits. In the post-invasion context, a weak, tottering regime could not be expected to protest an invasion of its territory by its principal "friend." Without U.S. support the Lon Nol regime would have no prospect whatsoever of maintaining power.

III. THE FUNDAMENTAL LEGAL ANALYSIS: AGGRESSION OR COLLECTIVE SELF-DEFENSE

Under modern international law an invasion of a foreign country that is not authorized by a competent international institution is either an act of aggression or an exercise of self-defense. Under most circumstances, states that initiate large-scale, overt violence across an international boundary have been identified as "the aggressor." It is almost impossible for the invading government to make out a persuasive case of self-defense. Possibly the only recent counterexample was the Israeli initiation of the June War in 1967 under conditions of evident and imminent provocation and danger.

The obligations of international law can be divided into two categories: *substantive norms that restrain behavior of governments,* and *procedural norms applicable to situations of alleged violation of substantive norms.* In the area of war and peace, the procedural norms are as important as the substantive norms.

Substantive Norms: The U.N. Charter provides a convenient starting-point for an analysis of the norms governing recourse to force in international affairs. Article 2 of the Charter has the following key paragraph:

(4) All Members shall refrain in their international relations from the threat or use of force against the territorial integrity or political independence of any state, or in any other manner inconsistent with the Purposes of the United Nations.

Article 51 qualifies this prohibition upon force by its limited authorization of self-defense:

Nothing in the present Charter shall impair the inherent right of self-defense if an armed attack occurs against a Member of the United Nations, until the Security Council has taken the measures necessary to maintain international peace and security. . . .

The prohibition and the exception have not been defined, despite numerous international efforts, in any more specific way.

The Charter law is fairly clear: it is not permissible to use force against a foreign territory except in response to an armed attack.[4] This Charter conception expresses general international law, except that a literal reading of its language might be taken to prevent nonmembers of the United Nations from claiming self-defense. North Vietnam and South Vietnam are not members of the organization, but this analysis will proceed on the assumption that any *state* is legally entitled to act in self-defense, whether or not a member of the United Nations. Although there are some difficulties associated with treating South Vietnam as a *state*, given the language and proclaimed intentions of the Geneva Accords of 1954 to create a unified Vietnam no later than July 1956, nevertheless, for purposes of this essay, South Vietnam will be treated as a sovereign state entitled to exercise rights of self-defense.

Especially, as far as the United States is concerned, the invasion of Cambodia rests on a claim of *collective* self-defense. Such a claim places a heavier burden of demonstration on the claimant as its own territory and political independence are not at stake. Some experts even argue that under no circumstances can a state satisfy the requirements of self-defense merely by associating its action with a state that is acting in valid individual self-defense; *alliance relations* are not sufficient to vindicate the claim of the non-attacked state to participate in the exercise of rights of collective self-defense. The infringement of some more direct legal interest must serve as the basis of the claim to join in the defense of an attacked state.[5] The United States has no such distinct legal interest in relation to the defense of South Vietnam—neither regional, cultural, historical, nor even ideological—such as would justify its participation in the Cambodian invasion even if South Vietnam could validly claim to be acting in self-defense. Professor Derek Bowett, who argues in favor of this restrictive view of collective self-defense, concludes that "the requirements of the right of collective self-defense are two in number; firstly, that each participating state has an individual right of self-defense, and secondly that there exists an agreement between the participating states to exercise their rights collectively"[6] In the context of the Cambodian Operation it is clear that the first requirement of collective self-defense has not been met. Since the Charter fails to authorize states to uphold international law as a separate justification for the use of force, then it seems clear that the United States could not, under any circumstances, associate itself with a South Vietnamese claim of self-defense unless the exercise of the right of self-defense were converted into a U.N. action, as happened, of course, in relation to the defense of South Korea in 1950.

Such a conception of self-defense has been criticized as unduly restrictive and unrealistic given the evolution of collective security arrangements. For instance, Myres S. McDougal and Florentino P. Feliciano, in a major work on the modern international law of force, contend that collective self-defense can be validly claimed "whenever a number of traditional bodies-politic asserting certain common demands for security as well as common expectations that such security can be achieved only by larger cooperative efforts . . . present themselves to the rest of the general community as one unified group or collectivity for purposes of security and defense."[7] This broader conception of collective self-defense underlies the various regional security pacts that the United States organized during the Dulles era as part of its containment policy directed at what was conceived to be a monolithic Communist movement intent upon world conquest.[8] Under this broader view of collective self-defense, which is probably more descriptive of practice and is generally accepted as being compatible with modern international law, the United States would be entitled to join in the Cambodian Operation *provided* the facts validated the underlying claim by South Vietnam. Even McDougal and Feliciano place a *higher* burden of demonstration for claims of collective than for individual self-defense: ". . . it may be appropriate to require a higher imminence of attack and more exacting evidence of compelling necessity for coercive response by the group as such than would be reasonably demanded if the responding participant were a single state."[9] As it is, "the traditional requirements imposed upon resort to self-defense" are most exacting: ". . . a realistic expectation of instant, imminent military attack and carefully calculated proportionality in response."[10] There was nothing about the events in Cambodia that could qualify as satisfying these conditions, nothing that could justify a claim of individual self-defense. Since it is more difficult to establish a claim of collective self-defense, the demonstration that no basis for individual self-defense exists also entails a rejection of the official U.S. plea based on collective self-defense.

Prior to May 1, 1970, the invasion date, there was no report of increased fighting along the border, and there were no indications of increased South Vietnamese or American casualties as a result of harassment from across the Cambodian border. Mr. Nixon never claimed more than that the expansion of the Cambodian base area might place American troops in great jeopardy by April 1971 (or almost a year after the invasion). Such a contention overlooks the prospects for interim changes either by way of negotiated settlement or successful Vietnamization of the war. The Cambodian base areas were sanctuaries used to provide logistic support to the antiregime side in the war to control South Vietnam. In this sense, and to a far greater extent, the United States has relied upon external base areas in Japan, South Korea, Thailand, Okinawa, and Guam to conduct its belligerent operations in South Vietnam. Would the United States regard a Soviet air strike against these base areas a legitimate exercise of the right of collective self-defense by North Vietnam or the Provisional Revolutionary Government? Consideration of a hypothetical reciprocal claim helps to expose the unreasonableness of the U.S. position and the utter absurdity of the administration contention that expanding the combat area across the Cambodian border is not a major escalation of the war. Note also that this same unreasonableness pertains to the South Vietnamese claim of self-defense which is put forward in more extravagant terms, relating itself to the internal Cambodian struggle for control, to the treatment of Vietnamese inhabitants by the Cambodian regime, and to the presence of North Vietnamese military personnel in any part of Cambodia. Any objective reading of the facts amply demonstrates that there was no *instant necessity* that might lend legal support to the Cambodian Operation as an exercise of the right of individual or collective self-defense.

There is, in addition, no relationship of proportionality between the claim to invade Cambodia and the alleged danger to South Vietnam. Indeed, it was the buildup of pressure by the Lon Nol regime to alter the long persisting status quo in the base areas that appeared to be the initial unsettling force. The Lon Nol regime insisted that the North Vietnamese cease to use these base areas altogether, and as we have already mentioned, also brought provocative pressure to bear on Vietnamese residents living in Cambodia. Such tactics, presumably a dual consequence of the weakness of the regime and the strength of American pressure, were part of the effort by the Lon Nol regime to mobilize support in the building struggle against the forces supporting the deposed Prince Sihanouk, who has in recent months joined dynastic with revolutionary legitimacy, a potent political linkage in any developing country. Therefore, the main precipitating event seems to be the consequence of changes in the political situation in Cambodia, rather than any *imminent* threat to South Vietnam; these changes were supported, not resisted, by American action. The American claim to destroy base area camps within the 21.7 mile border strip has had the predictable consequence of pushing North Vietnamese and NLF troops back toward the center of Cambodia, intensifying the struggle for political control of Cambodia, and utterly destroying any prospect for the resumption of the precarious, if stable, condition of relative neutrality that Cambodia had managed to maintain under Sihanouk's rule. Therefore, the Cambodian Operation seemed ill-conceived in relation to the principal alleged danger, the collapse of a pro-Western regime in Phnom Penh and its replacement by a radical anti-Western regime.

Mr. Nixon's report to the nation on June 4 stated that "all of our major military objectives have been achieved" in the Cambodian Operation.[11] These objectives were described in terms of the capture of war materiel. But reports from the field suggested that probably only about half of the war materiel stored in the base areas would have been discovered and captured by the pledged June 30th withdrawal. In that event, the alleged success of the operation would seem virtually unrelated to the level of future military activity in South Vietnam. There is no evidence that equipment shortages are likely to result for North Vietnam or the NLF if as much as one-half or more of the war materiel captured will still remain in the Cambodian base areas. In addition, the North Vietnamese, especially during the heavy bombardment of North Vietnam between February 1965 and October 1968, demonstrated great resourcefulness in circumventing efforts to interdict their supply routes. The element of proportionality seems absent from the claim of self-defense whether the claim is considered from the angle of the United States or from the perspective of the Saigon regime. Indeed, the invasion seems to have aggravated the very conditions it was designed to cure. Even long-term supporters of American military action have tended to criticize the invasion as lacking any rational relationship to its proclaimed goals. Certainly, Mr. Nixon's assertion that the Cambodian Operation would shorten the war seems without any foundation. The arena of violence has been widened, a new country has become a theater of military operations, and its people a victim of invasion, and taken in conjunction with the stepped-up American military operations in Laos, an all-Indochina War has emerged in place of the Vietnam War. Such an enlargement of the arena of violence and an expansion of principal actors involved in the combat greatly complicate the search for a negotiated settlement, which remains the proclaimed end of U.S. policy.

The Cambodian Operation is properly compared to the earlier extension of the war to North Vietnam, and much of the legal analysis of self-defense claims in the earlier setting fits the Cambodian Operation as well.[12] From the point of view of legal doctrine, the assertion of a claim of self-defense against Cambodia has even less merit than did the earlier assertion against North Vietnam. To cross the Cambodian boundary with large armies and supporting air force bombardments is to make a unilateral decision to attack the territory of a foreign country under circumstances where an armed attack on South Vietnam was neither imminent nor probable. The most that can be said is that political changes taking place in Cambodia were jeopardizing its neutrality from both sides. This kind of circumstance may involve competing claims of limited intervention, but it certainly doesn't support a claim of self-defense.

Such a conclusion needs to be understood in relation to the entire effort of international law to remove from national governments the discretion to initiate or expand warfare across boundaries on the basis of a calculation of national advantage. Central to this endeavor is the restriction of occasions upon which it is permissible to cross openly the boundary of a foreign country with armed force. The United States, until the Vietnam War, had played a central role in using international law to build up an external framework of restraint based on widely shared normative conceptions.[13] Although it is true that no agreed definitions of self-defense exist, there has been a general acknowledgment that the core meaning of self-defense relates to responses against either *an actual armed attack* or a credible impression of *imminent armed attack*. The diplomatic practice of the U.S. government lends support to this interpretation—the U.S. government has condemned as aggression the attacks by North Korea on South Korea in 1950, by Israel on Egypt in 1956, and by Belgium on the Congo in 1960, in which instances there was considerable provocation by the attacks' victims. Egypt, for example, was being used as a base area for persistent and *officially sanctioned* attacks by para-military forces upon Israeli security, with the scale and frequency of attacks mounting in the months before the invasion. Nevertheless, the United States interpreted the Suez Operation as a violation of the U.N. Charter and of general international law. In other words, the mere use of foreign territory as a base area has not been previously claimed by the United States to constitute such a violation of rights as to validate a claim of self-defense. Under these circumstances the assertion of such a claim is itself an illegal act of aggression that may amount, if on a sufficient scale, to an armed attack upon Cambodia giving rise to a right of self-defense on the part of the state of Cambodia (even if this right is not claimed by the presently constituted regime).

In summary, then, the American contention that the Cambodian Operation is a valid exercise of the right of collective self-defense seems without foundation in international law for reasons of *doctrine, diplomatic practice,* and *public policy.*

A Special Limited Claim. The American legal position has also been asserted in terms of a special limited claim to eliminate the base areas on Cambodian territory. This position has not been developed in a serious fashion by the U.S. government. The Deputy Secretary of Defense, David Packard, did allude to this line of justification in the course of a virtually unreported speech given to the Rotary Club in Fort

Worth, Texas. On that occasion Mr. Packard did say: "Under international law we had every right to strike the enemy in areas put to such uses. The inability of Cambodia over a period of years to live up to its legal obligations as a neutral state freed us from the obligation to stay out of these areas. They were not under Cambodian control. They were not neutral." Interestingly, Mr. Packard attributed the timing of the invasion to the changed political situation: "Our failure to disrupt the Cambodian bases earlier was dictated by political considerations which, as long as Prince Sihanouk remained in power, it was felt overrode military considerations." Mr. Packard went on to say, "With the downfall of Sihanouk, there was no longer any reason to believe that the action by South Vietnam or the United States in the occupied border areas would be objectionable to the government of Cambodia."[14] Note that Mr. Packard does not rest the case on any imminent threat to the security of American forces or on any building up of North Vietnamese capabilities. He did, in passing, mention the expansion of base area operations by "occupying enemy forces" as increasing "the potential danger faced by American forces." What is important here is that in the context of arguing on behalf of the alternate theory of enforcing Cambodia's neutral duties, Mr. Packard undercuts any assertion that conditions of imminent attack created an emergency justifying recourse to self-defense.

On its own grounds, however, the claimed right to take limited force to remedy the failure by Cambodia to uphold its neutral duties vis-à-vis North Vietnam encountered formidable difficulties.[15] First, the South Vietnamese claim is clearly not limited to the enforcement of Cambodia's neutral duties; it takes precedence over the American definition of the mission and provides the primary legal measure of what is being claimed. Second, sustained use of overt force against foreign territory by governments for purposes other than self-defense is not compatible with the language of the Charter or the practice of the United Nations.[16] Third, the United States has consistently condemned as illegal much more modest claims to use force against base areas across boundaries.

During the Algerian War of Independence, French forces in 1957 attacked Sakret-Sidi-Youssef, a town in Tunisia being used as a sanctuary and staging area by Algerian insurgents. The United States rejected the French claim that it was permissible to destroy cross-border base areas and supply depots and expressed its public displeasure, even though France was an American ally at the time. Similarly, Adlai Stevenson as U.S. representative in the Security Council condemned Britain's 1964 raid against Habir in Yemen, which was in reprisal for the town's use as a base for operations against the British occupation of Aden. Finally, the United States has on numerous occasions joined in criticizing and censuring Israel for attacking external base areas. The expansion of the theater of violent acts across a boundary by overt and official action has been consistently regarded as illegal under modern international law.

Mr. Packard's assertion that the Lon Nol government would probably not find an invasion objectionable is also a very fragile basis upon which to launch a large-scale invasion. No U.S. official even contends that Cambodia requested or even authorized the invasion, nor was there evident any attempt to secure consent in advance.

Furthermore, contrary to Mr. Nixon's contention on April 30 that "American policy" since 1954 has been "to scrupulously respect the neutrality of the Cambodian people," the number of border-crossing and air-space violations has been extensive ever since the intensification of the Vietnam War in 1964. Prince Sihanouk complained frequently about American violations of Cambodian neutrality, displayed captured American equipment, complained to the International Control Commission, and invited American citizens to visit Cambodia and inspect for themselves evidence of U.S. raids against border areas. These American incursions, although more disruptive for Cambodians than the North Vietnamese use of Cambodian territory as a sanctuary, did not draw Cambodia into the war and were generally consistent with the maintenance of Cambodian peace and security and the confinement of the war to the territory of South Vietnam.

Furthermore, there seems to be something peculiarly perverse about widening the war at a time when the official claim is that American involvement is being diminished. Casualties have been far lower during the withdrawal process initiated by Nixon than at other times during the war. If these base areas could be tolerated for so many years—even when

American objectives were being set forth in more ambitious terms—then what was the reason to assert suddenly a claim based on Cambodia's failure to uphold neutral duties? The only partially satisfactory explanation of the timing of the Cambodian Operation has to do with the fear that the Lon Nol regime was on the verge of collapse. Such explanation lacks much plausibility because the invasion is likely to push the regime closer to collapse, and may encourage the virtual partition of the country between South Vietnam, North Vietnam, Laos, and Thailand. Such an outcome has nothing to do with the enforcement of neutral rights, or, for that matter, with self-defense.

As with the claim of self-defense, there is no support in doctrine, practice, or policy to vindicate an American claim of the proportions of the Cambodian Operation. In the past, the organs of the world community have consistently condemned *lesser* claims—single raids lasting a few hours—to attack or destroy external base areas relied upon by the insurgent side in an internal war. Here, the limits are not narrow—a 21.7 mile territorial belt and a period of two months, besides less restrictive time and space zones for air attacks. Mr. Packard reports that even these limits were imposed on the operation by the President "because he wants the American people to understand that this is a temporary and limited operation."[17] What about respect for norms prohibiting border-crossing uses of force? What about the welfare and autonomy of the Cambodian people, who are the most permanent victims of the claim? Again, we are left with an *imperial* impression, the President giving an *internal* account, without any sense of obligation toward world standards. Such a peremptory claim to enforce neutral rights is the essence of unilateralism which it has been the overriding purpose of modern international law to discourage and moderate in the area of war and peace.

Procedural Norms. One of the most disturbing features of the American role in the Cambodian Operation is the evidence that the U.S. government has acted without any sense of respect for the rules and procedures of law and order on an international level. The minimum legal burden imposed on a head of state is to provide a legal justification to the international community for undertaking action that raises fundamental issues of international law as manifestly as does the invasion of a foreign country. Yet, the American claim to undertake the Cambodian Operation was made in peremptory form. American policy was put forward as an exhibition of sovereign discretion, moderated by some sense of limits, but not subject to review or challenge. In this spirit it is necessary to recall Mr. Nixon's forewarning foreign governments on April 30 that any effort to regard our invasion of Cambodia as a serious breach of international order—or as a flagrant violation of the Charter—would be entirely unacceptable to us.

Beyond the obligation to justify to the Security Council recourse to international force is the obligation to seek a peaceful settlement of an international dispute. Articles 2(3) and 33 of the Charter express this obligation in clear form. The Cambodian Operation is only the latest instance of a continuing American refusal to seek a peaceful settlement of the conflicts that exist in Indochina. It is not possible here to make a detailed analysis of the failure by the United States to respond to the NLF proposal of May 1969 for a settlement of the Vietnam War, the American failure to offer any counterproposal, and the failure to appoint a negotiator of prestige and stature from November 1969, when Henry Cabot Lodge resigned, through June 1970. The Thieu-Ky government has never made a secret of its opposition to a negotiated end to the war; its presence in Paris is a result of American pressure. Indeed, President Nixon's initial appointment of Mr. Lodge—known as an ardent supporter of the Saigon regime—and his subsequent nonreplacement for more than seven months seemed designed to *reassure* the Thieu-Ky group that the United States had no intention of encouraging serious negotiations in Paris.

The Cambodian Operation, then, illustrates a refusal on the part of the United States to comply with minimum procedural norms of international law:

(1) There has been no indication of any willingness to submit to community review the claim to attack a foreign state;

(2) There has been no official effort to reconcile the invasion with the requirements of international law beyond the nominal letter of report to the Security Council; this failure to provide an external explanation of recourse to force

against a foreign country violates Charter norms, at least as these norms have been interpreted on past occasions by the United States in relation to foreign states;

(3) There has been a failure to comply with the legal duty to seek a peaceful solution to the conflicts taking place in Indochina;

(4) South Vietnam has also provided no accounting for its more extensive claims to occupy Cambodian territory, and the United States seems legally responsible to the full extent of these wider claims—claims which even its own legal arguments developed since April 30 have not tried to justify.

IV. SOME CONCLUDING WORLD-ORDER COMMENTS

The development of international law is very much a consequence of the effective assertion of claims by principal states. Such claims create legal precedents that can be relied upon on subsequent occasions by other states. The Cambodian Operation, in this sense, represents both a violation of existing procedural and substantive rules of international law and a very unfortunate legislative claim for the future. It will now be possible for states to rely on the Cambodian Operation in carrying out raids against external base areas or even when invading a foreign country allegedly being used as a sanctuary. It will also no longer be possible for the U.S. government to make credible objections to such claims. The consequences of such a precedent for the Middle East and Southern Africa seem to be highly destabilizing.

In this case, the precedent was established without any effort to justify the claim from the point of view of international public policy. One of the important thresholds of restraint had involved respect for international boundaries, especially with regard to the initiation of full-scale armed attacks. International law has relied on second-order restraints to limit the combat area, even when the wider prohibition on recourse to violence has failed. The precedent set by the Cambodian Operation seriously erodes this second-order restraint, and appears to increase the discretion of national governments as to the permissible limits of force in international affairs.

Covert and sporadic uses of force across international boundaries have been part of the way in which a balance has been reached between the use of external sanctuaries by insurgent groups and the security of the target state. Peremptory strikes against these external base areas have been generally condemned, but the short duration of these claims and the direct response to provocative actions by groups operating from the target state have usually meant that such retaliatory force has not greatly nor indefinitely expanded the theater of combat operations. The Cambodian Operation involves a campaign that concerned at its height more than 50,000 men, heavy air support, and the occupation of foreign territory for an indefinite period of time. As such, it widens considerably the prior understanding of the limits of retaliatory force. Such widening is of serious consequence for at least three reasons:

(1) There are many conflict situations in which one or both contending factions can claim the need to attack external base areas;

(2) The claim to destroy the external base areas of the insurgent will undoubtedly generate counterclaims to destroy the external base areas of incumbent factions;

(3) The unilateral character of a determination as to when it is appropriate to attack external base areas is very subjective, tends to be self-serving, and is difficult to appraise.

In essence, then, the Cambodian Operation represents a step backward in the struggle to impose restraints on the use of force in the conduct of foreign relations. In the specific setting of the Vietnam War, the Cambodian Operation is a further extension of the United States' illegal involvement in Indochina. It has widened the theater of combat, complicated the task of negotiating a settlement, brought additional governments into positions of active cobelligerency, and has been convincingly justified by neither a demonstration of military necessity nor a claim of legal prerogative.

The Cambodian Operation is, perhaps, the most blatant violation of international law by the U.S. government since World War II, but it represents only the most recent instance in a series of illegal uses of force to intervene in the internal affairs of a sovereign society. Until Cambodia, the U.S. government either disguised its interventions, as in Guatemala in 1954, or made a serious effort to justify them, as in relation to the Dominican intervention of 1965. The Cambodian Operation is a peremptory claim to take military action; such action violates the letter and spirit of general international law and the Charter of the United Nations and seems to vindicate the allegation that the United States is acting in Southeast Asia with imperial pretensions rather than as one among many states subject to a common framework of minimum restraint in its international conduct.

PART FOUR

THE INSTRUMENT OF WAR: ECOCIDE

14

War and Urbanization in Indochina[1]

by Laurence A. G. Moss and
Zmarak M. Shalizi

The horror of the war in Viet Nam and Laos has finally
been forced upon Cambodia; the result of a right-wing military coup and the invasion of the country by American and
South Vietnamese forces. With this escalation the "Indo-
China War" has been pulled from the ashes of the French
colonial empire in Southeast Asia and thrust on the American
people. Already the U.S. military decision-makers have begun
to apply to Cambodia what appears to be their present
strategy for "winning a just peace"—forced urbanization
through razing the rural countryside. In Viet Nam and Laos,
where the strategy is operational, mass dislocation of civilians
is causing an enormous increase in urban populations accompanied by tremendous suffering and death.

This article describes urban conditions in Indo-China, using
the most documented case, metropolitan Saigon, for detailed
exposition. An attempt is also made to identify and describe the primary cause of these conditions, and to consider
probable future outcomes.

FRENCH COLONIAL CITIES AND
INDEPENDENT PHNOM PENH

Under French domination the cities of Indo-China,
especially Hanoi and Saigon, had a reputation for picturesque
beauty. Hanoi in northern Viet Nam was developed as the
administrative center of French Indo-Chinese holdings, while
Saigon in the south was built as the entrepot. The European

Laurence A. G. Moss is a Research City Planner of the Department of
City and Regional Planning, University of California, Berkeley, and
specializes in the study of Asian urbanization.

Zmarak M. Shalizi is a graduate student and Mellon Fellow, Department of City and Regional Planning, University of California, Berkeley.

section of Saigon, planned by admirals to resemble a French provincial capital, was replete with tree-lined avenues, sidewalk cafes, a cathedral, European shops containing the choicest offerings of Paris, and fine colonial residences surrounded by gardens. In the early 1930s, this city had a population of about 110,000, of whom 8,500 were Europeans.

About 125 miles to the west of Saigon lies Phnom Penh, the capital of the Kingdom of Cambodia. Of less importance to France than the Vietnamese cities, Phnom Penh moved at a slower tempo. A British traveler in 1933 described it as "a pleasant and colorful city, admirably situated on the banks of the Mekong and dotted with picturesque pagodas and Cambodian palaces."[2] Some 400 miles to the north, also on the Mekong River, is Vientiane, the capital of Laos. Like Phnom Penh it served the French as a provincial capital. Today it has grown into an agglomeration of villages dominated by the disproportionally wide Boulevard Lan Xang that cuts a gash across the city.

With independence, Phnom Penh was upgraded to the capital of a nation. As the center for an expanding national administration and economy, Phnom Penh took on the characteristics of a developing metropolis. From a population of 103,000 in 1936, it grew rapidly to 450,000 in 1960, an annual increase of 14 percent. In the past decade, this rate decreased to 4 to 6 percent so that the city's present population is about 600,000.[3] The Cambodian government has enlarged and improved on the original French plan for the city; and as a consequence, it appears that facilities have been able to stay abreast of the growth, particularly in comparison to conditions in other metropoli of the region. However, there is evidence that in the past few years, while physically the city appeared well, there was economic stress. This was evident in the growing rate of unemployment, particularly among young white collar aspirants. The national capital is Cambodia's only large city. Provincial capitals have been attracting rural people, but in total they still account for less than 15 percent of the nation's population.

Phnom Penh, while no longer a placid colonial town, has maintained an air of luxuriant tranquility. The city's well-kept streets and pastel-colored residential and commercial buildings are shaded by avenues of lush trees. Not yet inundated by the automobile, the people of Phnom Penh rely on bicycles and pedicabs as major passenger modes. The streets, filled with people in the morning and evening, are given over to the sun in the afternoon. The military until recently was conspicuous by its absence, the only common uniformed dress being the brilliant saffron robes of the Buddhist monks.

THE URBANIZATION OF VIET NAM

There is no tranquility in the cities of Viet Nam. Continuous war has swollen the towns and coastal cities of South Viet Nam with refugees from rural villages and hamlets, while in North Viet Nam, the pattern of dislocation is quite different. In the North, the tons of American bombs dropped on the towns and cities, with the exception of Hanoi and Haiphong, have accelerated the government's earlier decision to decentralize the population.

There are no accurate figures on the numbers of people that inhabit the cities and garrisoned towns of South Viet Nam. It is estimated that subsequent to World War II and up to 1965, growth of urban places resumed at about the prewar rate with the exception of the short period after the partition of the country in 1954, when approximately one million people from the North were assimilated in rural and urban areas of South Viet Nam. In the early 1960s, only 15 to 20 percent of South Viet Nam's 16 million people lived in urban places; current estimates place the number at 40 to 45 percent. Early in 1970, one expert on Viet Nam placed the figure at 60 percent.[4] Estimates for the Saigon metropolitan area converge on 4 million people, and a reasonable number for the total of other urban places would be 3.5 to 4 million people.[5] Coastal cities like Da Nang, Nha Trang, and Qui Nhon have doubled and tripled their population, as have many smaller places. Even the conservative Saigon government figures show the coastal city of Nha Trang increasing its population by 138 percent in the short period between 1964 and mid-1968.[6]

Most of this enormous increase has occurred since the escalation of the war in 1965, following Lyndon Johnson's increased commitment of U.S. ground troops and air power. Almost all these migrants to the urban areas are fleeing from U.S. bombing, from search and destroy missions, and from food shortages caused by defoliation. Most of these people are women and children. The men, for the most part, are dead, missing, or fighting.

Metropolitan Saigon, the largest single location of the rural exodus, is a magnification of the problems of the other urban places of South Viet Nam. Of the 4 million people now living in the metropolitan area, approximately 2.8 million are crowded into the 21 square miles of Saigon city. With the doubling of the city's population between 1962 and 1968, the average density has reached 148 persons per acre (compared to Tokyo's 63 persons per acre), and in some areas of the city, it is as high as 830 persons per acre.[7] Saigon may now claim to have the highest density of any city in the world; a reputation that offers no consolation to the unfortunate peasants that have established it.

Much of the overcrowding in the city is concealed behind the pretentious facades of older buildings that define the boundaries of city blocks. The interior of these blocks once served as utility yards and recreation spaces, but are now packed with the shacks of refugees. As space within the blocks became saturated, squatters put up their shelters anywhere they were able to find a space; on road or railroad rights of way, next to or over the canals, and so on. Already by the end of 1966 there was no obvious space left for squatting in Saigon, on either public or private land:

> Today the mayor cannot even find the land on which to build a bus repair station or to move the squatters who block the major road to the park. Though the government possesses a law of eminent domain, it does not use it because no one has enough confidence in the future of the piaster—or, indeed, in the future of the government to begin proceedings that are certain to last for eighteen months. An enforcement of the zoning laws, ancient as they are, is equally out of the question.[8]

Subsequently, densities passed the point of being comprehensible. In 1968, the U.S. Senate Judiciary Subcommittee on Refugees described the city's condition as follows:

> In large sections of Saigon, there are hundreds of thousands of people living in squalor, in subhuman conditions.

They sleep in the alleys and in the streets, in courtyards and halls, even in graveyards and mausoleums where bodies have been removed to allow more room. Most have no work, the children run wild; there is little food, little to sustain them both physically and mentally. The areas they live in are breeding grounds for disease and illness and VC recruitment.[9]

Beyond the city's boundaries, the surrounding Gia Dinh province has also been inundated by people fleeing the razed countryside. Within the past 20 years the metropolitan area has approximately tripled its physical size as a ring of suburban slums expands outward from the city. To the north, the squatters' shacks now stretch toward Bien Hoa, 12 miles distant.

The squatters build their shelters from scraps of wood, metal, thatch, cardboard, and poles they have been able to buy, scavenge, or pilfer. The means of access in these settlements are labyrinths of narrow alleys about three feet in width. Mud, rancid cesspools, stagnant canals, rotting garbage, and human excrement make up the environment of the inhabitants. Around everything there is the constant buzz of flies. Empty artillery shells are used as stoves, and napalm containers are fabricated into family pots and pans. Periodically, fires sweep through these squalid settlements, wiping out 40 to 50 shelters at a time. Fire fighting facilities are too limited and ineffective to assist. The people are left to scrounge and then rebuild.

Some of the migrants locate in government refugee camps. However, the distinction between these camps and the squatter settlements is dubious. Physically, some camps can be distinguished by the comparative regularity of construction. But internal conditions are parallel.

Since responsible officials have been unable to keep pace with the refugee flow, the result has been camps with 10 families in units suitable for only one family; shortages in supplies and foods; inadequate school and sanitation facilities; and an almost total lack of work.[10]

The conditions in these government camps, with the exception of "show pieces," appear to be uniformly appalling, whether in Saigon, a smaller provincial capital, or a garrisoned town. In one refugee camp adjacent to a town in Quang Ngai province, there were 242 families (911 people) left from the hamlet of Nhoc Loc. The median age was 14, the median male age was 12. The shelters they were living in were approximately 9 by 15 feet each, and the average number of persons in each shelter was 13.[11]

The enormous magnitude of the forced migration from the countryside is no doubt far greater than officials have been able to handle, but there has also been little effort made to deal with the problem. While there are officials who are genuinely concerned, the prevailing attitude is one of callous indifference. The excuse is often given that if the refugees are treated too well, they won't leave the cities after cessation of hostilities. The Senate Subcommittee on Refugees found that:

> The refugees were not receiving a minimum of care and the belief that the refugee was a burden permeated the thinking of both the U.S. and GVN. The fear of providing such plush conditions as to create a refugee class was so far from reality as to be almost ludicrous.[12]

Registered refugees, whether living in the camps or not, are theoretically entitled to some compensation and subsistence. However, corruption is rampant. In the staff interviews of the Senate Subcommittee on Refugees, it was repeatedly estimated that less than half the supplies for refugees reached them. Cash payments meet with a similar fate. While those who are registered have some hope of obtaining aid, the majority, who are unregistered or "unofficial," can expect nothing.

> A refugee may be "unofficial" for a number of reasons. Those in camps with a government administration may receive unofficial status because the administrator received no kickback, or because the official arbitrarily decided that certain refugees were politically suspect, or because he just couldn't be bothered with registering them.[13]

Others who hear of this corruption, indifference, and lack of due process do not even attempt to register for assistance.

It is difficult to say just how many Vietnamese are victims of these wretched conditions. Official figures are unreliable as they are based on registered refugees only. An American Friends Service Committee report of 1969 states that in total there are over 4 million displaced persons in South Viet Nam, of which over 1 million people, three-quarters of them children, are living in refugee camps.[14] For Saigon, even as late as 1968, official maps of the city listed zero refugees, yet in the same year the South Vietnamese official in charge of refugees estimated that Saigon had in excess of 300,000 refugees. A more realistic estimate for the same year states over 500,000, and for early 1970, approximately 1,300,000.[15] Another report, of December 1969, says that more than 2 million people live in Saigon's slums.[16]

Not all the migrants to the city are in dire straits; many have their own means or established relatives and friends. Even some of those living in squatter shacks have greater incomes than they had in their villages. Some may even prefer their present situation, but for the satisfaction of these few the cost to the majority of the Vietnamese people, and their culture, has been devastating.

The French planned the city of Saigon for a population of 300,000 people; however, under the weight of the present population, the French-built facilities have all but collapsed. The situation is the same in the smaller centers of South Viet Nam, particularly in the provincial capitals where U.S. military personnel and mercenaries, such as the Korean troops, are garrisoned. What is in general a miserable condition for the inhabitants is tragic for the poor migrants.

There is little of Saigon today that conjures up the image of a French provincial capital; perhaps some of the remaining elegant enclaves of the wealthy, part of central Tu Do Street, and the zoological gardens. The once beautiful shade trees that lined the avenues are grotesque amputees, replaced by garbage, sandbags, and rolls of barbed wire. Streets are now a snarl of honking and belching trucks, jeeps, cars, and Hondas. Saigon has 2,770 "registered" civilian vehicles per mile of street. This includes 7,000 cars and 125,000 motorbikes and scooters; the spoils of a war economy for the fortunate few.[17] The resulting traffic condition becomes completely incomprehensible when one adds military vehicles. The capital had the semblance of a public transportation system until January 1969, when Premier Tran Van Huong retired the few remaining decrepit buses. Now the Saigonese are left to their own means or the gouging taxi and jitney drivers.

The sewage system has all but collapsed. What remains of the old French system still manages to serve some of the inhabitants, but the canals that have always serviced a large number of the city's inhabitants are now full and overflow their putrid banks. They can no longer be dredged, and there is no plan to build new sewers.

Disposal facilities cannot keep pace with the amount of refuse being generated. In some areas of the city, water cannot be seen in the canals as the surface is covered with a layer of decomposed garbage. Americans in particular seem to exacerbate the situation: ". . . no group produces more garbage than Americans, and nothing adds to the garbage problem like army cooking. . . . Huge mounds of beer cans, banana peels, stale food, and torn army undershirts line the streets for dogs, flies, rats, children, and beggars to pick over."[18] The refuse from the refugees, while meager on a one-to-one ratio, grows daily as their numbers compound. The fleet of 160 garbage trucks the city obtained after months of negotiating with U.S. officials scarcely makes a dent in the refuse problem.

Unable to isolate themselves physically from the impact of the grossly inadequate and disintegrating electrical and water systems, the U.S. officials have made some improvements in these facilities. While brownouts and blackouts still occur every other day, the air conditioners of the foreigners, consuming 25 to 30 percent of the city's electricity, now operate most of the time. Yet in the evening one sees few lights in the poor districts of the city. The inhabitants cannot afford to install the lines or pay for the electricity.

Saigon has always had a water problem. Five years ago, with a million extra people drawing on them, the 40 wells that supplied the city with water threatened to pull in brackish water underground from the sea. With a loan from the United States Agency for International Development (USAID) some new pipes were installed, and at the beginning of this year, a project to pipe more water from the Dong Nai River was near completion. But "engineers fear that the 30-year-old French-built mains that must carry the flow are so worn that the upshot will be the world's biggest sprinkler system."[19] Even if the mains survive, large areas of the city will remain waterless, and in areas with service, the poor will obtain little benefit. This situation was eloquently explained to an American by a Vietnamese taxi driver: "The problem with your water system is that the pipes all go to the cement houses. I live in a thatch house and have to buy my water from a rich man."[20]

"Given the topography and a climate like that of New York or Washington, in a perpetual summer, Saigon will never be a healthy city. Given the overcrowding, the lack of drainage, of sewage and garbage collection, it may rate as one of the least healthy cities in the world."[21] In 1968, half of all the city's deaths were among children under five.[22] According to a World Health Organization (WHO) report on tuberculosis prevalence: "It is estimated, through the low-dose standard tuberculosis test, that approximately 60 percent of the population in the city has been infected by tubercle bacilli."[23] Cholera, smallpox, and bubonic plague, as well as leprosy and typhoid, have become endemic in almost every population center in Viet Nam. In 1961, there were 8 cases of bubonic plague; in 1967, 5,500 cases were reported, and many others undoubtedly occurred.[24] The causes reported are an infected and rapidly growing rat population and crowded, unsanitary living conditions. USAID and WHO initiated an inoculation program to combat those diseases affected by vaccine. However, these diseases persist. Other diseases also exist for which there are no vaccines: malaria, amoebic dysentery, swamp fever, and so on. These diseases will thrive and continue to kill unless concern for civilians and their environmental conditions improves considerably. There are no signs of this occurring. Health services remain almost nonexistent. In this country of 16 million, there are only about 1,000 Vietnamese doctors, over half of whom are in the military and seldom treat civilians.[25] To help fill the enormous gap between medical needs and facilities, a number of Western voluntary organizations have committed themselves to health service, but in the aggregate their impact is small. In the face of increasingly critical conditions, the USAID budget for public-health assistance has decreased. Moreover, it is reported that since 1968 the U.S. military has also reduced its medical assistance, especially in the area of investigating and preventing disease among the civilian population.[26]

Little remains of an indigenous economy. Last year the South Vietnamese imported $US850 million worth of goods while exporting only $US16 million.[27] With the increasing amount of rural destruction, less and less is coming into Saigon and other centers for consumption or processing. Defoliation and bombing have turned what was once one of Asia's richest rice-exporting areas into an importer of rice. As late as 1964–65, Viet Nam was still self-sufficient in rice, but since 1968 the United States has been shipping in 700,000 tons annually, of which 70 percent is consumed in Saigon.[28] Only a few light industries have developed in the post-colonial period, and in the entire nation only 3 percent of the work force is employed in local industry. Even if all of this industry were located in metropolitan Saigon, it would scarcely cause a ripple in the city's labor pool. The economist's adage of a large city generating its living from everyone taking in each other's laundry is of minimal applicability to Saigon—where so few own laundry.

South Viet Nam now has one economic base: the U.S. presence and, more precisely, the U.S. military machine. In mid-1968, Americans were spending $600 million a year to float the South Vietnamese economy, exclusive of a $2 billion-a-month military expenditure. In 1970, the combined direct spending on local goods and services by USAID, the U.S. Department of Defense, and private American firms will be approximately $880 million.[29] Yet for all this input, civilian conditions appear to be worsening. Inflation is chronic and growing at an increasing rate. In Saigon in 1966, the black-market exchange rate was 150 piasters per U.S. dollar; in 1969, 220; and in May of 1970 it climbed to 350, and some people obtained 420. The official rate is held constant at 118 piasters per U.S. dollar. In the short period of time from the fall of 1969 to June 1970, the price of rice rose 80 percent. While Saigon has become as expensive a place to live as most Western cities, incomes are a pitiful fraction of their Western counterparts. Of those who have incomes, the hardest hit by spiraling costs is the salaried worker, particularly the government worker. "At about $70.00 per month, the average civil servant's salary comes to about half the income of an industrious cabdriver and barely a tenth of what a skilled bar girl takes home."[30] If this salaried worker doesn't join the ranks of the corrupt, he must take a second job, if available, in order to support his family. Of course, there are those who fare much better than most, particularly those in the military and government who have access to American favor and supplies.

The peasants pouring into the cities have no urban skills or the opportunity to develop them. Where farming land exists it is already fully cultivated by local people, and therefore, at best, the newcomers can locate only marginal land on which they can grow a few vegetables. The fortunate among the men and boys are able to make a living as short-term laborers for the U.S. military and construction firms. The rest must turn to menial tasks like shoeshining, begging, scavenging, stealing, or pimping. Some women are able to find acceptable work as maids, construction workers, and so on. However, many must degrade themselves, bringing shame to their families; already in 1965, a conservative estimate placed the number of prostitutes in Saigon alone at 29,000, the number of bar girls at 80,000.[31] The clientele is mainly American. While the elderly in many cases have died, unable to endure the hardships, those remaining, along with the very young, the infirmed, and the badly maimed, are a tremendous burden on the meager incomes of relatives and friends.

Since most of the migrant children are occupied scrounging a living, they would not have the time to attend school even if educational facilities did exist. "Education" is watching American cowboy movies in 10-cent theaters or crowding around a television set. What was the foundation of Vietnamese society, the family, is now little more than a dream; the role of father, mother, son, or daughter disintegrates under the pressure of survival.

One academic observer appears to be sanguine about South Viet Nam's economic structure. Professor Samuel Huntington of Harvard's Government Department, an adviser to the U.S. government on Viet Nam, to underscore his position points out how in one Saigon slum area, Xom Chua, "in early 1965 before the American build-up, the people lived at a depressed level, with 33 percent of the adult males unemployed. Eighteen months later, as a result of the military escalation, the total population of the slum had increased by 30 percent, but the unemployment rate had dropped to five percent and average income had doubled."[32] What is not pointed out is that with the 30 percent population increase in the slum, living conditions went from worse to unbearable and inflation cut the worth of earning by approximately half. And now that the military has cut back on construction projects and U.S. troops are being withdrawn, the economic base is disappearing. Recently, when a U.S. division headquartered in Phu Cuong withdrew, 8,000 to 10,000 Vietnamese found themselves out of work. These people cannot return to the countryside, as withdrawal is paralleled by continuous bombing of the rural areas. Moreover, their employment opportunities are even further diminished by new refugees that stream into the urban areas seeking shelter from the bombing.

One wonders if in fact there is anyone administering to this Kafkaesque condition, or what type of plans are being implemented to at least reduce the suffering of the millions caught in Viet Nam's tragic urban trap. Urban planning functions in South Viet Nam are sprinkled over a number of national ministries and agencies, bound together by red tape. "City Planning" in the country conforms closely to what is generally referred to as physical planning in the United States and is carried out by the Directorate General of Reconstruction and Urban Planning (DGRUP), a division of the National Ministry of Public Works.[33] All authority is centralized in the Saigon government, to the extent that a plan for a community must make its way up through the bureaucratic ladder to the Prime Minister for approval. In view of this stipulation alone it is easily understood why only ten community plans have been approved since 1962–63. Even these development plans (in fact, merely land use/street plans and programs of easement and construction) are of little worth, as there is neither the personnel nor the budget to implement them. This is not to mention the great changes in land use that occur during the long processing time; and any amendment must climb back up the ladder of authority.

In 1962, DGRUP had a budget of $US1,050,000. In 1968, while there had been a tremendous increase in urban problems, the budget had dropped to $US745,000. For all urban places in South Viet Nam in 1968, using an official figure of 4 million persons living in urban places, about U.S. 2.7 cents per family was spent for city-planning services.[34] When the urban refugees are considered, the actual urban per family expenditure would be half this amount. DGRUP in 1968 had a total of 136 "professionals" (architects and engineers) and "sub-professionals" (clerks and typists) in its employ. Seventy-eight of these were located around the country and 58 were in Saigon; however, only 20 were responsible for the physical planning of Saigon-Cholon. This unbelievable condition becomes ludicrous when delving deeper: the information reveals that of the 20 persons, only 3 were on hand, the others having been drafted![35] There were no replacements. This is a typical situation for government offices. " 'To build a million-man South Vietnamese Army,' says a U.S. civil affairs expert in Saigon, 'we've stripped teachers, engineers and administrators from civil service. This general mobilization is a tragedy.' "[36]

A plethora of government ministries and agencies seems to be involved in making decisions that theoretically affect Saigon, yet the results are negligible. There is no effective administration. "Despite the whirlwind of money passing through it, the city collects very little to spend on its residents."[37] In 1969, Saigon city's budget was $US14 million, which breaks down to a per capita expenditure of about $US4.00, of which two-thirds is deducted for police and official salaries. In sharp contrast, the much smaller city of Berkeley, California, with a $14.1 million budget for 1967, was spending about $125 per capita.

Americans have been involved in the urban planning task, but there is little more to be said about this aid. The few tangible results have come from direct contributions: the partial electricity and water development projects. USAID appears to have no clear or comprehensive plan for involvement. Under the guise of not wishing to offend the Vietnamese by taking over the problems, they have gone to the opposite extreme: supplying professionals to be plugged here and there into the existing system. A number of urban studies have been undertaken, the most extensive probably being the 1965 three-volume Doxiadis report on the Saigon metropolitan area. However, upon completion, the studies become expensive shelf decorations, as there are not the funds, personnel, or concern to implement them.

For a short time it appeared that Saigon's problems were perhaps going to be seriously considered. In 1968, a new American organ called Saigon Civil Assistance Group

(SCAG) was established with the primary purpose of coordinating U.S. advisers in the various government agencies. It also became involved in traffic problems, budget analysis, urban beautification, a housing program, and the creation of political identity among the Saigonese—in total a rather ambitious slate of projects for an agency with an annual budget of only $2 million. In operation, however, SCAG proved to be most interested in building up an image for Saigon's mayor (locally and internationally) and in keeping the lid on local emergency situations by such acts as doling out rice to a particularly depressed group of refugees. The director of SCAG, a retired army officer with no real professional qualifications, has a "public image that casts him as one of Saigon's busiest wheeler-dealers."[38]

Earlier this year, SCAG initiated professional personnel cutbacks and appears to be dropping its urban improvement program. At the same time, USAID has also cut back on urban planning aids and now seems to be primarily concerned with the development of an urban civilian surveillance system.[39] These developments and other cutbacks referred to earlier have ominous implications. It would seem that the United States has never seriously concerned itself with the tragic Vietnamese urban condition, which is primarily of its making; and now at a time when increased saturation bombing is forcing even more Vietnamese peasants into the already bursting cities, the United States is doing less to alleviate the misery and suffering of these people than previously. The goal is merely to *control* the civilians, not to assist them. There can be no excuses for this blatant inhumanity.

THE DEVELOPMENT OF A STRATEGY

The cause of the atrocious urban condition described above is a military strategy that has evolved over the past decade. What was a "side-effect" in 1965–66—the creation of a rural exodus through military operations—has become the strategy for winning in 1969–70 and is a primary component of the Nixon administration's "Vietnamization Policy."

The U.S. involvement in South Viet Nam up to 1960–61 was limited to supplying some advisers and shipping arms and money to the Diem regime. In 1961–62, the number of military advisers was considerably increased, and helicopter gunships were sent in an attempt to make the Army of South Viet Nam (ARVN) capable of combating the National Liberation Front (NLF). The "strategic hamlet" program was initiated in 1962–63 to facilitate the military control and defense of the rural population. Isolated houses in the fields were razed, and their inhabitants were forced to concentrate in barbed-wire-and-spike-surrounded villages. The prototype had been developed earlier as a counterinsurgency tool by the British in Malaya. This program, while a continuation of the French plan to control the Viet Minh by defensive strategies, was quite significant, as it was the first large-scale attempt to physically isolate the rural population from the NLF. The urban areas were virtually ignored, "because at that time the urban populations were smaller and relatively isolated from the country people and the ravages of war."[40]

Beginning with the massive U.S. involvement in 1965–66, there was a shift in military strategy in rural areas from defense to offense. The heavy bombing of northern South Viet Nam and the commitment of U.S. ground troops resulted in a dramatic increase in the flow of refugees from the rural interior to urban coastal places. The U.S. Senate Judiciary Subcommittee on Refugees and Escapees of 1968 found that between December 31, 1964, and December 31, 1965, the cumulative number of "official" refugees shot up from 40,000 to 735,000.[41]

In 1966, the U.S. military began large-scale search and destroy missions; and on July 14 of that year, Dean Rusk, Secretary of State, acknowledged that the "refugee is a *direct* result of the course of military operations" *(emphasis added)*.[42] Several days later, William Gaud, head of USAID, testifying before the Senate Subcommittee on Refugees, stated that "beginning in April, 1966 the refugee flow took a sharp jump upward, doubling the totals of previous months."[43] This coincided with specific search and destroy operations initiated between April 8 and June 20 in the northern and central provinces of South Viet Nam.[44] By August 1, 1966, officially registered refugees approximated 1,500,000, and estimates of nonregistered refugees who had fled to urban centers were unofficially put at another 900,000.[45]

These refugees fled from the countryside not only because of U.S. bombing and search and destroy missions, but also because of random air strikes called in response to sniper fire from villages which resulted in a substantial increase in village destruction. It would appear at this date that:

> The destruction of villages in large areas was not ordinarily an objective of the military operations but was viewed as, in the words of one official, a *side-effect* of hunting the enemy [emphasis added].[46]

In 1967, the military began a policy of large-scale forced "selective relocation" of the rural population:

> The U.S. command with adequate forces at hand for a major assault, faced two problems: how to drive out the enemy without inflicting heavy civilian casualties, and how to prevent the V.C.'s return without committing thousands of U.S. troops to an interminable holding action. The decision was to resort to an ancient and harsh tactic: scorched earth . . . the order was to flatten the jungle and sear it to ash. Included were the villages. . . .
> The scorched earth decision immediately posed another problem: What happens to the civilian population? The U.S. answer was a mass evacuation of 10,000 villagers.[47]

Lacking a coordinated policy on where and how to relocate the population, further aggravated by the lack of concern on the part of the Saigon government, military and civilian authorities' actions resulted in inadequate and negligent reception of the evacuated people. The situation was made even worse by an increasing number of peasants making their own way out of the devastated areas. The Senate Subcommittee on Refugees felt that in 1966 this was a result of the civilian U.S. and South Vietnamese officials not yet grasping the seriousness and extent of the refugee problem. However, even the Subcommittee's own findings indicate that Saigon's concern did not appreciably increase after 1966; and in 1968, the year the Subcommittee stated this opinion, the U.S. government's budget for Vietnamese refugee aid was still a mere $43 million.[48] Volunteer agencies attempted to supplement the inadequate U.S. financial contributions, but their relief efforts were and are still quite inadequate in view of the magnitude of the problem.

After the shattering "Tet Offensive" of 1968, the intensity

and brutality of the war increased considerably on both sides, and for the first time blatantly obvious priority was given to military aims over civilian needs. The senseless destruction of large sections of Hue, the old imperial city, is a grim monument to U.S. "overkill." Numerous other towns and sections of cities in the delta and coastal areas were also callously "destroyed [in order] to save them."[49] Thousands of civilians were killed and wounded. The ambitious U.S. civilian objective of nation-building had finally degenerated into the simplistic military objective of "population control" and "security."[50]

Search and destroy missions and selective forced relocation were greatly reduced in 1968 (the military claimed they were "discontinued"), allegedly because they proved too costly and cumbersome; and U.S. and Vietnamese officials working with refugees were objecting on the grounds that they couldn't deal with the volume of refugees already created by such tactics. Yet there has been a continuous increase in the number of refugees fleeing the countryside to towns and cities since 1968. This increase is the result of the escalation of saturation bombing in South Viet Nam (paralleled in Laos) that began shortly after the bombing halt went into effect for North Viet Nam in 1968, and the result of crop destruction and defoliation, which cause starvation and illness.

The purchase and use of herbicides by the military has grown annually, from $12.5 million in 1965–66 to $70.8 million in 1968–69. As with the American use of conventional weapons, noncombatants are the greatest victims. Dr. Jean Mayer, professor of nutrition at Harvard, concludes from his studies of attempts to starve populations during war conditions: children are struck first and hardest by starvation; then, the elderly, and pregnant and lactating women; last and least adult males, and least of all soldiers.[51] There has also been an increase in indiscriminate ground action and "sweeps," resulting in nonselective forced relocation and the killing of villagers, mainly women, children, and the aged, on location. The heinous massacre of My Lai civilians in 1968, the best known example of these murders, reflects the depths of inhumanity and moral bankruptcy reached in the prosecution of the war.[52]

According to a conservative estimate in *The New York Times,* December 6, 1969, and *The Nation,* April 21, 1969,

3,900 square miles have been completely destroyed by bomb-ings and herbicides; 6.25 percent of the total land area of South Viet Nam. A recent Pentagon release states that between February 1965 and August 1968 over 2.5 million tons of bombs were dropped on South Viet Nam (an area the size of Southern California), which is more than the total tonnage dropped on all the Axis powers during World War II.[53] The ultimate contrivance in conventional destruction—B-52 saturation bombing—has profoundly changed the land-scape in South Viet Nam. The bombs have torn out some 2.6 million craters, 45 feet in diameter and 30 feet deep, which fill with water to become breeding grounds for malarial mosquitoes and other insect disease producers.[54] Many areas of the country now resemble the cratered surface of the moon. One description of the rural devastation of northern South Viet Nam from bombing is by a reporter who saw it from the air:

Like most of the province, the valley of the Song Tra Khuc was spotted with craters of all sizes. Craters from artillery fire, which were a yard or two wide, peppered the rice fields and the former villages, and craters from delayed fuse bombs, which were as much as thirty feet across and seven feet deep, and many of which had filled with water, dotted the landscape with little ponds. Anti-personnel bombs, which explode on contact, had made shallow craters that spread out in rays across the fields, like giant yellow asterisks, and napalm strikes had blackened the fields in uneven splotches. What had for-merly been dense woods on the mountainsides that rose up from the cultivated valley in a series of delicate ridges were just as badly torn up.[55]

As early as 1968, before the increase in bombing intensity, the Senate Subcommittee on Refugees reported that 80 per-cent of the displaced people fled their villages because of the bombings.[56] Now with the deliberate destruction of villages throughout rural South Viet Nam, it should not be surprising that 4.5 to 5 million Vietnamese, or just under one-third of the total population, are refugees.

"We inadvertently stumbled on the solution to guerrilla warfare—urbanization." This is how John Paul Vaun, a retired U.S. Army colonel, now a senior civilian adviser in Viet Nam, describes the present wholesale destruction of rural South Viet Nam, and the killing or relocation of its population.[57] However, this "solution" may not be so inadvertent, for an earlier, less diabolical urbanization strategy had been proposed by General J. Gavin in 1966. His proposal, suggested as an alternative to the manpower-intensive military strategy the United States was pursuing in 1966, envisioned the development of "defensive enclaves" throughout South Viet Nam. Saigon, Da Nang, Cam Ranh Bay, and a few other key coastal areas would be secured with a smaller military effort and still serve the U.S. global strategy of containing Chinese expansion and thwarting a NLF victory. At the same time, General M. Ridgeway, a Korean War army veteran, came out in favor of the enclave strategy:

> A concept like the one discussed by General J. Gavin, for holding fast to our defensive enclaves, would enable us to fulfill our obligation to our Vietnamese allies, before committing ourselves to an unlimited military effort. . . .

This, of course, was basically a military proposal, and there was no elaboration on the nature of the enclaves other than their defensive military character—a magnified strategic hamlet system.

General Ridgeway was also strongly opposed to the air strategy that was to come into effect:

> It is my firm belief that there is nothing in the present situation or in our code that requires us to bomb a small Asian nation 'back into the Stone Age. . . .' A victory that would require the wholesale devastation of a country . . . would be the ultimate in immorality.[58]

Gavin's strategy was not adopted by the military and civilian decision-makers since it left the NLF forces in control of the countryside, a condition which could not be construed as a military victory. The long-standing battle between the military services to determine who wins the critical battles and the budgetary appropriations also probably contributed to the rejection of this strategy, which would have given a minor role to the U.S. Air Force. The destruction of rural Viet Nam continued unabated and at an increased level, with the air force using saturation bombing and chemical weapons and the army moving into a phase of greater destruction of villages and their civilian population.

From the considerable increase in saturation bombing that began late in 1968 and the reduction of ground operations, it would seem that support solidified behind a shift from a "manpower intensive" to a "capital intensive" strategy—pull out the ground troops and decimate the countryside from the air. As a result, the rural civilian population would either come out to the urban enclaves or die in their villages. In either case, the NLF and North Vietnamese forces would theoretically lose their bases of operation—the people. When this strategy is fully operational, the army's role is reduced to one of advising and helping ARVN to protect the new "defensive enclaves." The Nixon administration hopes that this new low posture—reducing the U.S. troop commitment and casualties—will appease the American public and allow the administration to continue to fight for a military victory. This is the essence of "Vietnamization."

Apologists, such as Professor Samuel Huntington, consider this massive American effort of destruction and dislocation not as bombing a country "back into the Stone Age," but as

> A *social* revolution in the Vietnamese way of life which will be of far greater consequence to the future of the country.[59]

To him this is "a war for the *control* of the population" [*emphasis added*], not the destruction of an army and supply routes, since the NLF is not a conventional army but an extension of the frustrated rural population:

> . . . with half the population still in the countryside, the VC will remain a powerful force which cannot be dislodged from its constituency so long as the constituency continues to exist.[60]

While he recognizes that peace is based on accommodation, the conclusion from the above is obvious, and he does not shrink from it. One can insure that the constituency ceases to exist by

"direct application of mechanical and conventional power . . ." on such a massive scale as to produce a massive migration from countryside to city. . . . [Thus, the] . . . *Maoist-inspired rural revolution is under-cut by the American sponsored urban revolution* [emphasis added].[61]

In the cities, the NLF constituency—the rural population—can, it is hoped, be controlled in refugee camps and slums in and around Saigon and other coastal "enclaves." Noam Chomsky comments on Huntington's position:

In other words, the answer to a people's war is to *eliminate the people.* The means to accomplish this end are the "modernizing instruments" of bombs and artillery. The U.S. can thus escalate the war by bombing the countryside, while pulling out some U.S. troops.[62]

And, conceivably, by this brute force, the United States may still "win" in Viet Nam—and in the rest of Indo-China.

LAOS AND CAMBODIA

The U.S. military decision-makers, in their belief that they have finally found a strategy to eliminate the revolutionary element from Asian societies, have not been satisfied with the destruction of Viet Nam. Their scorched earth strategy is also being applied in Laos. In fact, Laos may have been the original testing ground for the concept of annihilating the civilian base of the "enemy." Heavy U.S. bombing of the Pathet Lao controlled areas of Laos as early as 1965 had already created large numbers of refugees: between 250,000 and 430,000 by press estimates.[63]

In October 1969, *The New York Times* reported that in Laos, "the rebel economy and social fabric" were now the main target of American bombing:

Refugees from the Plaine des Jarres area say that during recent months most open spaces have been evacuated.

Both civilians and soldiers have retreated into the forests and hills and frequently spend most of the daylight hours in caves and tunnels. Refugees said they could only sow their fields at night because they were unsafe during the day. . . . The bombing, by creating refugees, deprives the Communists of their chief source of food and transport. The population of the Pathet Lao zone find it increasingly difficult to fight a "people's war" with fewer and fewer people.[64]

Noam Chomsky's comments on the *Times* reporting are worthy of serious consideration:

It is, incidentally, remarkable that the *Times* can so blandly announce that the rebel economy and social fabric are the main target of the American bombardment. It is remarkable that this claim, if correct, sets American policy at the moral level of Nazi Germany, can be merely noted in casual comment, with—so far as I know—no public reaction of horror and indignation.[65]

Large numbers of those who are not killed in the saturation bombing raids and who do not flee to the towns and cities under Royal Lao government control, are forcibly air evacuated by the United States. One such evacuation in February, reported in the *Washington Post*, March 2, 1970, included some 13,000 people from villages on the Plaine des Jarres. In an earlier evacuation on September 13, 1969, carried out in conjunction with the Royal Lao Army, a village on the north side of the plain was burned and looted, the livestock shot, and the Lao men drafted into the army.[66] The United States is said to be operating a continual airlift to "relocate" the population. Planes carry thousands of refugees daily out of bombing zones to government-controlled cities such as Pakse, Sayebourg, and Vientiane, where they are located in shacks euphemistically called "relocation camps."[67] These government-controlled centers, while smaller in proportion with the smaller Lao population, are rapidly coming to resemble their Vietnamese counterparts. Between early 1968 and late 1969, the population of the capital, Vientiane, increased approximately from 88,000 to 160,000.[68] As in Viet Nam, women, children, and the old predominate.

There is no employment for these refugees; they live from begging and the rice USAID doles out. In the camps "most of the people sit dozing, waiting listlessly—sometimes for months, sometimes for years—for jobs and new homes."[69]

At present over one quarter of the Lao population—about 700,000 persons—are refugees.[70] Not all are the direct result of U.S. bombing; however, bombing is the major cause. In 1965, American bombers were flying an average of 50 sorties per day over Laos, which was a hundredfold increase over 1964. In 1966, the number of sorties was doubled, and by the end of April 1970, U.S. bombers were flying approximately 900 sorties a day, each day dropping an average of 1,980 tons of bombs.[71] The cost of munitions dropped in one day alone approximates $2.9 million—over $1 billion annually.[72] In stark contrast is the meager $2 million annual budget of SCAG, the U.S. agency set up to aid in solving Saigon's urban problems.

What have been the political advantages of this killing and dislocation? For the United States, seemingly little. The Pathet Lao, pointing to the bombing attacks on innocent villagers, have no trouble convincing these people of the ruthlessness of Americans. "The message is sinking in; many refugees now say they hate Americans. Further, a significant portion of the population—the youth—is sticking with the Communists. Most of the refugees are either the very old or the very young."[73]

Despite these obvious political failures and the lack of tangible military gains, the United States continues to destroy Laos, and in May of this year began saturation bombing in Cambodia. B-52 bombing raids began in the first week of the American invasion and with them the familiar pattern began to emerge—the establishment of "free-fire zones," the razing of villages, and the flow of refugees. From recent U.S. administration statements there can be little doubt that the bombing of Cambodia will continue after the withdrawal of U.S. ground troops.[74] The American government has already committed itself financially to supporting the Lon Nol regime,[75] and with the regime's effective control limited to Phnom Penh and a few other urban places, the stage is set for the United States to move ahead with its urbanization strategy in Cambodia. However, there is a new development in the macabre strategy—it is indicated that Thai and South Vietnamese will take a considerable role in the bombing. Thus, through American planning, Phnom Penh may become the horror that Saigon is, unless there is immediate and substantial change in U.S. policies.

AFTER THE VILLAGES ARE EMPTIED

The urban "strategic hamlet" is a logical extension of an attempt to "control the population" which did not succeed in the rural "strategic hamlet." Both strategies evidence a decision-making style of short-term reaction to immediate problems, overlooking the long term, and apparently more costly, consequences of these strategies in the future. The maximization of military goals is given precedence over the optimization of social, economic, and political goals.

Speculating upon the U.S. action, it seems clear that a great deal of faith is being placed in contemporary history, and in an intelligence system that has proven quite inaccurate in the past: The Chinese revolution was rural based; therefore, the Vietnamese cannot be otherwise. The Tet Offensive failed to instigate a mass urban uprising, thus the NLF will be unable to carry one out in the future. These seem to be rather simplistic assumptions. It is doubtful that the NLF has to date ever made a major effort to organize mass urban support. This owes

perhaps, less to the bias of Maoist-doctrine than to their own emotional ties with the Vietnamese village. But they may learn better. Faced with a military stalemate, they can only hope to exploit urban unrest.[76]

Today, metropolitan Saigon is swollen with refugees. The Saigon administration and U.S. decision-makers made no preparation for this influx and are still not attempting to alleviate the problems it creates. With intolerable conditions daily growing worse under the pressure of existing and newly dislocated people, urban insurrection becomes a real possibility.

What a report in *U.S. News & World Report* considered to be the NLF strategy of 1968:

First, create as many refugees as possible, by forcing battles that destroy homes.

Second, wait for or touch off incidents among these unhappy people.

Third, exploit these incidents to create the appearance of the general uprising, for which Hanoi has called—but hasn't yet got.[77]

seems to be obtaining considerable assistance from the action and inaction of the Saigon government and its American advisers. An ironic twist to the urbanization strategy may be in the making: from Huntington's *"urban* revolution" to an NLF "urban *revolution."*

However, the United States appears to believe that the urban populations can be controlled regardless of their condition. As was pointed out earlier, USAID has recently embarked on a large National Security Police training program, with American "public safety" advisers devising a stringent surveillance network to govern movement into and within Saigon. Failing to isolate the strategic hamlet from the NLF, it would appear that the U.S. and the Saigon governments believe they will have more success with the strategic city.

Regardless of who wins the urban battles, it will be the Vietnamese people who continue to pay the high cost of America's vanity. Packed into the slums in their search for the safety of their lives and that of their loved ones, many more will die needlessly, unless the United States quits the Thieu-Ky regime. To understand why, one need only look to 1968 when, during and after the Tet Offensive, the U.S. military and ARVN demonstrated their willingness to destroy cities as well as villages. In 1968, Saigon's shantytown waterfront district housed close to a half million people; 18,500 shanties were destroyed in the battle. According to an American adviser:

First VC mortar shells hit the area and then our helicopter gunships came in and flattened it . . . and there was no VC here.[78]

Many of the delta towns were also heavily damaged:

One American with whom I spoke witnessed ARVN soldiers systematically putting houses to torch, forcing

residents out in order to facilitate wholesale looting.
Time and again I heard descriptions of how whole
blocks were cordoned off to isolate a couple of snipers,
after which planes were called to level the area.[79]

During that same period, the NLF did not shrink from
mortar attacks on towns throughout South Viet Nam, many
resulting in civilian death.

But whatever the reason for the apparently random
attacks, they are not driving the [urban] populace into
the arms of the government. Said one professor [com-
menting on the U.S. military reaction]: "To save us from
2, 20 are killed, to save us from 20, 200 are killed, and it
is all justified by calling the 200 'Viet Cong'."[80]

Regardless of one's position on the United States' Indo-
China War, in scrutinizing this urbanizing strategy and the
resulting urban condition, one can only be appalled by its
inhumanity and indifference to life and suffering. The country,
the society, and the people of Viet Nam have suffered
irreparably at the hands of the Americans. Hundreds of
thousands have been killed, and many times that number
maimed, physically and psychologically. Their countryside
has been devastated, and their social fabric torn apart. The
destruction of Laos, while less extensive, is equally appalling.
And now Cambodia is seriously threatened.

In 1965, at a meeting in Honolulu with Air Marshall Ky,
President Johnson committed the United States to the reconstruction and rehabilitation of Viet Nam (North and South).
The time to honor this commitment is now. The only "victory" for America will be in regaining her esteem, in her own
and the eyes of others, by withdrawing her military forces
from Indo-China immediately and then attempting to repair
the enormous damage she has inflicted. However, Americans
must realize that no amount of peaceful assistance will ever
compensate for the full extent of the damage inflicted on the
peoples of Indo-China. We may only hope that time will
cause the scars to become less painful.

15

Leaf Abscission*

by Ngô Vinh Long

"Leaf abscission" is a term used by American military men
to designate their chemical war in Viet Nam. The term, like
its sister word "defoliation," is meant to suggest that the
dumping of herbicides and other chemicals over a tiny piece
of land that has also been the victim of the most intense
bombing in world history[1] has helped to thin out a few
troublesome trees and shrubs while causing no significant
damage to anything else at all. On the contrary, the use of
herbicides and other chemicals sprayed by the American
military in Viet Nam has already caused untold misery to
thousands of innocent civilians.

From late 1959 till early 1963 I was involved in making
detailed military maps of the whole of South Viet Nam, and
thus had occasion to be at one time or another in virtually
every hamlet and village in the country. It was in 1959 that
the Diem regime began putting into effect its "pacification"
program. As for the Vietnamese majority living in the plains,
by February 1959, "relocation of families within communities had begun and, in contrast to land development and
refugee activities, these relocations were often forced."[2] The
restructured villages, surrounded by moats and barbed wire,
were euphemistically known as "agrovilles." (In Vietnamese
they were called *khu trù mât*, a term with Chinese roots
which was presumably supposed to carry a graceful connota-
tion, although it literally means something like "compacted

* This is a revised version of an article from the English language
edition of *Thời Báo Gà* (No. 5, November 1969), a monthly publication
by a group of Vietnamese students in the United States. For more information about the publication, write to *Thời Báo Gà*, 76a Pleasant Street,
Cambridge, Mass. 02139.

Ngô Vinh Long is a graduate student in Vietnamese and Chinese
History at Harvard University and Editor of *Thời Báo Gà*, a publication
of Vietnamese students in Canada and the United States.

area" or "concentration zone.") People were taken from their plots of ground, where their houses, their rice-fields, their ancestral tombs were located, and moved to totally unsuitable areas where they could be "protected."[3] As for the ethnic minorities living in the mountains (often referred to in Western writings as "montagnards"), the Diem regime forced them down into the lowlands and into concentration-camp-like compounds where they were to call themselves by the new name of *Viêt Nam Mói* (or "New Vietnamese") and were to dress like the Vietnamese majority—a "cultural revolution" of sorts! In both cases, the houses and fields of those who had been relocated were burned, in order to deny their use to the "Viet Cong." (As early as 1956, Diem was already making extravagant use of the term "Viet Cong"—which literally means "Vietnamese Communists"—to mean anybody who opposed him.)

By 1961, when the American defoliation program had begun against jungle growth along highways, railways, and in places considered to be Viet Cong areas, the Diem regime was not long in finding new uses for the chemicals: by the end of November 1961, American special warfare troops had begun teaching Vietnamese fliers how to spray "Communist-held areas with a chemical that turns the rice-fields yellow, killing *any crop* being grown in rebel strongholds."[4] The Diem regime began putting this training into practice within a month. The "rebel strongholds" were more often than not, as I have witnessed personally, simply communities in sparsely populated areas isolated from effective government control. For this reason the Diem government felt it had to resort to killing their crops as a means of driving the population more quickly into the new and overly ambitious "strategic hamlets" *(ap chien luoc)*, which had replaced the abortive "agro-villes" early in the year. It was easier to order fliers to spray crops from the air than to send ground soldiers into the villages to force the people out by setting fire to their fields and houses. It had been discovered that government soldiers, on coming face to face with the misery and tearful entreaties of the dispossessed, were very often inclined to resist orders. The combined effects of regrouping the population in totally unsuitable areas and of killing their crops brought hunger and starvation to thousands of people.[5]

The misery inflicted upon thousands of people through the

killing of their crops to force them into the "strategic hamlets," and the repression of Buddhists and students, among other factors, led to the downfall of the Diem regime. In an attempt to stabilize the situation, the U.S. government began sending its troops into South Viet Nam. But even before the collapse of the Diem government, the U.S. military had already taken over the task of spraying crops in what they referred to as "Viet Cong territory."[6] In September 1963, Rufus Philipps reported to the President of the United States, "giving [him] the estimates of USOM Rural Affairs that the Delta was falling under Viet Cong control in areas where pacification was supposedly complete."[7] The delta is the whole land mass south and southwest of Saigon where most of the crops in the country were planted. In 1963, "Viet Cong territory," as defined by the Americans, therefore comprised a very sizable part of the food-producing area of the country!

Beginning in 1965, the American military initiated still another version of "pacification" by sending the Marines to "secure villages" and to root out "Viet Cong infrastructures."[8] After two years of continuous effort, a *New York Times* report of August 7, 1967, citing official U.S. data on the loyalties of the hamlets, stated that the number of hamlets under total Saigon government control was a mere 168, while the number of those totally controlled by the Viet Cong was 3,978. The rest of the hamlets were listed as "contested." To win the contest, or as the new name for the pacification program put it: to be successful in "The War to Win the Hearts and Minds of the People," the U.S. military was finding new ways to "pacify" the villages. One way was to send out American troops with bulldozers and bombers to raze the villages to the ground, and subsequently to transport the inhabitants to the so-called "camps for refugees fleeing from Communism" in and around the larger towns and cities where they could be "protected."[9] Another way was the intensified use of chemicals, much in the same way Diem had used them before. The well-known journalist Seymour M. Hersh writes:

But by early 1967, Presidential advisers had a different reason for using herbicides, one that wasn't directly linked to cutting off Viet Cong food supplies. The rationale was presented to a group of scientists who met in February with Donald Hornig, President Johnson's chief scientific adviser, to protest the use of anticrop chemicals. According to one scientist who attended the session, Hornig explained that the anticrop program was aimed chiefly at moving the people. The source quoted Hornig as explaining that when the United States found a Viet Cong supporting area, it was faced with the alternatives of either bombing, bulldozing, and attacking it or dropping leaflets telling the people to move because the herbicides were coming. As Hornig expressed it, "it's all geared to moving people."

Mr. Hersh further states that the Pentagon used 60 million dollars' worth of defoliants and herbicides—12 million gallons—in Viet Nam in 1967, which was enough to cover "nearly half of the arable land in South Viet Nam." He also writes that, since Pentagon officials were arguing that the herbicides were more effective in killing crops than in stripping foliage,

> . . . by the end of 1966 more than half of the C-123 missions were admittedly directed at crops, and it is probable that any effort at a trebling of capability in 1967 was aimed not at the jungles of South Viet Nam but at its arable crop land.

In a study of American anticrop and defoliation methods, Yōichi Fukushima, head of the Agronomy Section of the Japan Science Council, claims that American chemical attacks by 1967 had ruined more than 3.8 million acres (or one-half) of the arable land in South Viet Nam, and were a direct cause of death for nearly 1,000 peasants and more than 13,000 head of livestock. The impact of the U.S. anticrop program upon those peasants who escaped being taken to the "camps for refugees fleeing from Communism" is not known. As for the "refugees," their situation was (and is) so bad that the editorial staffs of Saigon newspapers, in spite of the harsh government censorship, felt compelled to run long articles on the misery endured by these people. For in Viet Nam people say that "you can't cover an elephant's mouth with a basket." Certain facts are so well known that they simply cannot be hidden from view. Thus, even *Song* (a Saigon daily newspaper which was specifically created to justify the "pacification" program [of which the defoliation program is a part] and whose editor and staff were members and leaders of the Rural Development Cadre Teams sponsored by the joint cooperation of the CIA and the USOM) had this to say on December 10, 1967, in a long article entitled "Looking at the Faces of the Two Quang Provinces in War, Hunger, Misery, and Corruption":

This is a free area—free for depravity, corruption, irresponsibility, cowardice, obsequiousness, and loss of human dignity. What the devil is dignity when people sit there waiting to be thrown a few hundred piasters and allotted a few dozen kilos of rice a month? . . . I believe that even if a certain Communist had in his pockets several dozen "open-arms program" passes, after seeing the kind of humiliated life in a refugee camp he would run away without daring to look back.

But we seem to like this, and the Americans also like us to perform these kinds of activities so that they can have a lot of big statistics to present to both their houses of Congress. The Americans like to count, count people's heads, count square and cubic meters, and count the money they throw out. They think that the more they can count, the better is the proof of their success, the proof of their humanitarianism, and the proof of their legitimacy in this war. . . . How high a figure has the number of refugees who have to suffer and stay hungry reached? *Many statistics proudly present the number two million.* [*emphasis added*]

If the number two million only referred to the situation in 1967, then how many more people have been victimized since then?

In an article entitled "Military Uses of Herbicides in Vietnam" published in the British journal *New Scientist* on June 13, 1968, Arthur Galston, Professor of Biology at Yale University and President of the Botanical Society of America, wrote:

The Air Force is preparing to spray about ten million gallons of herbicides over South Vietnam in the year beginning July 1968. . . . It is estimated that this will be enough to treat almost four million acres, of which about one-third will be crop land.

Professor Galston went on to say:

. . . With respect to the deliberate killing of crops in order to deprive the Viet Cong military of food, it can only be remarked that whenever starvation is used as a weapon against an entire civilian population, the main sufferers are inevitably the aged, the infirm, pregnant women, and children under five years old. The fighting man almost always gets enough food to sustain himself. Thus in using hunger as a weapon we are attacking the part of South Vietnamese society which is least involved in military operations and whom we would least wish to injure.

In the June 29, 1966, issue of *Christian Century*, two Harvard physicians, Dr. Jean Mayer, Professor of Nutrition, and Dr. Victor W. Sidel, warned that the U.S. anticrop program in Viet Nam, like that of every food blockade or like some of the famines that they have witnessed, would create a process which begins with the death from starvation of small children first, then older children, and then the elderly. In the case of South Viet Nam, as rightly noted in a report by the Boston-based Physicians for Social Responsibility, dated January 1967, *malnutrition, even before the anticrop program, was already a serious problem*, and beriberi, night blindness, anemia, decayed or poor teeth, endemic goiter, and other nutritional diseases were found to be widespread in the country. How high is the percentage of people affected by the above diseases now, after the U.S. military has effectively destroyed perhaps half or more of the arable land in South Viet Nam? Nobody knows the exact figure.

Besides hunger and starvation and their accompanying effects, have the chemicals used by the American military in Viet Nam caused any direct harm, immediate or eventual, either to animal or human life? At least three basic types of chemicals have been in use: 1) Agent Orange, a 50-50 mixture of two defoliants, 2,4,5-T (trichlorophenoxyacetic acid) and 2,4-D (dichlorophenoxyacetic acid); 2) Agent Blue, a neutralized cacodylic acid; and 3) Agent White, also known as Tordon 101, a weaker mixture of "unknown chemicals."[10]

First of all, according to a report of the National Institute of Environmental Health Science, September 1969, which contains data on the effects of pesticides, collected during the period 1965-1968 by the Bionetics Research Laboratory of Litton Industries (under contract for the National Cancer Institute), both 2,4,5,-T and 2,4-D have been shown in tests on mice to produce significant increases in the incidence of malformation in fetuses and also in the incidence of cancer. The worst of the two is 2,4,5-T, which repeatedly produced test results of 100 percent in the proportion of abnormal litters.

In Viet Nam there has for a long time been talk linking an apparent alarming rise in the incidence of birth deformities to the chemicals sprayed by the Americans there. The Americans and the Saigon regime have repeatedly denied that the chemicals they use could cause any harm whatsoever to animal or human life. Last summer, several Saigon newspapers, in defiance of strict censorship and the possibility of having their offices closed down, printed stories and pictures of horribly deformed babies born in villages that had been "defoliated." For example, *Tin Sáng,* in its June 26, 1969, issue, printed an interview with an old woman who reported that her newly pregnant daughter was caught in a chemical strike and fainted, with blood coming out of her mouth and nostrils, and later from the vulva. She was taken to a hospital where she was later delivered of a deformed fetus. *Dông Nai,* another Saigon newspaper, printed on the same day a long article entitled "The Disease of Women Producing Stillborn Fetuses," which they said was a new phenomenon which was causing the "noisiest discussion" in the country. Next to the article is a photograph of a dead deformed baby with a face like that of a duck and the section around the stomach shrunken and twisted. The same newspaper, on the following day, reported a case of a woman giving birth, in Long An Hospital in Tan An District, to a deformed baby with two heads, three arms, and twenty fingers. Just above the article, the paper carried a picture of another deformed baby with a head that resembles that of a poodle or a sheep. Still another Saigon newspaper, *Tia Sáng,* on June 26, 1969, printed a picture of a baby with three legs, a head squeezed in close to the legs, and two arms wrapped around a big bag that replaced the lower section of the face. Under the picture there is a separate report of the deformed baby mentioned above with two heads, three arms, and twenty fingers.

The Saigon government's counterargument was that the birth defects were caused by what it called "Okinawa bacteria." But many Vietnamese and American scientists who have seen the kinds of birth deformities in Viet Nam either in person or in pictures disagree with this argument. They say that venereal diseases can only cause warps in the bones and skin boils on new-born infants, and not such complete change in bodily structures. Even in an interview reported in the Saigon Army Newspaper, *Tien Tuyen*, Dr. Pham Tu Chính, Director of the Hùng Vuong Government Obstetrics Clinic, asserted that the cases of birth deformities that were causing concern in the country definitely could not have been caused by venereal diseases.[11]

In the rural areas, where most such known cases of deformed fetuses have occurred, there is an extreme shortage of trained medical personnel or of professional obstetric services, at least in those areas not held by the NLF. Thus it is difficult to compile accurate statistics concerning this phenomenon.

When the report of the National Institute of Environmental Health Sciences and the news of birth deformities in Viet Nam came to the attention of some American scientists, they went to Washington to try to persuade the U.S. government to curb the use of the harmful chemicals. On October 31, 1969, the *Washington Post,* in an article entitled "New Curbs Won't Affect Defoliation in Viet Nam," reported:

New White House restrictions on the use of a powerful herbicide will not affect its military usefulness in Vietnam, the Defense Department said yesterday.

The Pentagon statement said no change would be made in policy governing military use of the defoliant 2,4,5-T because the Defense Department feels its present policy conforms to the new presidential directive.

Four days later, in an article entitled "Spray Earth Policy" in the New York *Post,* November 4, 1969, Frank Mankiewicz and Tom Braden had this to say:

Those who are concerned over a possible massacre—
even of women and children—in South Vietnam when
U.S. troops depart might consider the fact that we now
spray throughout South Vietnam enormous amounts of
an anticrop chemical which has been known for three
years to cause deformed births in test animals—at a rate
of 100 per cent.

At least four newspapers in South Vietnam printed
stories—and pictures—last summer of deformed babies
born in villages sprayed with the chemical (called 2,4,-
5-T), and the newspapers were promptly closed down by
the Thieu government for "interfering with the war
effort."

Use of the chemical, described by our government
as "probably dangerous," is now banned in "populated
areas" and on or near food products in the United
States, but the Pentagon announced last week that it
would continue to use it in Vietnam, where Army Service
Manuals set forth its appropriate use against food supplies.

In addition, it is widely used in areas where the population captures its drinking water from rain, by the use
of roof gutters and barrels, and where wells are sunk
into soil saturated with the chemical.

Just how high an "offensive potential" this chemical
warfare had was not really known until 1966 when, for
the first time, the National Institute of Health com-
missioned tests on pregnant animals. The study showed
that severe malformation of offspring occurred in rats
at the rate of 39 per cent[12] . . . when they were given a
small dose [of 2,4,5-T]. When this dose was increased
to the level a Vietnamese woman might consume in a
few days in her drinking water, the percentage of
fetal malformation rose to 90 and beyond.

Whether the rate of human malformation from contact with this chemical is greater or less than with rats
is, of course, unknown.

It was this that prompted the finding that 2,4,5-T was
seriously hazardous and "probably dangerous" and
caused its removal from the domestic market in the
United States. The President's science adviser, Dr. Lee
du Bridge, perhaps adumbrating the Pentagon's refusal

to cut down its use against Asians, said only that the rate of fetal malformation was "greater than expected."[13]

. . . Not since the Romans salted the land after destroying Carthage has a nation taken pains to visit the war on future generations.

As for Agent Blue, the *Merck Index of Chemicals and Drugs* says that it is an organic arsenical acid composed 54.29 percent of arsenic. Arthur W. Galston, the Yale biologist mentioned earlier, in an article in the August-September 1967 issue of *Science and Citizen*, wrote that the lethal dose of the above compound in dogs is one gram per kilogram body weight, when administered beneath the skin. He added that if the same toxicity held for man, then about 70 grams, or slightly over two ounces, would kill the average 150-pound man. In the article already quoted, Seymour M. Hersh pointed out that in cases of "emergency," which he learned were not infrequent (especially when American pilots are exposed to heavy ground fire), the high-pressure spray nozzles of a plane on a spraying mission can eject the entire 1,000-gallon cargo in just 30 seconds. In such cases, who knows what might happen to the people below!

In the already quoted study prepared by Yōichi Fukushima, there is a testimony by Cao Von Nguyên, a doctor, which included a description of a chemical attack near Saigon on October 3, 1964, in which nearly 2,500 acres of crop-producing land, a large number of livestock, and more than 1,000 inhabitants were affected:

. . . They had only breathed in the polluted air or the poison had touched their skin. At first, they felt sick and had some diarrhea; then they began to feel it hard to breathe and they had low blood pressure; some serious cases had trouble with their optic nerves and went blind. Pregnant women gave birth to stillborn or premature children. Most of the affected cattle died from serious diarrhea, and river fish floated on the surface of the water belly up, soon after the chemicals were spread.

At a press conference in New York on April 3, 1969, E. W. Pfeiffer, Professor of Zoology at the University of

Montana, and G. H. Orians, occupying the same position at the University of Washington, after returning from an official mission to Viet Nam to investigate the effects of the U.S. defoliation program, reported that while traveling in an armed naval vessel along a 65-mile strip of waterway linking Saigon with the sea, they observed that the mangroves on both sides had been denuded, that scarcely any living creatures were to be seen, and that bird life had apparently been greatly reduced.[14]

Cambodia is also a victim of U.S. defoliation. Later in 1969, Professor Pfeiffer returned to Indo-China as a member of an international scientific commission, this time to investigate herbicidal damage by the United States in southeastern Cambodia (the "Fishhook" area). There the commission found conditions similar to those in Viet Nam: about 173,000 acres had been damaged by defoliants, including extensive damage to precious rubber trees and food crops. The inhabitants suffered diarrhea and vomiting, particularly the children; animals had become ill, some of the smaller ones dying.[15]

The dumping of herbicides and other chemicals in Viet Nam, besides causing harm to people, animals, and crops, as we have seen, could also trigger changes in ecology that, according to the belief of many scientists, may permanently reduce the once-fertile fields in Viet Nam to dust bowls. Laterization, a process which occurs in tropical regions when the organic material and chemicals that normally enrich the soil are washed away because of lack of protective growth, thus resulting in a reddish soil that hardens irreversibly into a bricklike consistency upon exposure to sunlight, has begun in some areas in Viet Nam.

There is some evidence that even if the spraying were to be stopped now, the process of laterization would likely continue for some time in the future. Fred H. Tschirley, assistant chief of the Crops Protection Research Division of the U.S. Department of Agriculture and former adviser to the U.S. Department of State, in an article entitled "Defoliation in Vietnam" in the February 21 issue of *Science,* wrote:

> Strips of mangrove on both sides of the Ong Doc River, sprayed with Orange in 1962, were of particular interest. The treated strips were still plainly visible. Thus,

one must assume that the trees were not simply defoliated, but were killed . . . 20 years may be a reasonable estimate of the time needed for this forest to return to its original condition.

Also, Agent Blue (an arsenic compound) does not disintegrate or decompose in the soil but will keep on killing vegetation and soil microorganisms for a long time. Furthermore, as Representative McCarthy of New York pointed out in his book *The Ultimate Folly,* the herbicides used in Viet Nam are made ten times more potent than their normal dose, while the spray nozzles used to administer them have not been altered, resulting in a heavy overdose for the trees and vegetation sprayed.

As if all the above were not enough, some in the American military would "escalate" the anticrop war to new proportions. Professor Arthur W. Galston, in his article "Military Uses of Herbicides in Viet Nam" already cited, reported that some U.S. military men and their advisers would very much like to spread an especially virulent strain of rice-blast fungus developed at Fort Detrick, Maryland, "in the Vietnam theatre of war."

The U.S. government has again and again tried to tell the American people that it is in Viet Nam to protect freedom, democracy, and the right of self-determination for the Vietnamese. But the Vietnamese people understand very well what the U.S. government is in Viet Nam for.

An open letter of September 23, 1967, to President Johnson from the Student Unions of Can Tho University, Van Hanh University, Saigon University, and Dalat University (representing most of the university students in the country) begins with these words:

The American intervention in the Vietnamese internal situation since after the Geneva Accord in 1954 has made the Vietnamese people regard the United States as replacing the French colonizers. The American policy, instead of helping the Vietnamese people, only pushes them into a destructive and bloody war. . . .

At the beginning of this year [1970], Professor Ly Chánh Trung of the University of Saigon, an ardent Catholic intellectual, was compelled to say the following words in a speech entitled "Why Do I Want Peace," delivered before the Saigon Student Union:

> Being a Vietnamese I can no longer stand the sight of foreigners arrogantly destroying my country through the use of the most modern and most terrible means, and through the use of the slogan "In protecting the freedom" of the South Vietnamese population, a kind of freedom that the South Vietnamese population has had to throw up and vomit continuously during the last ten years or so without being able to swallow it successfully.

Apart from the "vocal minority," many other Vietnamese, perhaps finding it difficult to make public their views in so many words, choose to express themselves by continuing to fight.

Already, the war in Viet Nam has been the longest war in United States history, except perhaps, depending on just how one marks its duration, America's own War of Independence.

PART FIVE

AMERICA'S HARVEST

16

Nixon's Trap

by Franz Schurmann

Only a short time ago the anti-war movement was gripped by a despair that increasingly expressed itself in terrorism. Now the movement has a life and scope never before seen. Throughout the country, thousands of groups are *organizing* for a protracted struggle to end the war in Southeast Asia. No central committee shouted the call to action; no particular organization leads the drive to organize. The moment Nixon ordered American troops into Cambodia, spontaneous moves of extraordinary similarity erupted throughout the country. It appears that millions in the anti-war movement had been thinking along similar lines and needed only a provocation of proper magnitude to act. President Nixon provided that provocation on April 30.

The threatening tone of his speech that night implied a determination to seek military victory in Southeast Asia. Thus he reversed the entire thrust of his rhetoric on Vietnam since taking office. Nixon still does not understand that an obligation of a national leader, more important than decision-making, is to set guidelines for the country. People, whether they support or oppose a leader, expect him to define the environment in which they live. They want him to be decisive, one way or the other, so that they can order their individual and collective lives accordingly. During the first year of his Administration, Nixon appeared determined to get out of Vietnam. The anti-war movement was generally quiescent, except for the great demonstrations of October and November 1969. When his resolve began to wobble early this year, the movement stirred. Anxiety deepened among the silent ma-

Franz Schurmann is Professor of History and Sociology at the University of California, Berkeley, and Director of the Bay Area Institute, San Francisco, California. He is author of *Ideology and Organization in Communist China* and other publications, and co-author of *The Politics of Escalation in Vietnam*.

jority, malaise spread among the opponents of war, and terroristic violence erupted. On April 30, the President flatly reversed himself, and the movement exploded. The weak, contrite, conciliatory tone of his May 8 press conference only deepened the conviction that he lacks the capacity to be a leader.

Ever since the anti-war movement arose on a massive scale in March 1965, it has always acted in relationship to the country's leaders, and particularly to the President. The movement has no ideology, no unifying principles of its own. All attempts to transform it into an independent Left, such as the Peace and Freedom Party in California, have failed, and only small sectarian groups survive from the experiments. Until the demonstrations against the Chicago Democratic convention, it reacted in relationship to the liberals who then ruled in Washington. Whatever its rhetoric, it was crying for a return to the ideals of peace and freedom that had won Lyndon Baines Johnson the greatest electoral victory in American history. After the convention, the movement, except for the determined, suspicious, alienated radicals, declined. Many liberals came to believe that, one way or another, the war would end. The Nixon of the first year was impossible to relate to. Postures of benign neglect, coupled with an impression of competent professional workings behind the scenes, led many to believe that peace was in sight. After all, the message from Wall Street was clear—the war and defense spending are ruining the economy. Yet the Nixon rhetoric of that first year was not decisive enough to convince. And as the war dragged on, wariness turned into suspicion and finally despair. The radicals sensed that the war would take a turn for the worse, and ROTC, the most available symbol of American militarism on the campuses, became the natural target of political action. The revolutionaries moved on to terrorism.

The terrorism cannot be dismissed as the actions of a lunatic fringe. It has been the most extreme expression of a more general mood which became apparent last year, particularly in the ecology movement. While the Establishment cheerfully embraced ecology as a diversion from more dangerous anti-war and campus politics, it failed to recognize the spiritual convictions of the ecologists. Those convictions are apocalyptic and arise from a vision of the coming doom of all mankind. Not just the war in Vietnam but the entire system is plunging the world headlong into destruction; the crisis is so vast that only the most heroic efforts will save us —and they are unlikely. This vision of impending holocaust is utterly different from the clean-up-the-garbage reformism of the Establishment. While some of the leaders of the ecology movement advocated totalitarian planning as the only means to avert the holocaust, some of the young chose the ultra-individualistic path of terror. The apocalyptic visions of the Right see holocaust pouring in from without (Yellow Peril, Red Hordes), or from internal agents of the foreign enemy (the International Communist Conspiracy). The apocalyptic visions of the Left see the holocaust coming from the suicidal impulses of the system itself (nuclear war, destructive growth, pollution of all things material and spiritual). Out of that profound pessimism came the despair and the terrorism of the period preceding the Cambodia operation.

That mood ended on April 30. The moment Nixon spoke clearly as a war President, the millions in the anti-war movement had something tangible toward which to relate. It was no longer the system propelling us toward suicide but a single man ordering us into a bigger war. The movement had toppled one President—it could topple this one too. Similarities to the McCarthy campaign are evident. Everywhere small groups are organizing, going out into the community, leafleting, lobbying, arguing. Entire universities are being pushed by students and faculty to use their resources to end the war. Confrontation and violence are minimal. The liberals, only a short time ago in despair, have reawakened in huge numbers. Optimism reigns once again, and optimism has always been the badge of liberalism. Radicals and revolutionaries regard the system as hopeless, and urge struggle of one sort or another against it as the only possible form of political action. Yet it would be a mistake to see this renewed liberal optimism as a reversion to what once prevailed. The massiveness of the effort now being mounted is a last-ditch stand. Either we stop the war now or catastrophe will be at hand.

The fragments of evidence surrounding the Cambodia coup which have come out of Washington indicate that the liberals perceive the situation correctly. Either we nullify Nixon's decision on Cambodia now or we move inexorably in the direction of catastrophes the dimensions of which will become clear before the end of the year.

Since the movement erupted in reaction to Nixon's decision to extend the war, we must look at that step more closely. The stories out of Washington and Saigon bespeak utter amazement. Not only was Congress not consulted but people at the highest levels of the national security bureaucracy were in the dark until the decision was made. Moreover, men most closely involved with the conduct of the war, such men as Secretary of Defense Laird and Secretary of State Rogers, were said to have been opposed to sending American ground combat troops into Cambodia. Henry Kissinger was described as "equivocal." Some reports say even the CIA was opposed. Attorney General Mitchell alone is reported to have been "enthusiastic," but why should Nixon follow his advice on the war? Behind the President the Joint Chiefs of Staff lurk like the ancient Greek fates. The belief is widespread that Nixon caved in to the generals. Yet again, reports imply that some members of the Joint Chiefs didn't know of the decision, and not a single report from Saigon suggests that anyone there had foreknowledge of it. The invasion of the Fishhook region was hastily prepared, and launched at the moment of the April 30 speech. In his April 20 speech, Mr. Nixon expressed continued faith in his withdrawal program. Ten days later he seemed almost in panic, reiterating that America would never be defeated. Since Nixon is no Napoleon trusting to his inner military intuition, something must have happened to jolt him during those ten days, as Max Frankel of *The New York Times* suggested in his reflections on the considerations that led to the Cambodia invasion.

For weeks after the overthrow of Prince Sihanouk, American generals had been arguing that we should seize this "golden opportunity" to wipe out the NVA and Vietcong sanctuaries in Cambodia. On April 20, Nixon announced troop withdrawal plans that were widely regarded as a compromise between the views of the generals, who wanted a flat halt to withdrawals, and those of others, like Rogers and Laird, who wanted the President to announce another early round of withdrawals. The conservative San Francisco *Examiner* announced in headlines that Nixon had split with the Pentagon. Immediately after the speech, according to newspaper reports, intensive deliberations on the Cambodian situation began in Washington. By the following weekend, Nixon was said to have decided to let the South Vietnamese invade the Parrot's Beak, supported by American advisers and air power. The requisite orders went out to General Abrams. On April 27, Secretary of State Rogers came before the Senate Foreign Relations Committee, where he implied that there might be changes in Cambodian policy, but gave no indication of the magnitude of the action. When he appeared, only the plans for the Parrot's Beak had been settled; but that same night the fateful decision was made to invade the Fishhook region. That operation was to be carried out with American ground combat troops, in direct reversal of everything Nixon and his Cabinet members had been saying since the proclamation of the "Guam Doctrine." If the various published reports are to be believed, the decision to invade the Fishhook erupted as suddenly as a tornado in a clear sky.

But if one looks back at the escalation of the last years, the suddenness of the Fishhook move is no surprise. The air war over Laos began on May 17, 1964, after a crisis of little more than a day caused by the fall of a minuscule Laotian town called Tha Thom, apparently but not really, to the Pathet Lao. The most notoriously sudden decision of all was Tonkin Gulf. Hardly had the conflicting reports on the second clash with North Vietnamese PT boats come into Washington than the word went out to launch massive air strikes against North Vietnam. The most critical escalation of all, the February 7 air attack on North Vietnam which launched the bombing war, was decided on within twelve hours of the Vietcong attack on Pleiku.

Thus far only one report has suggested the kind of crisis President Nixon faced on the night of April 27. Flora Lewis of *Newsday* wrote that the Pentagon suddenly proposed to Nixon a seaborne attack against the port of Sihanoukville. For years the military had been claiming that the Vietcong were being supplied through Sihanoukville by Soviet and Chinese ships. If those supplies were cut off, the Vietcong in the southern provinces of South Vietnam would be dependent entirely on supplies brought down the Ho Chi Minh Trail. Intensive bombing of the trail and destruction of the Cambodian sanctuaries would make it extremely difficult for such supplies to come through. Thus one swift blow could seal the doom of the enemy. Why should such a proposal alarm Nixon and his advisers? An attack on Sihanoukville, like the bombardment of Haiphong that was so bitterly debated during the Johnson Administration, would mean a direct confrontation with the Russians and the Chinese. Obviously those who pushed for the attack did not fear such a confrontation, but there were others who did.

Since the end of World War II we have survived several crises which brought us to the brink of a third world war. In each case, they involved a confrontation with Russia or China or both. The Cuban missile crisis was the most publicized. Showdowns with Russia have been rare of late, though they may be developing again. Soviet pilots are flying in Egypt, and Soviet ships are in the Caribbean. During the bombing of North Vietnam, we had a number of confrontations with the Chinese, as American planes bombed closer and closer to the Chinese frontier. On April 27, 1970, we were rapidly approaching another crisis with the Chinese. Peking announced a summit conference of the North Vietnamese, the NLF government of South Vietnam, the Pathet Lao and Sihanouk. The Chinese thereby put their weight behind Sihanouk in his drive to regain power in Cambodia. This took on added importance with the launching of the first Chinese earth-orbiting satellite. But we were also moving toward a potential confrontation with Russia in the Middle East. If Russian pilots actively engage Israeli forces or if Israel, made desperate by a changing balance of power, launches a preventive strike against Russian installations in Egypt, America would immediately be drawn in.

But while Chinese actions vis-à-vis Cambodia and Russian actions in the Middle East understandably alarmed Washington, they cannot in themselves explain the sudden sense of crisis which gripped Nixon on the night of April 27 and which led so hurriedly to the decision to invade the Fishhook. A much more plausible cause is the Pentagon's plan to attack Sihanoukville. Intimations came from the Pentagon or segments thereof, such as CINCPAC (Commander-in-Chief, Pacific Area Command) in Honolulu, that the military intended to go ahead full speed with deployments, awaiting only the go-ahead signal to launch the attack. On August 5, 1964, at the time of Tonkin Gulf, the deployments were ready and the planes poised to take off before the decision to attack was made. That decision came fast.

I see no other explanation for the manner in which the decision to invade the Fishhook was made than that it was a quick compromise between the extremely dangerous plan to attack Sihanoukville and the more "moderate" tactics apparently advocated by Laird and Rogers. If Nixon had not acted, CINCPAC units might in any case have begun the attack, leaving to Washington the task of explaining why and how it had "authorized" it. As it was, the Navy and the Air Force resumed bombing of North Vietnam—"authorized" by Washington, it was subsequently announced. And even though the military leaders didn't get what they wanted on the night of April 27, Marshal Ky's blockade of a 100-mile stretch of Cambodian coast line, announced on May 13, indicates that the Sihanoukville plan is still alive. But the move into the Fishhook region at least did not involve an immediate confrontation with the Russians and the Chinese.

The military bureaucracy has one virtue—consistency. It has never accepted the notion of a *détente* with any of the forces of world communism. It fought bitterly against the 1963 Partial Test Ban Treaty, and now advocates a renewed arms race with the USSR, not to mention continuing pressure against China. Ever since President Kennedy muzzled the military, it is difficult to read or see their views in the media. A good substitute are the columns of Joseph Alsop, who of late has been mounting a crusade for the preservation of American power. From his own point of view he is right. Not since 1964, when the spirit of the Partial Test Ban Treaty led the Administration to cut down on defense spending, has the threat to the military been so great. Defense spending has declined and will decline even more if the SALT talks should succeed. It will decline if the war ends in Vietnam. Far stronger than in 1964 is the deep anti-military sentiment among youth, and the defection of scientists from the cause of military research. The great trauma of many generals, as revealed in their memoirs, was the incredible demobilization of American power after World War II. The U.S. Armed Forces literally self-disintegrated. The prospect of a repetition frightens them more than anything else. Taught to think in terms of the domino theory, they fear that they may be the dominoes to fall.

The military are unhappy, yet they are trained to follow orders, to accept the policies of their Commander in Chief. The military did not get us into Vietnam, but when Washington policy makers opened the doors of Laos and Vietnam, they rushed through. Their unhappiness gave them greater determination and speed. The door into Cambodia was not opened by the plan to attack Sihanoukville but by the "golden opportunity" which civilians and military urged Nixon to seize. The decision to let the South Vietnamese attack the Parrot's Beak with American advisers was taken before April 27. By allowing this seemingly minimal escalation, Nixon had made a profound policy decision which reversed his entire Vietnamization program. He probably sincerely wishes to limit the invasion of Cambodia, as he stated plaintively in his press conference, but others have different ideas. They have already shown what those ideas are by resuming the large-scale bombing of North Vietnam.

The Cambodia coup of April 30 is not a seizure of power by the military. Unlike the Greek colonels, the American military still believes that running the country is the business of its various governments, federal, state and local. (It may drop its present aloofness from domestic matters if "anarchy" prevails.) But the military has one cardinal belief—America must be supremely powerful, cost what it may. Secretary of Defense Laird shares this belief, but appears to be proposing a new arms race with the Russians as a substitute for the draining war in Vietnam. The Joint Chiefs of Staff, CINCPAC and Saigon do not agree with him. Their determination to win in Vietnam has not slackened; neither has their willingness to confront the great Communist powers. In the past, great crises had the effect of arousing the country's patriotic and supportive sentiments. It usually sufficed to give the military the hardware it wanted.

In the Vietnamese War, compromise escalations have eventually turned into the full escalations the military wanted. Nixon's prediction that all American forces will be out of Cambodia by the end of June may turn out to be correct. Once the monsoon rains come to Cambodia, the country turns into mud, and military actions are impossible. The more likely escalations are a renewal of bombing in North Vietnam, an attack against Sihanoukville and, perhaps most ominously, an action in Laos. Pathet Lao and North Vietnamese forces, in response to the invasion of Cambodia, have advanced across the cease-fire lines in Laos. Sam Thuong and Long Cheng, the last Armée Clandestine outposts on the Plaine des Jarres, remain under threat. It is said that the entire population has fled. Years ago, as Roger Hilsman reports in *To Move a Nation,* the military opposed ever again opening a land war on the Asian mainland—unless they could use nuclear weapons. Since the dispatch of American ground combat troops into the Plaine des Jarres does not seem feasible, it is permissible to wonder if some military minds are toying with the idea of using tactical nuclear weapons to stem a North Vietnamese advance toward the Mekong.

The dangers of the Cambodia invasion are very widely sensed, if not fully understood. The stock market has responded; the voices of the Establishment opposing the invasion are equally clear; those supporting Nixon are muted, even fearful. The voice of the campuses announces organized, protracted resistance. Few abroad support Nixon; even America's subservient ally, Britain, abstains. Millions suddenly sense that we stand on the crest of a watershed, and that a last supreme effort must be made if we are not to go over the other side.

The struggle now being waged in this country is ultimately an ideological one, cutting across conventional notions of class and interest. The ideologies in combat arise from two utterly opposed views of the world. One sees it as basically peaceful, with conflict an aberration; the other sees it riven in two, with struggle to the death the basic fact of life. For years, American leaders have proclaimed their commitment to peace, even while their actions contradicted their words. But people believed the rhetoric; they took it as the guideline for action, the definition of the world given them by their knowing leaders. On April 30 Nixon came close to abandoning that rhetoric and going back to the cold war. The military has never seen the world as essentially peaceful. Nor have large segments of the United States whose spokesman has been Barry Goldwater. Nixon's past puts him closer to Goldwater, but as the standard-bearer of the Republican Party he must straddle the ideological fence. After years of growth and affluence, a variety of forces are giving new power to the ideology of reactionary conservatism. The economy is shaky; youth is turbulent; black discontent is rising. And we are told that the great outside threats, the Russian and Chinese missiles, close in upon us.

A further escalation of the war in Southeast Asia will halt the downward trend in defense spending. But then, since defense spending is the major cause of the inflation, it is hard to see how the government can avoid wage-price controls— in short, economic dictatorship. A new escalation will deepen the turbulence of the discontented, leading to greater despair and greater terrorism. John Mitchell may already have foreseen certain police-state remedies for such a situation. Escalation now will mean confrontation with Russia and China, and that is the threshold of the third world war.

The cry for peace comes from large segments of the middle class, from students, professionals, scientists and many businessmen. It is not heard so widely from the poor or from the minorities whose militant spokesmen see struggle as the only escape from their misery. The radical current of the movement, which earlier had been pressed into the background by the revolutionaries and now by the liberal upsurge, accepts the view that struggle, not peace, must be the guideline of political action. In a different arena, that has been the key ideological difference between Russia and China. The Russians, under Khrushchev, committed themselves to peace as the supreme goal of their foreign policy; the Chinese, speaking for the poor of the world, demanded struggle. The enormous chasm between the Russians and the Chinese should warn us that the currents of the essentially white peace movement and of the black liberation struggle may not be running in the same courses. But as American militarism threatens both Russia and China, its domestic counterparts threaten the anti-war and black liberation movements. And reactionary conservatism sees them all as "communistic."

Today the chief threat to peace is the Joint Chiefs of Staff, and the chief force for domestic repression is Mitchell's Justice Department. As Justice and Defense have come closer together, so have the white peace movement and the black liberation struggle. The great happening at Yale, where the defense of the Black Panthers coincided with the Cambodia coup, shows this convergence. While anti-militarism and antifascism are still different thrusts, the gap has narrowed. As the crisis grows, the anti-war movement has shown more and more willingness to struggle. The movement is still basically nonviolent, but if the struggle goes badly, then the violence which so many fear will spread. The struggle will go badly when reactionary conservatism, which sees violence as the only instrument for coping with a threatening and disorderly world, starts coming to power.

People in the Establishment, both liberals and conservatives, warn the movement frantically against violence. They argue that violence will only harm the cause of peace and racial justice, so speeding the repression. There is truth in this argument, but there is an even more important truth: if the liberal establishment, now exemplified largely by the Senate, cannot halt the war and arrest the spread of reactionary conservatism, then the violence they fear so much will descend upon them from both Right and Left. Beyond that there will be war. The supreme responsibility and leadership of the anti-war movement rests today with the Congress, particularly the Senate. All forms of action against the war, ranging from the protest of the stock market to rock throwing, have failed to prevent the drift toward escalation. They have been effective in showing the range and depth of the opposition to the war, but have not been translatable into power. What little power is left to halt the military lies in Congress, in its constitutional right to grant or refuse appropriations. In 1914, the German and French parliamentary deputies assured the military unrestricted power when they voted the war credits. We face a similar situation now.

John Mitchell probably counseled Nixon that, when he escalated into Cambodia, the protest would blow over soon and Congress would never refuse to support our boys in the field. If Mitchell is correct, then we shall have war, to be followed by repression so severe that frustrated protest will turn to violence. The issue, however, has not yet been decided. The key lies with the Senate. If the Senate refuses appropriations for the Cambodian invasion, it will not thereby have defeated the threat from the military but will probably have prevented a massive explosion of violence from a frustrated anti-war movement.

We are in a constitutional crisis, as many are saying with greater frequency. But if my explanation of what happened on

April 27 is correct, then it is not a crisis arising out of Presidential despotism. Rather it is a crisis caused by the President's loss of power. Lyndon Johnson was once quoted as saying that the President has no power save that of using nuclear weapons, which he cannot use. He also said: "When the going gets tough, the toughs get going." While he was referring to hard-bitten radical militants, the phrase applies equally well to the military. Loss of control over a military which has the power to determine the fate of the entire society is the deepest constitutional crisis imaginable. The seriousness of this crisis is underscored by the June 14 report in *The New York Times* that Laird is trying to reassert his leadership over the Joint Chiefs before he loses control.

President Nixon's decision to go into Cambodia was evidently tailored to the Pentagon's desires. An AP report of May 20 disclosed that General Abrams and the Joint Chiefs had demanded that the Cambodian sanctuaries must be liquidated if the withdrawal of troops was to continue. This information, provided by a Pentagon informant, indicated that Abrams' demand was largely a response to the President's April 20 announcement of more troop pullouts, rather than a result of significant changes in the strategic situation. This latter point is underscored by the intelligence reports from Saigon before the invasion. Senator Fulbright's staff report, based on intelligence briefings in Saigon, confirms the fact that there was no increased activity in the sanctuaries which threatened Vietnam. But rather than reject the Pentagon's invasion plan, Nixon resorted to the transparent lie that the Communists were building up in the sanctuaries for an impending massive assault in South Vietnam.

Another facet of this constitutional crisis between the President and the military has recently come to light. The Pentagon, and hence the President, disregarded not only State Department but also CIA estimates of the Cambodia venture. The CIA predicted that the Communists would quickly withdraw and establish new bases in Cambodia and southern Laos to harass the Lon Nol government. The Pentagon claimed that the North Vietnamese were too weak to conduct simultaneous operations in South Vietnam and these areas. Central to this debate were contradictory intelligence estimates of the number of enemy forces in the Cambodian sanctuaries. The Pentagon insisted there were only 25,000 enemy troops, while the CIA put the figure at 63,000. But the military ruled, and the invasion was launched. Six weeks later, when half of Cambodia and most of southern Laos had fallen to the Communist forces, the military glibly announced that their earlier estimates of enemy strength were much too low. Yet in spite of this obvious bungling, the President plans to turn civilian aid programs in Indochina over to military management.

The lies that have been coming out of official quarters in Washington since the Cambodia invasion appear to be frantic attempts to preserve the illusion of Presidential command and control over foreign policy. Mr. Nixon's rapidly alternating moods—calm optimism on April 20, threats on April 30, contrition on May 8—show weakness where there should be strength. The weakness is exacerbated by his inability to choose between two diametrically opposed thrusts of his political make-up—one, a proclivity for reactionary conservatism which marked the beginnings of his political career, and the other a desire expressed in his campaign and in the first year of office to bring us all together. He cannot be a President of peace and of war at the same time. Johnson tried that by separating the two: he waged war abroad and preached peace at home. It worked for a while because the foreign and home fronts were not yet tightly linked. Today they are inextricably enmeshed, morally on the campuses and materially in the stock market. Nixon must make a move in one direction or another. Whichever way he moves, he will have a great fight on his hands. If he does not move, whatever power he has left will slip away. The decisive confrontation between the constitutionalists who want peace and the militarists who want war is close at hand.

17

Scars of the War

by Robert Jay Lifton

I have done psychiatric work at a number of Veterans hospitals and out-patient clinics and at the Walter Reed Army Institute of Research. During the Korean War I served as an Air Force Psychiatrist in Korea and Japan. I have spent almost seven years living and working in the Far East, and made visits to Vietnam in 1954 and in 1967.

I have done research on such "extreme situations" as the psychological aspects of Chinese thought reform (or "brainwashing"), and the psychological effects of the atomic bomb in Hiroshima. I have been greatly concerned with the application of psychological methods to the study of historical events, and with the general psychology of the *survivor*.

I would like to comment upon the psychological predicament of the Vietnam veteran, both from the standpoint of war in general and of the nature of this particular war.

For veterans of any war there is a difficult transition from the "extreme situation" of the war environment to the more ordinary civilian world. This was noted after World War I, World War II, and the Korean War, but only recently have we begun to appreciate the problem from the standpoint of the psychology of the survivor. The combat veteran of any war has survived the deaths of specific buddies, as well as the deaths of anonymous soldiers on his and on the enemy's side. He survives the general war environment, within which he was taught that killing was not only legitimate but proper and necessary.

Upon returning to civilian life the war veteran faces several important psychological tasks in relationship to the deaths he has witnessed. He must, first of all, struggle with anxiety he continues to feel, often in association with the indelible

Robert Jay Lifton is Foundation Fund Professor for Research in Psychiatry at Yale University. He is the author of *Death in Life; Survivors of Hiroshima, History and Survival,* and other publications.

images of death, dying and suffering that constitute the survivor's "death imprint." He must also struggle with feelings
of guilt and shame resulting directly from the war experience.
These guilt feelings can relate simply to the fact that he
survived while so many others died, or they may focus upon
the specific death of one particular buddy who in some way,
he feels, was sacrificed, so that he, the veteran, could go on
living. His sense of guilt may also relate to his having killed
enemy soldiers, or having done various other things in order
to stay alive. But his overall psychological task is that of
finding meaning and justification in having survived, and in
having fought and killed. That is, as a survivor he must, con-
sciously or unconsciously, give some form to the extreme
experience of war, in order to be able to find meaning in all
else he does afterward in civilian life.

These psychological tasks are never perfectly managed, and
as a result the veteran may experience anything from a mild
readjustment problem to disabling forms of psychiatric im-
pairment. Typically, the returning veteran manifests a certain
amount of withdrawal from civilian life, a measure of distrust
of the civilian environment—a feeling that what it offers him
may well be counterfeit—and some confusion and uncertainty about the meaning of his wartime experience and of his
future life. His overall adjustment is greatly influenced by the
extent to which he can become inwardly convinced that *his*
war, and *his* participation in that war, had purpose and significance.

All of this is true for the Vietnam veteran. But in addition
his psychological experience is influenced by certain characteristics of the war in Vietnam. The average Vietnam GI is
thrust into a strange, far-away, and very alien place. The
Vietnamese people and their culture are equally alien to him.
Finding himself in the middle of a guerrilla war in which the
guerrillas have intimate contact with ordinary people, the
environment to him is not only dangerous and unpredictable
but devoid of landmarks that might warn of danger or help
him to identify the enemy. He experiences a combination of
profound inner confusion, helplessness and terror.

Then he sees his buddies killed and mutilated. He may experience the soldier-survivor's impulse toward revenge, toward
overcoming his own emotional conflicts and giving meaning
to his buddies' sacrifices by getting back at the enemy. And

in an ordinary war there is a structure and ritual for doing just that—battle lines and established methods for contacting the enemy and carrying out individual and group battle tasks with aggressiveness and courage. But in Vietnam there is none of that—the enemy is everyone and no one, never still, rarely visible and usually indistinguishable from the ordinary peasant. The GI is therefore denied the minimal psychological satisfactions of war, and as a result, his fear, rage and frustration mount.

At the same time he notices that the South Vietnamese fight poorly or not at all; and rather than ask himself why this is so, he tends to associate them with the general corruption and deterioration he sees all about him. Any previous potential for racism is mobilized and he comes to look upon Vietnamese as inferior people or even nonhuman creatures.

This dehumanization of the Vietnamese by the individual GI is furthered by his participation in such everyday actions as the saturation of villages with bombs and artillery fire and the burning of entire hamlets. Observing the deaths and injuries of Vietnamese civilians on such a massive scale and the even more massive disruptions of village life and forced relocations, he cannot but feel that the Vietnamese have become more or less expendable.

That is why Vietnam veterans I have talked to were not really surprised by the recent disclosures of atrocities committed by American troops at My Lai and elsewhere. Virtually all of them had either witnessed or heard of similar incidents, if on a somewhat smaller scale. Hence Paul Medlo's public statement that what he and others did at My Lai "seemed like it was the natural thing to do at the time." Another former infantryman, Terry Reed, who described a similar incident elsewhere, made a public statement of even greater psychological significance. He said: "To me the war was being ambushed every three to five days, being left with scores of wounded GIs. Then come right back at the enemy by going into an innocent village, destroying and killing the people." What these words suggest is how, under the extraordinary stress of an impossible situation, GIs come to see all Vietnamese, whatever their age or sex or affiliation, as interchangeable with the enemy, so that killing any Vietnamese can become a way of "coming right back" at those responsible for wounding or killing their own buddies.

Medlo went on to say that immediately after killing a number of Vietnamese civilians he "felt good" and that "I was getting relieved from what I had seen earlier over there." Applicable here is an established psychological principle that killing can relieve fear of being killed. But there is something more operating in connection with these massacres: the momentary illusion on the part of GIs that, by gunning down these figures now equated with the enemy—even little babies and women and old men—they were finally involved in a genuine "military action," their elusive adversaries had finally been located, made to stand still, and annihilated—an illusion, in other words, that they had finally put their world back in order.

Other veterans have reported witnessing or participating in killings of civilians without even the need for such an illusion. Sometimes these killings have been performed with the spirit of the hunter or the indiscriminate executioner—pot shots at random Vietnamese taken from helicopters, heavy fire directed at populated villages for no more reason than a commanding officer's feeling that he "didn't like their looks." In addition there have been many accounts of such things as the shoving of suspects out of helicopters, the beheadings of Vietcong or Vietcong suspects and of various forms of dismembering the bodies of dead Vietnamese.

Actions such as these require an advanced state of what I have called psychic numbing—the loss of the capacity to feel—and of general brutalization. Where such actions are committed in a direct face-to-face fashion—without even the psychological protection of distance that is available to those who drop bombs from the sky or direct long-range artillery fire—the psychological aberration and the moral disintegration are very advanced indeed. For while there is little ethical difference between killing someone far away whom one cannot see, and looking directly into the victim's eyes from five or ten feet away while pulling the trigger, there is a considerable psychological difference between the two acts.

The Vietnam GI also is profoundly affected by atrocities committed by the Vietcong, by South Vietnamese soldiers and by South Korean forces. All of these contribute both to his numbing and his brutalization. But it is one's own atrocities that haunt one most. And no one can emerge from that environment without profound inner questions concerning

the American mission in Vietnam and the ostensibly democratic nature of our allies there—even if, as is often the case,
the GI resists these questions and keeps them from his own
consciousness.

Whatever kind of adjustment the returning Vietnam veteran
appears to be making, he must continue to carry images of
these experiences inside of him. Survivors of a special kind
of war, these men constitute a special kind of veterans' group.
Murray Polner, a historian who has now interviewed more
than two hundred Vietnam veterans as part of an investigation of their experiences, has found that none of the men he
talked to—not one of them—was entirely free from doubt
about the nature of the American involvement in Vietnam.
This does not mean that all of them actively oppose the war,
but rather that as a group they have grave difficulty finding
inner justification for what they have experienced and what
they have done.

That is exactly what former Army Captain Max Cleland,
a triple-amputee, meant when he told this Subcommittee last
month: "To the devastating psychological effect of getting
maimed, paralyzed, or in some way unable to reenter American life as you left it, is the added psychological weight that
it may not have been worth it; that the war may have been
a cruel hoax, an American tragedy, that left a small minority
of young American males holding the bag." It is also what a
19-year-old marine who had lost part of his leg and was
awaiting medical discharge meant when he told Polner (as
quoted in *Trans-action* magazine, November 1968): "I think
any other war would have been worth my foot. But not this
one. One day, someone has got to explain to me why I was
there." This inability to find significance or meaning in their
extreme experience leaves many Vietnam veterans with a ter-
rible burden of survivor guilt. And this sense of guilt can
become associated with deep distrust of the society that sent
them to their ordeal in Vietnam. They then retain a strong
and deeply disturbing feeling of having been victimized and
betrayed by their own country.

As a result many continue to be numbed as civilians, the
numbing now taking the form of a refusal to talk or think
about the war. Some become almost phobic toward television
broadcasts or newspaper reports having anything to do with
the war. A number of those I spoke to could only take jobs

permitting them to remain isolated from most of their fellow Americans, often night jobs. One Vietnam veteran told me, "I worked at night because I couldn't stand looking at those nine-to-five people who sent me to Vietnam." Yet these men are also affected by the deep ambivalence of the general American population about the war in general, an ambivalence which extends to those who have fought it. It is difficult for most Americans to make into heroes the men who have fought in this filthy, ambiguous war, and if they try to do so with a particular veteran there is likely to be a great deal of conflict and embarrassment all around. There is in fact an unspoken feeling on the part of many Americans that returning veterans carry some of the taint of that dirty and unsuccessful war.

From work that I and a number of others have done on related forms of war experience and survival, we can expect various kinds of psychological disturbance to appear in Vietnam veterans, ranging from mild withdrawal to periodic depression to severe psychosomatic disorder to disabling psychosis. Some are likely to seek continuing outlets for a pattern of violence to which they have become habituated, whether by indulging in antisocial or criminal behavior, or by, almost in the fashion of mercenaries, offering their services to the highest bidder. Similarly, many will hold onto a related habituation to racism and the need to victimize others. Any of these patterns may appear very quickly in some, but in others lie dormant for a period of months or even years and then emerge in response to various internal or external pressures.

What I have been saying is that we cannot separate the larger historical contradictions surrounding the American involvement in Vietnam from the individual psychological responses of our soldiers. Indeed, the Vietnam veteran serves as a psychological crucible of the entire country's doubts and misgivings about the war. He has been the agent and victim of that confusion—of on the one hand our general desensitization to indiscriminate killing, and on the other our accumulating guilt and deep suspicion concerning our own actions. We sent him as an intruder in a revolution taking place in a small Asian society, and he returns as a tainted intruder in our own society. Albert Camus urged that men be neither victims nor executioners. In Vietnam we have made our young men into both.

Of course Vietnam veterans need and deserve improved medical and psychiatric facilities, as well as better opportunities for education and employment. But if we are really concerned about the psychological and spiritual health of America's young men—and, indeed, about our own as well—we shall cease victimizing and brutalizing them in this war.

18

Economic Impacts of the War in Indochina: A Primer

by Douglass B. Lee, Jr., and John W. Dyckman

In the past, we Americans have been willing to make the sacrifices necessary to support a major war, and today we find ourselves in a similar but diminished situation. The present conflict in Indochina is a war of moderate size, but one that is very expensive. This paper is an attempt to make the true costs of the war in Indochina clearer to the American public. In it we do not deal with the war itself, its immorality, its dangers of expanded world conflict, or even its constitutionality. We do not treat its impact on dividing the nation politically, on alienating American youth, and on distorting the political process. Our concern is with the immediate and long-run economic interests of the American people. In particular, we briefly examine the direct impacts of the war on individuals, its cost in social programs foregone, its role in the paradoxical squeeze of inflation and unemployment, its diversion of national resources and energies, and its relative economic irreversibility, resulting from the structural changes produced by warping the productive system.

DIRECT COSTS OF THE WAR

Over the last three years, the war in Indochina has cost the United States about $30 billion a year, above and beyond the normal cost of maintaining our national defense. At the

John W. Dyckman is Professor and Chairman of the Department of City and Regional Planning at the University of California, Berkeley. Among his many publications are "Defense Expenditures in Forecasts of California's Economic Growth," "Social Planning, Social Planners, and Planned Society," and his forthcoming volume edited with Richard Burton, *Readings in Metropolitan Economic Analysis*.

Douglass B. Lee, Jr., is Assistant Professor in the Department of City and Regional Planning at the University of California, Berkeley.

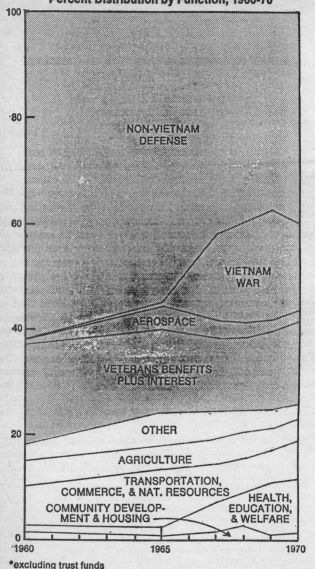

FEDERAL BUDGET OUTLAYS*
Percent Distribution by Function, 1960-70

NON-VIETNAM DEFENSE

VIETNAM WAR

AEROSPACE

VETERANS BENEFITS PLUS INTEREST

OTHER

AGRICULTURE

TRANSPORTATION, COMMERCE, & NAT. RESOURCES

COMMUNITY DEVELOPMENT & HOUSING

HEALTH, EDUCATION, & WELFARE

1960   1965   1970

*excluding trust funds

Manifest national priorities are revealed by comparing expenditures for different purposes in the federal budget (trust funds such as social security are included in the federal budget even though they are independent of it; these funds have been removed from the data presented here). Defense alone accounts for a full 55 to 60 percent of the budget, and to a large extent the war has been taken out of the defense budget rather than being added on. If aerospace, veterans' benefits, and interest on the national debt are added to the defense budget, the military-aerospace portion of the federal budget absorbs almost 80 percent (veterans' benefits and interest on the national debt are primarily a result of past and present wars).

The remaining 20 percent is then available for all other national programs, including physical resources, human resources, and the general operation of the government. Agricultural subsidies eat up almost twice as much as the entire HUD budget. Transportation, commerce, and resources includes national parks and recreation, highway and transit programs, the postal service, business loans, regional development, and the business regulatory functions. Health, education, and welfare includes manpower training, various aids to education, science and other research. Community development includes model cities, urban renewal, poverty programs, community planning, housing, and rehabilitation and mortgage programs.

rate of $26 billion per year this comes to half a billion dollars a week, $71 million per day, or $3 million an hour, twenty-four hours a day, seven days a week. Yet this underestimates the *direct* cost of the war to the United States alone. If it were possible to add up all the *indirect* costs (where we *could* be in terms of private production, personal welfare, social betterment), nonpriceable costs (loss of lives, social unrest, governmental conflicts, and loss of world esteem) and costs to the rest of the world (the destruction of Indochina, disruption of trade, expansion of military costs in other countries), these costs would make our direct expenses appear insignificant.

Direct costs can be estimated and compared with other types of dollar measurements, such as Gross National Product. (Defense gets about 10 percent of the GNP, and from one-third to one-half of that goes for Indoch'na.) Cost may also be allocated in terms of who pays (the average taxpayer contributes about $600 per year toward defense). Translated into dollar equivalent alternatives, three weeks of the war would cover the entire Model Cities program budgeted for 1967–68 and, at the same time, cover the construction costs for the Bay Area Rapid Transit system in the San Francisco region.

Indirect effects can be documented as well. Unemployment has turned sharply upward in the last year, after eight years of steady decline, largely as a by-product of efforts to curb the inflation caused by the war. The war taxes the consumer by restricting potential consumption output and raising prices. If 4 percent of the current 7 percent annual inflation rate is attributed to the war, that is equivalent to increasing personal income taxes by 30 percent. (The average taxpayer contributes about 13 percent of his income to the federal government.) Opportunity costs can be inferred from consideration of alternative uses of these resources, but this is mere speculation, for the performance of our society without war is a matter for conjecture. Having mentioned the nonprice costs, we must put them aside. This does not imply that these costs are less important than the measurable costs, or the cause of less concern. In fact, direct and indirect costs that are verifiable are themselves sufficient reasons to question the wisdom of the war. Economics in this case are on the side of ethics and humanitarianism.

INFLATION AND UNEMPLOYMENT

The single most dramatic economic impact of the war has been its striking inflationary push, accompanied by its counterpart demand-pull. The sources of this runaway inflation, which in the past months has been "flattening out" at a rate of about 6 to 7 percent per year, are examined below.

(1) Cost-Push

One conception of inflationary origins that has been accorded a high place by recent administrations is that which has prices rising as a result of the price increases in basic factors of production, particularly labor. In this reasoning, automobiles become more costly because of higher costs for steel, which in turn are due to higher wages for steelworkers. Auto workers then get on the bandwagon and demand higher wages, accelerating the effect and passing the increase to the consumer. Hence the cries for "restraint" and "wage guidelines."

Since real wages (dollar wages corrected for price levels) decline in inflationary periods, workers will make claims for higher wages in order to maintain purchasing power. (In certain industries, wage levels are tied to cost-of-living contracts, making the push "automatic.") This makes the separation of cause and effect difficult, because neither inflation nor wages will sit still very long while the other increases. Responsibility for setting off the chain is difficult to determine and would require that extended observations show that one effect followed the other cause, with appropriate lag. In fact, the causality may be less important than the result. In the aggregate, wages have not kept pace with inflation. These and other data suggest that inflation in the United States since World War II has had a very small cost-push component, although the size of this push is difficult to estimate.

(2) Demand-Pull

The alternative to cost-push as an explanation of inflation is demand-pull, but this concept subsumes several variations. Too many dollars chasing too few goods is the immediate cause of inflation, with the possibility of an oversupply of money, insufficient investment in productive capacity, or immobility of factors being underlying causes.

Current inflation can be attributed to all three of these influences, but in reverse order. Monetary theorists such as Milton Friedman emphasize the importance of the money supply, but they would not deny the importance of the other variables. There is some evidence that the money supply has not played a major role in this inflation, largely due to Federal Reserve policies in 1969–70. That supply, as measured by demand deposits and currency and including the flow of "Eurodollars," has been increasing at a substantially declining rate since 1968 (from 6 percent per annum to about 3.5 percent per annum in early 1970), without appreciably affecting the rate of inflation. But a consequence of the efforts to curb inflation by controlling the money supply has been high interest rates, which in turn have severely affected sectors such as housing.

Insufficient investment, in a general way, is a major cause of the inflation. Growth in real Gross National Product (in constant dollars) was approximately 4 to 5 percent per year during the sixties. Measured in current dollars this same growth was about 10 percent annually, which means that over half the measured growth was due solely to price increases. When growth in disposable income is not matched by increase in productive output, unless the difference is saved, inflation results. The federal government contributed to this inflation in two major ways: (1) personal and corporate taxes were not high enough to siphon off the excess of income over output while at the same time (2) the government was stimulating, directly and indirectly, investment in military and aerospace goods and services that could not be purchased by private consumers. In effect, tax dollars have been competing with private consumption dollars for the same scarce resources, thus bidding up the prices of those resources.

Underinvestment also hit the supply of labor. The shift of labor into military production maintains the disposable income of those workers shifted, but cuts the production of consumer goods which can be bought with that income. The fact that war expenditures were piled on relatively full employment insured that this result would occur, and government's bidding for skilled labor worsened the effect. The

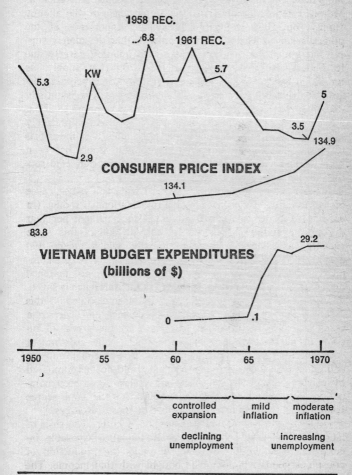

CIVILIAN LABOR FORCE UNEMPLOYED (percent)

1958 REC.
6.8
1961 REC.
5.7
5.3
KW
5
2.9
3.5
134.9

CONSUMER PRICE INDEX

134.1
83.8

VIETNAM BUDGET EXPENDITURES (billions of $)

29.2
0
.1

| 1950 | 55 | 60 | 65 | 1970 |

| controlled expansion | mild inflation | moderate inflation |

| declining unemployment | increasing unemployment |

The unemployment rate series begins in a recession following the post-war inflation, dropping rapidly during the Korean War. With the termination of the Korean War, the government

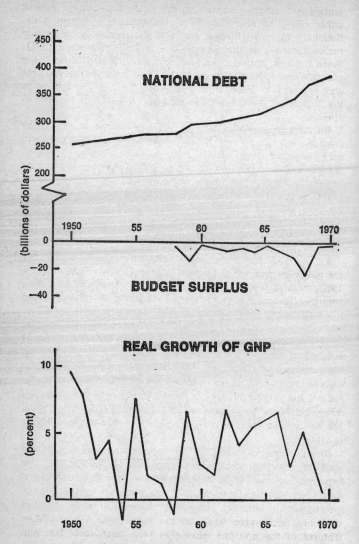

immediately stopped a major portion of defense outlays without either offsetting expenditures or tax cuts, resulting in a deflationary (surplus) budget and a sharp recession. Two other recessions have occurred since, one in 1958 and one in 1961. Since the last of these, we have enjoyed a period of declining unemployment, controlled expansion, and general stability. This was reversed in 1968, and unemployment has risen back to the 5 percent level, from the post-war low of 3.5 percent in 1968.

Inflation is indicated by the consumer price index, which gives the relative price of a representative bundle of goods and services based on an arbitrary starting year. The index moved gradually upward through the fifties, occasionally responding to one of the recessions (consumer spending is not strongly influenced by mild recessions due to built-in stabilizing mechanisms such as transfer payments, including welfare), at a rate of about 2 percent a year. This rate continued up until 1965, when it began accelerating. At present, inflation has reached an annual rate of about 7 percent a year.

Expenditures for the Vietnam War began around 1960, but the major escalations in the war have come since 1965. Since 1967, outlays for the war alone have approached $30 billion annually (the exact amount is not available; government figures may understate the true amount by as much as $10 billion, since they exclude such items as the CIA, which employs over 15,000 persons, and military aid). War expenditures alone would not cause the current inflation if it were not for the fact that the government has chosen to finance the war out of borrowing, rather than increased taxation. This can be seen in the federal budget deficit, which remained close to zero through 1965, but which had grown to $25 billion by 1968. In that year, the deficit was approximately equal to the direct expenditures in Vietnam.

Major increases in the national debt normally occur during wartime, with the debt remaining stable in peacetime. The expansion of the 1960s contributed gradually to the national debt, but achieved stability, full employment, and economic growth without inflation. Since 1967, the rate of increase in the debt has accelerated while at the same time the desirable features of the previous expansion have been lost. The real rate of growth (correcting for inflation) of GNP—quite volatile up until 1960—was maintained at over 5 percent for most of the decade, but has recently declined to almost zero.

$9,000 engineer in the private sector hired by a defense industry for $11,000 has an increase in usable dollars at the same time that his contribution to the "consumables" economy is reduced to zero.

Even if aggregate demand were equal to aggregate supply, heavy emphasis on a limited number of industries utilizing specialized resources could cause short-run inflation. Commercial shipbuilding men and equipment are not easily shifted into production of warships; and to the extent that this is so, Navy ships are built with high-cost factors that are relatively scarce.

Whatever these effects, the economy is so interconnected that inflation is transmitted from sector to sector despite immobilities in resources. These structural effects have sometimes been neglected by the conservative neo-Keynesians, a fact that may explain Lyndon Johnson's insistence that we could have unlimited guns without sacrifice of butter.

USE OF CORRECTIVES

To blunt the inflationary pressure, the government has tried or considered a number of steps. None of these has been fully effective, and some have had undesirable side-effects. Let us consider some of the main instruments for economic management, and their records.

(1) Fiscal Policy

Since the early 1960s the federal government has accepted the fact that it has the responsibility for maintaining economic stability in the nation. Growth, controlled inflation, and the gradual reduction of unemployment have replaced the balanced budget as the neo-Keynesian federal fiscal policy (though President Nixon seems to have revived the budget issue). The mechanisms employed are taxation and expenditure by the federal government; taxation dampens inflation while expenditures stimulate a sluggish economy. Other things being equal, a deficit budget is inflationary or expansionary while a surplus will have a contracting effect. From this standpoint, the appropriate policy in a demand-pull inflation is to increase personal and corporate income taxes, while encouraging investment to expand industrial capacity.

Current fiscal policy has done the opposite. Federal budgets have been running in the red, investment in consumption industries has been stifled, and investment funds diverted to nonmarket war industries. The failure of the government to increase taxes sufficiently to control inflation is a result of (a) the unwillingness of both Congress and the administration to pass on the real costs of the war to the taxpayer for fear of his reaction, and (b) the difficulty of planning a budget when the future costs of the war are unknown, either because of unforeseen events or Department of Defense dissembling. Instead, the cost of the war is passed on through inflation, and the taxpayer is deluded into thinking that the inflation is caused by greedy workers or expensive social programs.

(2) Monetary Policy

The Nixon administration has chosen to rely more heavily, thus far, on restraining the money supply and raising interest rates. This limits the amount of money created through credit and reduces the demand for investment goods. The policy is deflationary in the short run, but dampens output in the productive domestic sectors resulting in a growing deficit in needed production of housing and nondefense plants and equipment. Investment in defense industries is maintained—despite tight credit and inflation—by government demand. The attractiveness of this monetary policy to the administration is enhanced by the fact that it shores the government debt and balance-of-payments position by attracting short-term credit from outside the country while avoiding tax increases. But since this money must be repaid shortly at inflated interest rates, it is a costly way of buying time.

(3) Wage and Price Controls

Arthur Burns, Chairman of the Federal Reserve Board, has recently hinted at direct control of wages and prices, reinforcing the impression that the inflation is of the cost-push type. Only a complete set of wartime controls would be adequate to contain present inflation, and if controls are to be effective, they must be accompanied by rationing. The result is a high level of forced savings of the World War II type. After that war, savings were quickly dissipated by inflation; the savers paid double. Partial wage and price controls would exacerbate the inequities produced by the current war. While Burns's suggestion was probably a feeler, or propaganda, in view of the administration's response, the possibility remains that controls could be used to suppress the symptoms of disequilibrium induced by the war economy.

CONSEQUENCES OF INFLATION

Inflation is not necessary, even in wartime. Indirect monetary and fiscal policy instruments are capable of keeping inflation within reasonable bounds—around 3 percent a year. Our current crisis is due to the political and mechanical difficulties in applying the correct policies and to the extreme strain placed on the economy by the war effort. The traditional trade-off between inflation and employment—so that price stability is reached at high levels of unemployment—has not occurred. Rising unemployment in the past year has not dampened inflation, and the coincidence of accelerating unemployment and inflation is remarkable evidence of the structural imbalances in the economy.

If all prices and wages rise or fall proportionately, distribution effects are minimal, and the result is merely a change in scale of the economy. In practice, inflation is never so neutral. Persons on fixed incomes, such as pensioners and welfare recipients, suffer declining real incomes while owners of wealth or fluid assets keep pace with prices. High interest rates and inflation together favor the well-endowed. The resulting redistribution favors the rich at the expense of the poor, worsening income distribution. The rich increase their holdings, the middle classes run faster on the treadmill, and the poor experience hardship. And where money incomes rise with inflation, keeping real income constant, a further tax on consumers results from the fact that taxes are related to *money* incomes.

Even if domestic inflation were perfectly distributed so that its effects were completely neutral, its international effects would be serious. Unless all other countries are experiencing the same, or higher, rates of inflation, exchange rates between the United States and other countries must be adjusted by devaluing the dollar. For most countries this is not a serious problem, but for large nations whose stability is essential for world trade, the unit of devaluation causes international trade crises. Strong pressures now exist on the dollar, both from our balance of payments deficit and from declining confidence in the American economy.

UNEMPLOYMENT

It is widely believed, especially by certain trade union leaders, that defense spending creates jobs. This notion should be subjected to close scrutiny. Growth of defense industries has had an important impact on the distribution of skill levels among the employed and on the regional redistribution of jobs. When these factors are taken together, it can be shown that military spending has had perverse effects on certain aspects of employment.

During World War II, defense production served to stimulate the economy and create jobs. (The arms boom did more in this respect than the New Deal programs.) At that time there were many idle resources and much unused capacity after a decade of depression. War spending drew these resources into production and the unemployed and underemployed into productive jobs. But the present war spending splurge took off from relatively full employment in an economy operating close to capacity. The result was inflation rather than growth. Defense industries had to hire persons who were already employed in productive jobs, and they mobilized capital that would otherwise have gone into production for the private market. Moreover, these employees were often working at high skill levels; defense industries use proportionately fewer unskilled than the private sector as a whole, and are less likely to hire from the ranks of the unemployed.

Regional redistribution resulting from defense contract patterns creates residual problems. California and Texas are the heaviest recipients of defense contracts, and with it employment migration. (The Los Angeles-Long Beach SMSA, for example, has 17.6 percent of all mathematicians and 14.7 percent of the physicists in the National Register of Scientific and Technical Personnel, and three California SMSAs have 28.8 percent of the astronomers, 25.4 percent of the mathematicians, and 24.8 percent of the physicists in that register.) California has recently been feeling the pangs of cutbacks in

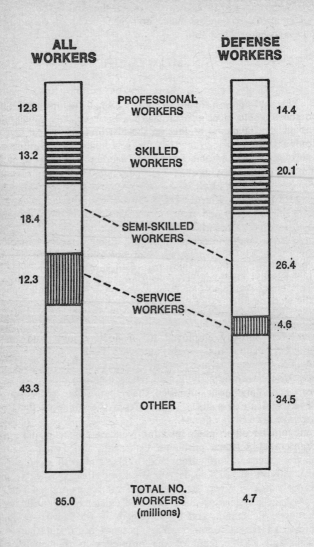

ALL WORKERS

DEFENSE WORKERS

PROFESSIONAL WORKERS

SKILLED WORKERS

SEMI-SKILLED WORKERS

SERVICE WORKERS

OTHER

12.8

13.2

18.4

12.3

43.3

14.4

20.1

26.4

4.6

34.5

TOTAL NO. WORKERS (millions)

85.0

4.7

The distribution of skills in defense employment versus non-defense employment has some subtle but revealing implications about the structure of the economy. Professionals appear in only slightly higher proportions in defense firms, but are probably more highly paid than their nondefense counterparts. Skilled workers and semiskilled workers are much more heavily represented in defense work (46.5 percent versus 31.6 percent for the two combined), and at the expense of service workers— the relatively low skilled. (This effect would probably be even more pronounced if laborers could be separated from farm workers, who would not be expected to participate strongly in defense production.) Thus the jobs that defense "creates" are in skilled occupations where labor was already scarce. The new jobs are not for the poor, and in fact, their jobs are sacrificed. This effect may also help to explain why a large proportion of the working middle class believes that the war has helped them and the economy.

Lack of demand for unskilled workers has been partially offset by the war itself, which has used some 700,000 new men to do the fighting, mostly those from the 18 to 23 age bracket. Since the armed forces selected the best of the group (almost 50 percent were rejected on physical or mental grounds), much of the competition was removed from the low-skill job market. The war has had the effect, on the one hand, of structuring the private market to offer fewer jobs to the young and the poor, and on the other, postponed the time when the deeper problems must be faced.

aerospace, which employs many of these high-level technicians. The largest defense contractor, Lockheed Corporation,
is in danger of heavy cutbacks due to cash-flow problems. The
costs of this over-concentration are felt not only by the
regions left out of the contracting and losing by migration,
but also by the recipients, who are dangerously vulnerable to
changing conditions. As the economy grows and changes, it
is likely that some regions will prosper and others will decline;
but there is need to ease the transitions, rather than exacerbate them.

BALANCE OF PAYMENTS EFFECTS

For the last two decades the United States has had a minor
but nagging deficit in its aggregated balance of payments, i.e.,
more money left the country than came in. Like many mac-
roeconomic indicators (including GNP), there are some
conceptual problems in measuring the balance of payments,
and there is more than one operational definition. There are
also questions as to how the measure is to be interpreted,
since it summarizes a lot of diverse information. There is no
doubt about the central fact, however, which is that we have
consistently run at a deficit for a long period of time.

No one questions the undesirability of operating at a deficit
indefinitely, since the situation is analogous to an individual
who spends more than he earns. Eventually his savings are
used up or his credit is terminated. The international implications of these consequences—using up our gold reserves
and devaluing the dollar—are perhaps relatively more cata-
strophic for the nation than they are for the individual. Apologists for the balance of payments deficit claim that the
reasons for the imbalance are essentially short run, and will
correct themselves or can be corrected by measures short of
devaluation. Some of these reasons are (a) our trade balance
is favorable and the deficit is caused by foreign aid (b) the
deficit is caused by U.S. investment in foreign countries,
which is helping them and will eventually return a surplus to
us, (c) the strength of the dollar is dependent upon confidence in our economy, not on how much gold we have. These
arguments are at best misleading. Our economic relationships
with the rest of the world are in critical condition, and our

defense expenditures enter into the imbalance in many ways, both direct and indirect.

BALANCE OF PAYMENTS, 1963 (BILLIONS)

	payments	receipts	balance
current account	29.787	27.007	—2.780
capital account	5.278	5.398	.120
total	35.065	32.405	—2.660

Source: *U.S. Balance of Payments,*
Dept. of Commerce, 1964.

Further discussion will be under two headings, which break the components of the balance of payments into current account transactions and capital account. Current transactions involve imports and exports, foreign aid, military expenditures, and other items that are more or less in the nature of consumption, and hence are not cumulative (they do not augment a stock, or increase wealth); capital account transactions include private investment, credit, money, and gold. This breakdown is less common in the balance of payments field, but the items within each category are so interrelated that not much can be gained in considering each one independently.

(1) Current Account

Until recently it was true that the United States exported more goods and services than it imported, but this was largely an accounting fiction. If merchandise only is considered, excluding military goods, the balance is approximately zero. But this includes a substantial volume of exports that is the result of foreign aid, since 80 percent of foreign aid is tied to American exports. How much of this would have occurred without the ties or without the aid is open to debate, but it is certainly much less. Thus if foreign aid is included in the balance, it is negative and has been so for some time. Add in transportation, military expenditures, and travel—all of which earn deficits—and the balance on current account for 1963 is $2.780 billion, payments over receipts. Our position since then has continued to weaken.

Bombs are produced in the United States, are purchased by the government, and are neither exports nor imports. They are a form of domestic consumption that we choose to consume by exploding them (reasonably enough) in some other country, and they are not entered into the balance of payments. Military expenditures abroad are of three types: (a) money spent by military and civilian personnel working overseas; (b) purchases by the military of foreign supplies and equipment; and (c) purchases by the military of foreign utilities, transportation, and other services. The sum of these expenditures ($2.88 billion in 1963) is enough to completely offset the current account deficit, but would mean no bases or military personnel abroad and would probably reduce our exports (both supplies and military goods) in addition.

It is interesting to note that these expenditures have already been heavily adjusted to minimize their payments effects. Military personnel and their families are encouraged to buy (imported) American products and are often provided with subsidized goods (the military buys and sells them at a loss). In military procurement, if the cost of U.S. goods and services is less than 50 percent more than equivalent local products, U.S. goods are purchased. Deals are made with some of our allies to sell them U.S. military goods and services equal to or in some proportion of our expenditures in their country. The result is that the cost of maintaining a foreign military extension is much higher than it needs to be, simply to reduce the negative balance of payments effect.

Other components of the current account are also interesting. Transportation services, while only 4 percent of GNP, contribute almost 11 percent of our payments deficit, making it a relatively big loser. It is also symptomatic of much of the payments problem. We took a $422 million loss on air and ship passenger fares, which means Americans traveled heavily on foreign lines. In the case of ships, we rarely either make or run them; and in the case of planes, we support our aircraft industry by selling sophisticated planes to foreign countries who desire a glamorous airline. Freight charges and charter fees, plus other payments, added $389 million to the deficit, largely because of our limited shipping capability. The American shipbuilding industry does not exist in the world market for two reasons: (a) the majority of its resources, including research and development, are employed by the navy, which builds very high cost ships; and (b) the federal government will pay up to 33 percent of the price of a ship in order to keep the industry alive in commercial vessels. The effect of this subsidy, however, is to keep the industry from having to make the necessary technological advances to be competitive. While Japanese ships dominate the world market, American shipbuilders ask for higher subsidies.

The transportation deficit is partly offset by expenditures on port services, which produced a surplus of $505 million. A final important component in the current account is travel —essentially tourism—which loses us $1.13 billion a year. Encouraging both Americans and foreigners to travel in the United States and restricting travel and expenditures abroad only partially offset the basic difficulty—U.S. prices are high for foreigners and foreign prices are cheap for Americans. Inflation, of course, makes the situation worse.

(2) Capital Account

Many opportunities for investment exist in foreign countries, and U.S. capital has been generally eager to take advantage of them. These investments are, in general, justifiable transfers of the location of capital to improve its efficiency and can cause a slight payments deficit only in the short run. The present situation is not so simple. Over the last two decades, American capital has chosen to leave the country and seek higher and easier returns rather than develop new techniques for improving American labor productivity, and this process has been aided by the government's use of political devices to enhance private economic objectives abroad. This has led to a market distortion that has often earned the label of exploitation or economic imperialism. A good case can be made for saying that in Latin America we have taken out more than we have put in.

More recent domestic policies have aggravated this problem. Instead of applying higher taxes to pay for the war (the appropriate policy), the government has tried to cool the economy through tighter money and higher interest rates. This has the effect of throttling domestic private investment, particularly in consumer goods and construction, while attracting foreign short-term capital, i.e., loans. These loans are taken mostly by the government, representing a borrowing to

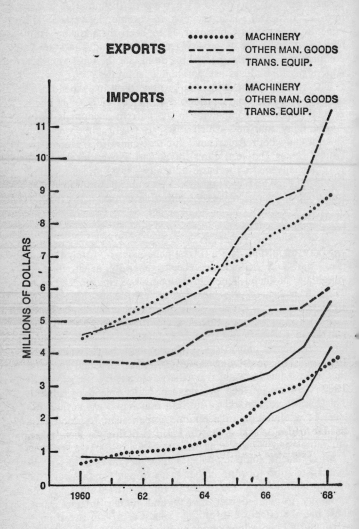

EXPORTS AND IMPORTS,
SELECTED COMMODITY GROUPS 1960-1968

year	machinery	(exports/imports) transportation equipment	other manufactured goods
1960	4476	2517	3815
	724	742	4575
1962	5447	2579	3766
	954	720	5215
1963	5702	2540	4046
	1054	764	5546
1964	6525	2844	4795
	1314	902	6188
1965	6934	3214	4890
	1800	1148	7528
1966	7678	3478	5388
	2688	2135	8668
1967	8280	4294	5468
	3099	2695	9004
1968	8597	5850	6083
	3688	4298	11508
1969	9865	6515	6999
	4489	5289	12021

Source: U.S. Bureau of the Census, **Statistical Abstract of the United States: 1969**; Office of Business Economics, **Survey of Current Business**, March 1970.

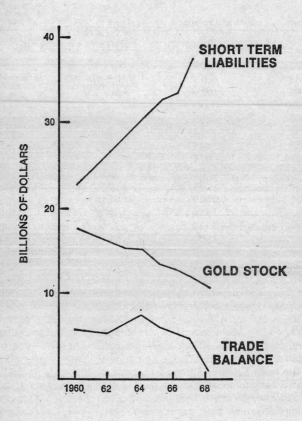

BALANCE OF PAYMENTS INDICATORS 1960–1969

year	trade balance	gold stock	short-term federal government liabilities (marketable interest bearing) maturity of one year or less
1960	4.0	17.8	70.5
1961	5.5	16.9	
1962	4.9	16.0	
1963	5.6	15.5	
1964	8.3	15.4	
1965	7.0	13.7	87.6
1966	5.1	13.1	
1967	4.8	12.0	
1968	2.0	10.4	106.4
1969	(1.0)	10.4	

Sources: gold stock—**Federal Reserve Bulletin**
trade balance—**Survey of Current Business**
short-term liabilities—**Treasury Bulletin**

Two indicators of our balance of payments problem are the level of our gold reserves and the amount of short-term (less than one year for repayment) loans the government has owing. The gold stock has dwindled inexorably since 1950, particularly since 1955, and is now approaching statutory limits. Short-term liabilities have risen rapidly over this same period, with an even more rapid increase since the escalation of the war. Currently, these notes must be refinanced at unusually high interest rates, adding unnecessarily to the burden of the national debt.

Another indicator of our trade position is the difference between exports of merchandise and general imports, referred to as the trade balance. Although we have maintained a favorable (somewhat spurious) balance in this component, even it has eroded away to almost nothing. In most of the major manufacturing categories both exports and imports are increasing in current dollar volume, but imports are increasing proportionately faster while still smaller in magnitude (machinery, transportation equipment) or are both larger in magnitude and increasing faster (other manufactured goods). The deterioration is due partly to inflation and partly to stagnation, with the major changes occurring since 1965.

pay for the war, and the loans must be paid off fairly quickly at the high interest rates—hence a request to raise the debt ceiling. The influx of short-term capital temporarily offsets, to some extent, the balance of payments deficit, but will make it worse in the long run.

As the inflation progresses, our balance of payments position worsens and confidence in the dollar and this country's ability to correct its mistakes is reduced. This means even higher interest rates since any kind of investment becomes more risky under these conditions. American long-term capital will increasingly go abroad, and the trade balance will deteriorate even further. A run on our gold reserves would produce an international monetary crisis, making devaluation both inevitable and extremely costly in terms of speculation and stability in the entire free world. Strenuous efforts are required very soon to keep the situation under control.

The balance of payments problem is less important in itself than as a symptom of the structural changes in our economy brought about by the war. Our failure to keep pace, technologically, in such industries as typewriters, sewing machines, machine tools, and rail transportation means that domestic labor productivity is low and capital investment lagging. When and if the United States returns to a peacetime economy, the structural problems, including their important counterpart unemployment, will emerge as a painful assignment. The major symbol of these structural shifts, which have been taking place over two decades, is the emergence of the "military-industrial complex" which President Eisenhower saw as imminent.

THE MILITARY-INDUSTRIAL COMPLEX

The elitist view that a handful of very powerful men make all the important decisions in the private and public economies (and that these men are not elected) is probably not true in the narrow sense, but a good deal of evidence supports the contention that power and wealth are heavily concentrated in this country. It is not necessary to subscribe to this argument, however, to acknowledge the existence of a group of firms and government agencies that behave in an observably consistent fashion. Whether the cause is interlocking directorates, personal relationships, common values, the institutional framework in which they all operate, or some other structural characteristics of our economic system is not of immediate consequence in establishing the existence of a military-industrial complex.

Unfortunately, a number of simplistic notions (such as world exploitation and corporate war profiteering) have served to obscure what is a complex and little understood set of relationships. We will present the issues of excess profits on the part of defense contractors, impacts of defense spending on private research and development, and an emerging form of socialism (referred to as "state capitalism") which characterizes part of the defense industry, without developing or evaluating the arguments in a very thorough manner.

WAR PROFITEERING

Looked at in terms of earnings per share of stock, the largest defense contractors do not stand out as strong performers. Many have clearly had difficulties, and those that have done well seem to have relied more heavily on nondefense markets. Douglas Aircraft was acquired by McDonnell; Lockheed and General Dynamics have had cost overruns and faulty products; General Electric has recently sold its computer business just when it was returning a profit in order to obtain working capital; United Aircraft and Raytheon have maintained their profits primarily through diversification into nondefense lines. Whether the second-rank defense contractors or the welter of minor contractors and sub-contractors have profited unduly is hard to say in the aggregate, but it is clear that receiving defense contracts does not automatically mean enormous profits.

A number of explanations can be offered. First is the lumpiness and riskiness of defense work, aggravated by the government's overt and covert reinforcement of the impression that the war has been almost over for the past five years. Firms never get tooled up to the appropriate scale of production, since additional fixed capital requires time to amortize and this is not worthwhile in the short run. Aerospace and weapons system research firms may have done much better in this respect, since the expenditures have been fairly steady over some period of time. Many firms, however, have been forced into uneconomic production schedules (requiring over-time and overuse of facilities) by the demands of the war.

Secondly, some firms appear healthier, measured by return on investment, but this is due to the fact that these firms are using government capital, both fixed capital (land, plant, and equipment) and working capital. (Lockheed's request for a government grant of half a billion dollars was of this type.) While this should lead to a higher paper return on investment, the direct managerial control exerted by the Department of Defense on these firms does not allow them to operate as efficiently as they would if they were competing in a private market. Because there is only a very small open market for defense products, this control may be necessary. Present procurement policies, nonetheless, are less than perfect.

This suggests the other side of the coin from profits: whether we are getting the best we can for what we pay, or simple efficiency in expenditure. Waste and mismanagement, both in the public and in the private sector, can make a weapons system extremely expensive without showing large profits for the contractor. This kind of inefficiency seems to be widespread in the entire war effort, and even extends to black market activities by military personnel in foreign countries.

RESEARCH AND DEVELOPMENT

The war has drained off funds from a wide range of research areas, including social research programs, cancer research, work in the physical and natural sciences, aerospace, military weapons systems, and private industry. (The National Institutes of Health are allowed to spend $1.3 billion per year, while Edgewood Arsenal gets $2.6 billion for chemical and biological warfare.) To the extent that new research is gen-erated, it is directed at defense production problems and is imbedded in production contracts. Thus we are presently sacrificing long-run productive capacity in favor of short-run output, since research and the development of technology constitute essential investment, in addition to plant, equip-ment, and social overhead capital (such as transportation and education).

Beyond the intertemporal effects of the war, there is the question of the balance between different areas in research and development, regardless of the total expenditures. While the military has given up some of its research funding, no projects have been eliminated; if the war stops, DOD will be ready and able to allocate the surplus funds to weapons systems and aerospace research and development without leaving much to either the private sector or what is left of the public sector. Altering research priorities will require more than simply ending the war.

Even without the war, the private sector has not been keeping pace with the rest of the world in developing and applying research. Industry by industry, the competitive position of the United States in world markets is being eroded and replaced by foreign producers. Steel and automobiles are hard hit. American management has become very conservative in developing new production techniques and new designs, yet investment of U.S. private capital in foreign markets has been very high. We have become experts in managing large conglomerates and other kinds of complex systems, but our productive capacity has deteriorated. Our most sophisticated products for export are aerospace and weapons systems and specific areas like computers and road-building equipment. What it will take to revitalize American entrepreneurship while retaining American management capacities is impossible to say at this point.

STATE CAPITALISM

When the national government provides a large share of the capital used in a large sector of the economy and controls not only the quantity and quality of the output but the management and production process itself, then the result is obviously much closer to socialism than it is to capitalism. Independent of whether this form of economic organization is appropriate for the particular industry or for this particular country, public policy should not be based on the assumption of a free market private enterprise system. (The DOD owned $196 billion worth of property in 1967, of which $40 billion was real property.) Because of the dominance of the defense sector over the economy as a whole, structural relationships developed in that sector will tend to characterize the economy.

In its characteristics, the defense industry is far from our free enterprise ideal. It is a "monopsonistic" industry, in that

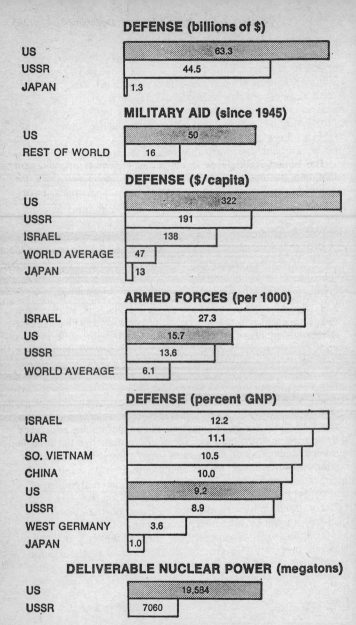

DEFENSE (billions of $)

US — 63.3
USSR — 44.5
JAPAN — 1.3

MILITARY AID (since 1945)

US — 50
REST OF WORLD — 16

DEFENSE ($/capita)

US — 322
USSR — 191
ISRAEL — 138
WORLD AVERAGE — 47
JAPAN — 13

ARMED FORCES (per 1000)

ISRAEL — 27.3
US — 15.7
USSR — 13.6
WORLD AVERAGE — 6.1

DEFENSE (percent GNP)

ISRAEL — 12.2
UAR — 11.1
SO. VIETNAM — 10.5
CHINA — 10.0
US — 9.2
USSR — 8.9
WEST GERMANY — 3.6
JAPAN — 1.0

DELIVERABLE NUCLEAR POWER (megatons)

US — 19,584
USSR — 7060

The United States leads in almost all indicators of militarism that can be measured or estimated. We spend far more for defense, whether measured in total or in per capita terms, than the Russians, who are in second place. We have more men per capita under arms. We give more military aid and have the largest arms exporting business. Because the United States is the most fully industrialized large country in the world, we are relatively more wealthy and can support such a heavy defense effort with less sacrifice, although the sacrifice is larger than is presently perceived in this country.

Israel—a country for whom national security is an immediate and urgent problem—devotes approximately the same share of resources to defense as the United States. Japan and West Germany—countries that are rapidly cutting into our foreign and domestic markets, despite their small size—are not wasting their economies on defense. An impartial observer looking at these data would conclude that (a) the United States is irrationally worried about external attack, or (b) the United States is determined to be the world leader in the technology and production of weapons systems and military hardware. The United States has, in fact, supplied most of the arms used by both sides in almost all of the 56 wars that have occurred in the world since 1945. Since the data are for 1966, they understate the current U.S. advantage.

it has only one buyer, the government. The path to government sales is not through advertising, marketing, salesmanship, or product differentiation. The path, rather, is strewn with influence-peddling, lobbying, wire-pulling, and control of key committees. Markets are hard to hold, for the industry is vulnerable to strategic shifts, electoral results, and personal whims of politicians. To secure every advantage in this dangerous game, defense firms employ as officers ex-generals, colonels, and purchasing agents. Yet despite personal setbacks and the losses of particular firms, the industry as a whole hangs together. In part this is because of the virtual interchangeability of industry personnel. Executives switch companies freely, and technicians belong to the floating defense-aerospace labor pool, centered on Los Angeles, rather than to any one company which tomorrow might lose out to a competitor on a big contract. The danger is that this mode of doing business, however inefficient and wasteful, has become the dominant mode for American business. If it persists, our historic industrial superiority will be a hollow shell.

PROSPECTS FOR CONVERSION

In view of the deep structural changes in our economy produced by our "permanent" wartime footing, what are the prospects for converting our economic system to a full peacetime economy? For whatever the prospects, we see no long-run alternative to peace. If the Nixon administration were to end the war, as promised, it would need to take charge of the economy and direct resources so that the war's corrosive effect on the economy could be diminished without sudden instability or hardship. Some sacrifices would necessarily attend this set of moves, but they need not be more than those occurring through normal growth and change in the economy. Personal consumption might be cut back for a time, while investment was shifted into nondefense industries, and taxes should be raised in the interim. The redirection of resources would harm some individuals while benefiting others. Since employment-maintaining expenditures are a necessary component of a war-reduction program, the government would still be competing with private capital for a time. None of these effects need be of serious magnitude.

If the government should begin by reducing the commitment of resources to Indochina, it would follow as soon as possible with full withdrawal. In the transition, the government must seek to prevent either inflation or recession, especially the latter. Taxes should favor investment in consumer goods. Strong efforts should be made to reduce costs of exports, and to induce application of new technologies in private production. Since technology will continue to be labor-saving, investment in education, manpower training, housing, the services sector, and especially public services, must be encouraged.

Indeed, a major problem of the transition is that of diverting resources from the military, largely into the public sector. The DOD has projects underway or in planning that would use up all the savings that might result from ending the war. It will be difficult to pry loose these funds, given the strength of the military in the public budget. But the government would have a golden opportunity to show its commitment to ending poverty, racism, urban decay, environmental pollution, and defects in public services. (An income maintenance program that would eliminate poverty in that 13 percent of our population would cost about $16 billion per year. The fiscal year 1967–68 budget for the poverty program was $1.7 billion.) In these programs, real income must be given priority over money income. Many services in these categories are outside the market mechanism. The government might consider ways to transfer funds directly to consumers of these services, and to build up "markets" for them.

The prospects for effective administration of such funds are not now good. There is nothing in the performance of existing public bureaucracies, inside and outside of the war apparatus, to give us optimism. Present delivery systems are full of inflexibilities, inequities, waste, and leakage. Nothing short of a massive reconstitution of government service would make possible the effective application of huge new programs. The problem is not one of lack of targets. In a work conducted in 1958 and published in 1960, Dyckman and Isaacs estimated the potential development and redevelopment bill for American cities at about a trillion dollars, to be spent over twelve years. In the twelve years since that book was written, the military establishment has spent more than that amount. But the military delivery system is simplified by the fact that it is delivered to "clients" outside the country. The institutional and behavioral shifts necessary for effective application of such funds in domestic programs are formidable. Our internal divisions of interest and values stand in the way almost as much as does the power of the military.

To make matters worse, the problem has been regionalized. Impact of conversion would fall unequally on states in the federal system. No simple block grant formula based on population would be equitable compensation. Whole industries would be expected to lobby for their lives. In fiscal year 1962, 72 percent of the value of the military prime contracts was awarded to 100 corporate contractors. The number accounting for this share has since been reduced by almost a quarter. These remaining firms and institutions, moreover, are the economic "base" of their communities. While the relationship of Boeing to Seattle is notorious, other contractors are in much the same local situation. Whole regions, notably the Gulf Crescent and Southern California, would be disaster areas if war contracting shut down without replacement. We should remember that California and Texas have powerful congressional delegations. It is not wholly accidental that they have produced the last two presidents.

Yet in the face of the alternatives, should we not risk these costs? The uncounted costs of the Vietnam war probably exceed the direct expenditures. The official kill of "Vietcong" since the war began is over half a million, which includes, as we now know, many old men, women, and children. The cost of this killing, out of our pockets, is about $115 billion. But to this should be added the costs of some 45,000 American lives lost, 100,000 South Vietnamese soldiers killed, plus at least 1,000,000 "friendly" civilians "accidentally" killed. At cost, a Vietcong is worth $207,000, since we pay more than that to kill him. At that price, and we cannot conceive that American lives are worth less, the cost in lives to the United States has been $9.3 billion—not much in reference to the cost of planes lost. At the capitalized value of life earnings of these young men, the price would be much higher.

Over 150,000 U.S. soldiers have been hospitalized as a result of the war, at unknown cost to them. Some 500,000 troops are fighting in Indochina; this represents earnings foregone of about $3 billion annually. Working in the domestic peacetime economy these earnings would increase national welfare and might make a dent in poverty. It costs $90,000 per year to train, equip, and support a front line soldier in Vietnam; it might cost as much as $45,000 to pay the full cost of an eight-year education for a high-school graduate, and he could have a Ph.D. at the completion. An infantryman in Indochina for eight years would have cost $720,000, after which time he might well be ready for a mental institution or for permanent custody.

At least 10,000 American young men of draft age have gone to Canada to escape the war. Another several thousand have refused induction and accepted the penalty (imposing costs on the courts and jails) when the local boards could get around to prosecution (they sometimes cannot). The desertion rate of U.S. soldiers in Vietnam is about 80,000 per year, of whom 10 percent fail to return. But the widespread disaffection of youth is even more costly. The "drop-out" from an America in whom they have lost faith is staggeringly high in economic costs. Loss of the future contributions of many of these people, who are often the promising and talented youth, is priceless.

In the face of these considerations, we have much to gain and little to lose, even in that least sensitive of measurements, economic cost, by reconstituting the U.S. economy on a peaceful, non-garrison basis.

APPENDICES
NOTES
BIBLIOGRAPHY
INDEX

APPENDIX I

A. President Nixon's Address to the Nation on Cambodia, April 30, 1970

Good evening, my fellow Americans:

Ten days ago, in my report to the nation on Vietnam, I announced the decision to withdraw an additional 150,000 Americans from Vietnam over the next year. I said then that I was making that decision despite our concern over increased enemy activity in Laos, in Cambodia and in South Vietnam.

And at that time I warned that if I concluded that increased enemy activity in any of these areas endangered the lives of Americans remaining in Vietnam, I would not hesitate to take strong and effective measures to deal with that situation.

Despite that warning, North Vietnam has increased its military aggression in all these areas—and particularly in Cambodia.

After full consultation with the National Security Council, Ambassador Bunker, General Abrams and my other advisers, I have concluded that the actions of the enemy in the last 10 days clearly endanger the lives of Americans who are in Vietnam now and would constitute an unacceptable risk to those who will be there after withdrawal of another 150,000.

To protect our men who are in Vietnam and to guarantee the continued success of our withdrawal and Vietnamization programs, I have concluded that the time has come for action.

Tonight I shall describe the actions of the enemy, the actions I have ordered to deal with that situation and the reasons for my decision.

Cambodia, a small country of 7 million people, has been a neutral nation since the Geneva Agreement of 1954—an agreement, incidentally, which was signed by the Government of North Vietnam.

American policy since then has been to scrupulously respect the neutrality of the Cambodian people. We have maintained a skeleton diplomatic mission of fewer than 15 in Cambodia's capital—and that only since last August. For the previous four years—from 1965 to 1969—we did not have any diplomatic mission whatever in Cambodia. And for the past five years, we have provided no military assistance whatever and no economic assistance to Cambodia.

North Vietnam, however, has not respected that neutrality.

For the past five years—as indicated on this map that you see here—North Vietnam has occupied military sanctuaries all along the Cambodian frontier with South Vietnam. Some of these extend up to 20 miles into Cambodia. The sanctuaries are in red, and, as you note, they are on both sides of the border. They are used for hit-and-run attacks on American and South Vietnamese forces in South Vietnam.

These Communist-occupied territories contain major base camps, training sites, logistics facilities, weapons and ammunition factories, airstrips and prisoner-of-war compounds.

And for five years, neither the United States nor South Vietnam has moved against these enemy sanctuaries, because we did not wish to violate the territory of a neutral nation. Even after the Vietnamese Communists began to expand these sanctuaries four weeks ago, we counseled patience to our South Vietnamese allies and imposed restraints on our own commanders.

In contrast to our policy, the enemy in the past two weeks has stepped up his guerrilla actions, and he is concentrating his main forces in these sanctuaries that you see on this map, where they are building up to launch massive attacks on our forces and those of South Vietnam.

North Vietnam in the last two weeks has stripped away all pretense of respecting the sovereignty or the neutrality of Cambodia. Thousands of their soldiers are invading the country from the sanctuaries; they are encircling the capital of Pnompenh. Coming from these sanctuaries, as you see here, they have moved into Cambodia and are encircling the capital.

Cambodia, as a result of this, has sent out a call to the United States—to a number of other nations—for assistance, because if this enemy effort succeeds, Cambodia would become a vast enemy staging area and a springboard for attacks on South Vietnam along 600 miles of frontier—a refuge where enemy troops could return from combat without fear of retaliation.

North Vietnamese men and supplies could then be poured into that country, jeopardizing not only the lives of our own men but the people of South Vietnam as well.

Now, confronted with this situation, we have three options:

First, we can do nothing. The ultimate result of that course of action is clear. Unless we indulge in wishful thinking, the lives of Americans remaining in Vietnam after our next withdrawal of 150,000 would be gravely threatened.

Let us go to the map again. Here is South Vietnam. Here is North Vietnam. North Vietnam already occupies this part of Laos. If North Vietnam also occupied this whole band in Cambodia, or the entire country, it would mean that South Vietnam was completely outflanked and the forces of Americans in this area, as well as the South Vietnamese, would be in an untenable military position.

Our second choice is to provide massive military assistance to Cambodia itself. Now, unfortunately, while we deeply sympathize with the plight of 7 million Cambodians whose country is being invaded, massive amounts of military assistance could not be rapidly and effectively utilized by the small Cambodian Army against the immediate threat. With other nations, we shall do our best to provide the small arms and other equipment which the Cambodian Army of 40,000 needs and can use for its defense. But the aid we will provide will be limited to the purpose of enabling Cambodia to defend its neutrality—and not for the purpose of making it an active belligerent on one side or the other.

Our third choice is to go to the heart of the trouble. And that means cleaning out major North Vietnamese and Viet Cong-occupied territories—these sanctuaries which serve as bases for attacks on both Cambodia, and American and South Vietnamese forces in South Vietnam.

Some of these, incidentally, are as close to Saigon as Baltimore is to Washington. This one, for example, is called the Parrot's Beak. It's only 33 miles from Saigon.

Now, faced with these three options, this is the decision I have made:

In cooperation with the armed forces of South Vietnam, attacks are being launched this week to clean out major enemy sanctuaries on the Cambodian-Vietnam border.

A major responsibility for the ground operations is being assumed by South Vietnamese forces. For example, the attacks in several areas, including the Parrot's Beak that I referred to a moment ago, are exclusively South Vietnamese ground operations under South Vietnamese command, with the United States providing air and logistical support.

There is one area, however—immediately above Parrot's Beak—where I have concluded that a combined American and South Vietnamese operation is necessary. Tonight American and South Vietnamese units will attack the headquarters for the entire Communist military operation in South Vietnam. This key control center has been occupied by the North Vietnamese and Viet Cong for five years, in blatant violation of Cambodia's neutrality.

This is not an invasion of Cambodia. The areas in which these attacks will be launched are completely occupied and controlled by North Vietnamese forces. Our purpose is not to occupy the areas. Once enemy forces are driven out of these sanctuaries and once their military supplies destroyed, we will withdraw.

These actions are in no way directed to the security interests of any nation. Any government that chooses to use these actions as a pretext for harming relations with the United States will be doing so on its own responsibility and on its own initiative, and we will draw the appropriate conclusions.

And now let me give you the reasons for my decision:

A majority of the American people, a majority of you listening to me, are for the withdrawal of our forces from Vietnam. The action I have taken tonight is indispensable for the continuing success of that withdrawal program.

A majority of the American people want to end this war rather than to have it drag on interminably. The action I take tonight will serve that purpose.

A majority of the American people want to keep the casualties of our brave men in Vietnam at an absolute minimum. The action I take tonight is essential if we are to accomplish that goal.

We take this action not for the purpose of expanding the war into Cambodia but for the purpose of ending the war in Vietnam and winning the just peace we all desire. We have made, we will continue to make every possible effort to end this war through negotiation at the conference table rather than through more fighting on the battlefield.

Let's look again at the record:

We've stopped the bombing of North Vietnam. We have cut air operations by over 20 percent. We've announced the withdrawal of over 250,000 of our men. We have offered to withdraw all of our men if they withdraw theirs. We've offered to negotiate all issues with only one condition—and that is that the future of South Vietnam be determined not by North Vietnam and not by the United States, but by the people of South Vietnam themselves.

The answer of the enemy has been intransigence at the conference table, belligerence in Hanoi, massive military aggression in Laos and Cambodia, and stepped-up attacks in South Vietnam designed to increase American casualties.

This attitude has become intolerable. We will not react to this threat to American lives merely by plaintive diplomatic protests. If we did, the credibility of the United States would be destroyed in every area of the world where only the power of the United States deters aggression.

Tonight I again warn the North Vietnamese that if they continue to escalate the fighting when the United States is withdrawing its forces, I shall meet my responsibility as Commander in Chief of our armed forces to take the action I consider necessary to defend the security of our American men.

The action that I have announced tonight puts the leaders of North Vietnam on notice that we will be patient in working for peace, we will be conciliatory at the conference table—but we will not be humiliated, we will not be defeated, we will not allow American men by the thousands to be killed by an enemy from privileged sanctuaries.

The time came long ago to end this war through peaceful negotiations. We stand ready for these negotiations. We have made major efforts, many of which must remain secret. I say tonight: All the offers and approaches made previously remain on the conference table whenever Hanoi is ready to negotiate seriously.

But if the enemy response to our most conciliatory efforts for peaceful negotiation continues to be to increase its attacks and humiliate and defeat us, we shall react accordingly.

My fellow Americans, we live in an age of anarchy both

abroad and at home. We see mindless attacks on all the great institutions which have been created by free civilizations in the last 500 years. Even here in the United States, great universities are being systematically destroyed. Small nations all over the world find themselves under attack from within and from without.

If, when the chips are down, the world's most powerful nation—the United States of America—acts like a pitiful, helpless giant, the forces of totalitarianism and anarchy will threaten free nations and free institutions throughout the world.

It is not our power but our will and character that is being tested tonight. The question all Americans must ask and answer tonight is this:

Does the richest and strongest nation in the history of the world have the character to meet a direct challenge by a group which rejects every effort to win a just peace, ignores our warning, tramples on solemn agreements, violates the neutrality of an unarmed people and uses our prisoners as hostages?

If we fail to meet this challenge, all other nations will be on notice that despite its overwhelming power the United States, when a real crisis comes, will be found wanting.

During my campaign for the Presidency, I pledged to bring Americans home from Vietnam; they are coming home. I promised to end this war; I shall keep that promise. I promised to win a just peace; I shall keep that promise.

We shall avoid a wider war—but we are also determined to put an end to this war.

In this room Woodrow Wilson made the great decisions which led to victory in World War I; Franklin Roosevelt made the decisions which led to our victory in World War II; Dwight D. Eisenhower made decisions which ended the war in Korea and avoided war in the Middle East; John F. Kennedy, in his finest hour, made the great decision which removed Soviet nuclear missiles from Cuba and the Western Hemisphere.

I have noted that there has been a great deal of discussion with regard to this decision that I have made, and I should point out that I do not contend that it is in the same magnitude as these decisions that I have just mentioned. But between those decisions and this decision there is a difference that is very fundamental: In those decisions, the American people were not assailed by counsels of doubt and defeat from some of the most widely known opinion leaders of the nation.

I have noted, for example, that a Republican Senator has said that this action I have taken means that my party has lost all chance of winning the November elections. And others are saying today that this move against the enemy sanctuaries will make me a one-term President.

No one is more aware than I am of the political consequences of the action I have taken.

It is tempting to take the easy political path: to blame this war on previous Administrations and to bring all of our men home immediately—regardless of the consequences—even though that would mean defeat for the United States; to desert 18 million South Vietnamese people who have put their trust in us, to expose them to the same slaughter and savagery which the leaders of North Vietnam inflicted on hundreds of thousands of North Vietnamese who chose freedom when the Communists took over North Vietnam in 1954; to get peace at any price now even though I know that a peace of humiliation for the United States would lead to a bigger war or surrender later.

I have rejected all political considerations in making this decision.

Whether my party gains in November is nothing compared to the lives of 400,000 brave Americans fighting for our country and for the cause of peace and freedom in Vietnam. Whether I may be a one-term President is insignificant compared to whether, by our failure to act in this crisis, the United States proves itself to be unworthy to lead the forces of freedom in this critical period in world history. I would rather be a one-term President and do what I believe is right than to be a two-term President at the cost of seeing America become a second-rate power and to see this nation accept the first defeat in its proud 190-year history.

I realize that in this war there are honest and deep differences in this country about whether we should have become involved, that there are differences as to how the war should have been conducted.

But the decision I announce tonight transcends those differences:

For the lives of American men are involved. The opportunity for 150,000 Americans to come home in the next 12 months is involved. The future of 18 million people in South Vietnam and 7 million people in Cambodia is involved. The possibility of winning a just peace in Vietnam and in the Pacific is at stake.

It is customary to conclude a speech from the White House by asking support for the President of the United States. Tonight I depart from that precedent. What I ask is far more important.

I ask for your support for our brave men fighting tonight halfway around the world—not for territory, not for glory, but so that their younger brothers and their sons and your sons can have a chance to grow up in a world of peace and freedom and justice.

Thank you, and good night.

B. Proclamation of the Royal Government of National Union Under the Leadership of the National United Front of Kampuchea

Samdech Norodom Sihanouk, Head of State of Cambodia and Chairman of the National United Front of Kampuchea, made public at a press conference in Peking on May 5 a proclamation of the Royal Government of National Union Under the Leadership of the National United Front of Kampuchea. Full text follows:

In his solemn message to the Khmer nation, dated March 23, 1970, Samdech Norodom Sihanouk, Head of State of Cambodia, announced the forming of a new Royal Government of National Union Under the Leadership of the N.U.F.K.

Today, following the extraordinary congress which brought together in Peking the qualified representatives of different circles of Khmer society, the new Royal Government of National Union Under the Leadership of the N.U.F.K., of which Mr. Penn Nouth is the Prime Minister, is formed.

Just as it was defined in the aforesaid message of the Head of State, the essential mission of the new Government is to faithfully and entirely execute the Political Programme of the N.U.F.K.:

1. Unite all our people for fighting against all the manoeuvres and aggression by the American imperialists and overthrowing the dictatorship of their valets headed by Lon Nol–Sirik Matak.

2. After complete victory, build an independent, peaceful, neutral, democratic and prosperous Cambodia.

On this occasion, the new Government of National Union Under the Leadership of the N.U.F.K. reaffirms solemnly its qualifications as the sole legal and legitimate government of the entire Khmer nation excluding the fascist and racist reactionary regime of Phnom Penh.

On this score, it proclaims solemnly:

1. The condemnation of the Khmer people of the traitorous Lon Nol–Sirik Matak clique which has sabotaged and destroyed the independence, peace and neutrality of Cambodia for the benefit of American imperialism whose troops, supported by those of Saigon, have invaded and occupied on a large scale the national territory, in defiance of all the international laws, in order to repress our people.

2. That the foreign policy of Cambodia is and will remain that of national independence, peace, neutrality and nonalignment, of solidarity and friendship with all the peaceloving and justice-loving peoples and governments.

In this spirit, the new Royal Government of National Union Under the Leadership of the N.U.F.K. proclaims its absolute respect for all the international treaties, accords and conventions which Cambodia has signed before the date of March 18, 1970.

Considering moreover that the Cambodian people are in the struggle for the recovery of its sacred rights of independence and national sovereignty, against oppression by the American imperialists and their lackeys of Phnom Penh, and that this struggle is common to all the Indo-Chinese peoples, victims of American imperialism, and confident of the correctness of the struggle being waged at present against the open and massive aggression by the armed forces of the American imperialists, and of final victory, the Royal Government of National Union Under the Leadership of the N.U.F.K. is certain of the encouragement, militant sympathy and fraternal support, as from today, on the part of all the peoples and governments in the world who uphold independence, peace and justice.

This encouragement, sympathy and support would find expression in the recognition of our Government as the sole legal and legitimate Government of Cambodia by more and more friendly peoples and governments.

For their part, the Khmer people, under the leadership of the N.U.F.K. and its Chairman Samdech Norodom Sihanouk, are ready to make all sacrifices for achieving final victory over the American imperialists and their lackeys, the Lon Nol–Sirik Matak clique, for the present struggle determines the liberty and dignity of our future generations and it is fundamental for the independence, liberty and progress of the Indo-Chinese peoples and the peoples of the world.

Long live the N.U.F.K.!

Long live Samdech Norodom Sihanouk, Head of State and Chairman of the N.U.F.K.!

The Khmer people will win!

May 4, 1970, *Peking Review, No. 20*

Political Programme of National United Front of Kampuchea

The Cambodian people established an organized society more than 2,000 years ago, and the light of the Angkor civilization shone throughout Southeast Asia for many centuries, making an appreciable contribution to world civilization.

During that period, Cambodian society honoured moral and intellectual values, cultivated traditions of struggle and the sense of honour and of dignity and looked upon state power as a mission to serve the people and placed the general interest in priority over the interests of the individual. The happiness and well-being of the people were the aim of all state power. The evidences of this civilization, the marks of a popular conception of state responsibilities and the refinement of philosophy are perceptible everywhere, on the bas-reliefs of historical monuments, in inscriptions, on gravestones, on the remains of hospitals, barrages, causeways, bridges, etc. . . . and in all the details of the habits and customs in the life of our people.

As with other peoples, through the centuries the Cambodian people passed in the course of their historical development crises, accidents and misfortunes as well as periods of prosperity, victorious struggles and splendour. During the past century, just as the other peoples on the Indo-China Peninsula, the Cambodian people suffered from the rule of French colonialism. But loyal to their long tradition of struggle and inspired by the heritage of Angkor splendour, the Cambodian people never ceased, even during the darkest moments of their history, to carry on a stubborn fight against colonialist occupation and to undergo supreme sacrifices in order to safeguard their national independence. Our history is filled with glorious pages and the lineage of our ancestors is rich in heroes. That is why, guided by the noble traditions of their ancestors and inspired by their rich national heritage, the entire Cambodian people, united as one in a heroic struggle against the French colonialists who were already supported by the American interventionists, finally won complete national independence recognized and guaranteed by the Geneva Agreements of 1954.

Since then, the Cambodian people, in conformity with their temperament and profound aspirations, chose a policy of national independence, peace and neutrality, and adopted the Five Principles of Peaceful Coexistence of Bandung of 1955 in international relations. But experience has shown that the American imperialists are the most dangerous, the most implacable and the most treacherous enemy of our people and our policy. As a matter of fact, they fomented a number of plots, of which the most important were that in 1959 with the participation of the Cambodian general Dap Chuon, Sam Sary and a member of the Embassy of the United States of America in Phnom Penh, which was followed by the sending of a time-bomb to the Royal Palace; the plot in 1963 organized by Songsak, a banker and an agent of the C.I.A., with the complicity of Sirik Matak, aimed at sabotaging our economy and our policy. During the past ten years, the armed forces of the Saigon government serving the United States and often supported by American troops and planes have been openly and on an intensive scale committing aggression against our frontier villages and inhabitants, causing major losses in property and the death of hundreds of our compatriots, the greater part of whom are defenceless civilians, men, women and children. But seeing the political maturity of the Khmer people who were able to defeat all the plots and acts of aggression, the agents of the American imperialists and their flunkeys consisting of a group of traitors headed by Lon Nol and Sirik Matak, manoeuvred to undermine openly the nationalized sector of our economy and increased arrests, arbitrary detentions and assassinations of patriots and stepped up vilifications and distortions of the truth against honest intellectuals, monks, partisan elements standing firmly for neutrality and progressive patriots, and excluded them from serving the state. The culmination of this plot was the military coup d'etat of March 18, 1970 which permitted the American imperialists to install in Phnom Penh a fascist and racist regime headed by the traitors Lon Nol–Sirik Matak. And the fact is, one month after that event, the entire world has come to know that the policy of national independence, peace and neutrality of our country is dead and that the traitors Lon Nol–Sirik Matak are more and more openly associating themselves with the other flunkeys of the American imperialists in Indo-China and in Asia in order to impose on the Cambodian people a fascist and racist dictatorship. The whole world also knows that Cambodia has become a new "Viet Nam" where the American forces are openly and savagely intervening in order to suppress our people.

Responding to the historic call of March 23, 1970 of Samdech Norodom Sihanouk, Head of State, the Cambodian people of one mind have conducted with enthusiasm and ardour political, armed and other forms of struggles both at home and abroad, in the capital, urban centres and in the countryside, including the most remote places, shaking the morale and the already precarious authority of the traitors in the country. The aim of the present Political Programme of the N.U.F.K. is to realize the broadest national union for fighting against all the manoeuvres and aggression of the American imperialists, overthrowing the dictatorship of their flunkeys headed by Lon Nol–Sirik Matak and for defending the national independence, peace, neutrality, sovereignty and territorial integrity of the country within her present frontiers and for building a free and democratic regime of the people progressing toward the construction of a prosperous Cambodia conforming to the profound aspirations of our people.

PART ONE

Unite the Entire People for Fighting Against All the Manoeuvres and Aggression of the American Imperialists and Overthrowing the Dictatorship of Their Flunkeys Headed by Lon Nol–Sirik Matak and for Building an Independent, Peaceful, Neutral, Democratic and Prosperous Cambodia

During the last 15 years, the Khmer people have been able to safeguard an independent, peaceful and neutral Cambodia,

they have defeated all the manoeuvres of encirclement, provocation, subversion and aggression by the American imperialists
and thus have frustrated their plans of aggression aimed at
establishing a system of military bases from south Viet Nam
to Thailand, including Laos and Cambodia and transforming
our country into a new-type colony. The coup d'etat of March
18, 1970 engineered by the American imperialists brutally
destroyed the independence, peace and neutrality of our
country. That is why, responding to the historic call made by
Head of State Samdech Norodom Sihanouk on March 23,
1970, the Khmer people, deeply adhering to these ideas and
to their traditions, rose en masse to carry out political, armed
and all other forms of struggles against the American
imperialists, their satellites and particularly those of south
Viet Nam and their Cambodian flunkeys headed by Lon Nol–
Sirik Matak. In these circumstances, desiring to develop the
five-point declaration of Samdech, the Head of State, the
N.U.F.K. proposes the following tasks:

—Unite and mobilize all social classes and strata,
all political parties, all professional or religious organizations, all patriotic personages either at home or abroad,
irrespective of their political opinion, sex and religious
belief, so as to safeguard Cambodia's national independence, peace, neutrality and territorial integrity
within her present frontiers, oppose American imperialist
schemes and aggression, and overthrow the fascist and
racist dictatorship of the American imperialists' flunkeys
headed by Lon Nol–Sirik Matak.
—Welcome as brothers the masses of the people, and
all functionaries, policemen, officers, non-commissioned
officers and men in the armed forces of the Lon Nol–
Sirik Matak clique, intellectuals, students and other
personages, who have decided to join the N.U.F.K.
Those people who for various reasons cannot as yet
join the N.U.F.K. but oppose the American imperialists
and their flunkeys can co-ordinate their efforts with
those of the N.U.F.K., and they will also be welcomed
with understanding by the N.U.F.K.
—As the American aggression against Cambodia is
a component of the plan for the expansion of the war
which the American imperialists are losing in south

Viet Nam and Laos, the N.U.F.K. co-ordinates its struggle with that of the fraternal peoples of Viet Nam and Laos on the principle that the liberation and defence of each country are the affairs of its own people and the principle that the mutual support among the three peoples must be based on mutual respect and the legitimate aspirations of each people concerned.

—Create and strengthen the National Liberation Army (N.L.A.) comprising guerrilla units, partisans, those elements in the Royal Khmer Army who refuse to submit to the dictatorship of Lon Nol–Sirik Matak, flunkeys of the American imperialists, and those elements in the mercenary troops of the traitors Lon Nol and Sirik Matak who will decide in the future to join the ranks of the N.L.A.

—The mission of the N.L.A. is to destroy to the maximum the enemy armed forces and to defend and expand the liberated areas, the solid rear for our struggle. In the course of struggle, the N.L.A. must develop the spirit of patriotism, raise its political level and foster utter devotion to the cause of the people.

—Those army units now serving the reactionary regime, which for various reasons cannot join the N.L.A. at present but which are struggling against the American imperialists, can co-ordinate their actions with those of the N.L.A. in striking at the American imperialists and their flunkeys.

—Severely punish the reactionaries guilty of crimes against the people, but show leniency to those criminals who have sincerely repented.

—The wounded and the prisoners of war will be looked after and treated humanely.

PART TWO

Build a Democratic and Prosperous Cambodia

The Cambodian people are unanimously determined to liberate the country from the dictatorship of Lon Nol–Sirik Matak, valets of the American imperialists, and from all other forms of American imperialist domination.

The Cambodian society, which will be established in the liberated zone and then in the whole country, will be rid of all defects impeding its rapid and full bloom: elimination of depraving customs, corruption, all sorts of illicit trading, smuggling and means of inhuman exploitation of the people. The N.U.F.K. declares that "power is, and will always be, in the hands of the progressive, industrious and genuine working people who will ensure our motherland a bright future on the basis of social justice, equality and fraternity among all the Khmers" (Solemn Declaration of Samdech, Head of State, on March 23, 1970). The people are the source of all power.

The democratization of Cambodian society is being carried out in the liberated zone at present and will be carried out in the whole country later in the following ways:

—Guarantee to all Cambodians, except traitors known to the country, the freedom of vote, the freedom of standing for election, the freedom of speech, the press, opinion, association, demonstration, residence, travel at home and going abroad, etc. . . . Safeguard the inviolability of the person, property, wealth and privacy of correspondence.

—Guarantee effective equality to both sexes, strive to wipe out backward traditions discriminating against women. Encourage by all means the cultural and professional development of women to enable them fully to participate in the common struggle. Give primary importance to training and educating women cadres at all levels in the national life. Abolish polygamy.

—Buddhism is and will remain to be the state religion. But the N.U.F.K. recognizes and guarantees the freedom of all other religions and beliefs: Islamism, Brahmanism, the belief of the Khmers-Loeur, Catholicism, Protestantism, Caodaism, etc. . . . Places of worship are protected.

—Look after with greatest solicitude the needs of our disabled servicemen and the families of our fighters who gave their lives for the country, and reserve privileged treatment for them.

—Ensure the protection of the legitimate rights and interests of foreign nationals who respect our laws and customs, the independence and sovereignty of Cambodia.

—See to it that the legitimate rights and interests of the minority nationalities and Cambodian nationals living abroad are respected.

The N.U.F.K. is devoted to building up and developing an independent national economy by relying principally on the resources and productive forces of Cambodia.

This economic policy finds concrete expression in:

—Freeing the national economy from persons who engage in profiteering, smuggling, blackmarketeering and inhuman exploitation of the people.

—Protecting and guaranteeing the rights of ownership of land and property in accordance with the laws of the state.

—Confiscating the land and property of traitors who are active accomplices in the pay of the American imperialists and who have committed crimes against the people. The land and property seized will be distributed among the needy peasants.

—Guaranteeing to the peasants the right of ownership of the land they cultivate. Establishing a fair system on land rent and rates of interest on loans.

—Helping the peasants resolve the agrarian problem through a fair solution of unreasonable debts.

—Helping the peasants increase production and labour productivity. Protecting and developing co-operation and the good customs of mutual aid in the countryside.

—Ensuring conditions of safe and rational management and ensuring the marketing and economical transportation of products.

—Encouraging the formation of trade unions. Guaranteeing security of employment and reasonable remuneration to the labouring classes. Improving working conditions. Ensuring a system of social insurance.

—Developing the industrialization of the country and carrying out a rational industrial policy so that production will meet the principal needs of the people to the maximum. Studying adequate measures for the elimination of faults in the administration of state or joint enterprises.

—Encouraging the national bourgeoisie to run well and set up enterprises beneficial to the people in conformity with the laws concerning wage-earners. Ensuring rational and uninterrupted sale of manufactured goods.

—Helping the handicraftsmen raise labour productivity and diversify their products and ensuring the sale of their products on the best conditions.

—Developing communication lines and the means of transportation.

—Safeguarding the interests of school and university students, intellectuals and functionaries; providing employment for "those without occupation" and the unemployed in accordance with their ability and helping them develop further their ability to serve the motherland.

—Maintaining the nationalization of the banks and foreign trade.

—With regard to foreign trade, encouraging and developing export, limiting imports to equipment and products necessary to the national economy. Protecting national products from foreign competition.

—Safeguarding the purchasing power of the *riel* and paying attention to improving the public finance.

Alongside with the democratization and the realization of the above-mentioned economic policies, the N.U.F.K. pays attention to the training of persons capable of correctly applying these objectives. The policy of the N.U.F.K. concerning education and culture is based on the following points:

—Develop the good traditions of the Angkor civilization handed down to us till now. Build a national culture on the basis of patriotism and love for work well done and love for art. Protect historical relics and monuments.

—Khmerize gradually the curricula for the different stages of education, including higher education.

—Adopt the national language as the sole official language in the public services.

—Adapt the educational programmes and methods to the needs of the country.

—Encourage and assist scientific research and experimentation and encourage the efforts of those who wish to deepen their studies.

—Promote the research in our national history which is often distorted by foreign authors, and include our national history in the educational programmes.

—Ensure continuous education through regular school terms or practical training.

—Develop pre-school education: nurseries, kindergartens and pre-school classes.

—Ensure free education and provide scholarships for the needy children and youth.

—Ensure and support an extensive political, civic and cultural education among the people and the youth. Help every citizen realize his duties to himself, to society and to the people. Instil actively the ideas of public interests and love for service to the community and of making himself useful to the people. This political, civic and cultural education should be carried out at all levels, in the ministries, public services and administrations, factories, shops, co-operatives, in the capital, provinces, districts, villages and families. Develop the ideas of morality, honour, national dignity, patriotism, mutual aid, usefulness of collective labour, the sense and nobleness of rendering sacrifices for the people's cause, the spirit of working conscientiously and practising economy, and the respect for public property.

PART THREE

Foreign Policy

The foreign policy of the N.U.F.K. is one of national independence, peace, neutrality, non-alignment, solidarity and friendship with all peace-loving and justice-loving peoples and governments. The N.U.F.K. maintains relations of friendship and co-operation with all countries according to the Five Principles of Peaceful Co-existence and the spirit of the Charter of the United Nations irrespective of their political system and ideology. It will not participate in any military alliance, nor does it allow any foreign country to set up military bases or station troops and military personnel on the territory of Cambodia for the purpose of aggression against other countries. The N.U.F.K. does not accept the protection of any country or of any military alliance. In the common struggle against American imperialism, the N.U.F.K. pursues a policy of friendship, militant solidarity and co-operation with Laos and Viet Nam according to the principle that the liberation and the defence of each country are the affair of her own people and that the three peoples pledge to do their best to support one another according to the desire of the interested country on the basis of mutual respect. In addition, Cambodia is ready to make concerted efforts with Laos and Viet Nam to make Indo-China genuinely a zone of independence, peace and progress, where each nation preserves its integral sovereignty with the sympathy and support of the peoples and governments of the socialist countries, non-aligned countries and peace-loving and justice-loving countries in the world, including the American people.

The N.U.F.K. expresses full support for the struggle of the peoples of the world for peace, independence, democracy and social progress, against the aggressive and warlike American imperialists, against old and new colonialism in all its forms; it expresses full support for the struggle of the peoples of Asia, Africa and Latin America for independence and freedom, the struggle of the Chinese people for the recovery of Taiwan, an integral part of the People's Republic of China, the struggle of the Korean people against the American imperialist aggressors and for the liberation of the southern part of their country and the reunification of Korea, the struggle of the Arab people, the Palestinian people in particular, for their fundamental national rights against the Israeli aggressors in the pay of the American imperialists, the struggle of the American people against the war of aggression, against racial discrimination and for peace and their genuine interests, etc. . . . .

The Khmer people, under the leadership of the N.U.F.K., are prepared to make all sacrifices to win final victory over the American imperialists and their lackey, the Lon Nol–Sirik Matak clique, for the present struggle is decisive to the freedom and dignity of our future generations and is essential to the independence, freedom and progress of the peoples of Indo-China and the rest of the world.

In this spirit, the N.U.F.K. pays warm tribute to the political organizations, the various religious and cultural organizations, patriots and progressives who have approved or will approve the five-point declaration of Samdech, Head of State, dated March 23, 1970, and who have joined or will join the organizations of the N.U.F.K. or remain outside these organizations to fight against the aggression of the American imperialists and their local flunkeys.

For its part the N.U.F.K. strengthens and unfolds political activities with a view to raising the patriotic level and the determination of the Khmer people in the current struggle for national salvation. Our whole people will certainly rise like one man to march gloriously toward final victory over the American aggressors and the Lon Nol–Sirik Matak clique in their pay.

The N.U.F.K. will certainly prove itself worthy of the confidence and sympathy of all the Khmer patriots and their foreign friends in the world.

Long live the N.U.F.K.!

Long live independent, peaceful, neutral, democratic and prosperous Cambodia!

Adopted unanimously by the congress held in Peking on Sunday, May 3, 1970.

Members of the Bureau   *Chairman of the Session*
   Thiounn Mumm   Penn Nouth
   Chan Youran
   Hak Seang Layny

C. Mao Tse-tung's Statement on the Cambodian Invasion

A new upsurge in the struggle against U.S. imperialism is now emerging throughout the world. Ever since World War II, U.S. imperialism and its followers have been continuously launching wars of aggression and the people in various countries have been continuously waging revolutionary wars to defeat the aggressors. The danger of a new world war still exists, and the people of all countries must get prepared. But revolution is the main trend in the world today.*

Unable to win in Viet Nam and Laos, the U.S. aggressors treacherously engineered the reactionary coup d'etat by the Lon Nol–Sirik Matak clique, brazenly dispatched their troops to invade Cambodia and resumed the bombing of north Viet Nam, and this has aroused the furious resistance of the three Indo-Chinese peoples. I warmly support the fighting spirit of Samdech Norodom Sihanouk, Head of State of Cambodia, in opposing U.S. imperialism and its lackeys. I warmly support the Joint Declaration of the Summit Conference of the Indo-Chinese Peoples. I warmly support the establishment of the Royal Government of National Union Under the Leadership of the National United Front of Kampuchea. Strengthening their unity, supporting each other and persevering in a protracted people's war, the three Indo-Chinese peoples will certainly overcome all difficulties and win complete victory.

While massacring the people in other countries, U.S. imperialism is slaughtering the white and black people in its own country. Nixon's fascist atrocities have kindled the raging flames of the revolutionary mass movement in the United States. The Chinese people firmly support the revolutionary struggle of the American people. I am convinced that the American people who are fighting valiantly will

---

* Editor's note: One of China's 1970 New Year's slogans was "Be Prepared against War" which was intended to convey to the Russian leadership and the Chinese populace that China was not overawed by Russia's nuclear weaponry. Here, Mao intimates that China's resolve has not weakened, but that her attention has shifted to what Mao believes is a favorable tide in Indochina and elsewhere.

ultimately win victory and that the fascist rule in the United States will inevitably be defeated.

The Nixon government is beset with troubles internally and externally, with utter chaos at home and extreme isolation abroad. The mass movement of protest against U.S. aggression in Cambodia has swept the globe. Less than ten days after its establishment, the Royal Government of National Union of Cambodia was recognized by nearly 20 countries. The situation is getting better and better in the war of resistance against U.S. aggression and for national salvation waged by the people of Viet Nam, Laos and Cambodia. The revolutionary armed struggles of the people of the Southeast Asian countries, the struggles of the people of Korea, Japan and other Asian countries against the revival of Japanese militarism by the U.S. and Japanese reactionaries, the struggles of the Palestinian and other Arab peoples against the U.S.-Israeli aggressors, the national-liberation struggles of the Asian, African and Latin American peoples and the revolutionary struggles of the peoples of North America, Europe and Oceania are all developing vigorously. The Chinese people firmly support the people of the three Indo-Chinese countries and of other countries of the world in their revolutionary struggles against U.S. imperialism and its lackeys.

U.S. imperialism, which looks like a huge monster, is in essence a paper tiger, now in the throes of its death-bed struggle. In the world of today, who actually fears whom? It is not the Vietnamese people, the Laotian people, the Cambodian people, the Palestinian people, the Arab people or the people of other countries who fear U.S. imperialism: it is U.S. imperialism which fears the people of the world. It becomes panic-stricken at the mere rustle of leaves in the wind. Innumerable facts prove that a just cause enjoys abundant support while an unjust cause finds little support. A weak nation can defeat a strong, a small nation can defeat a big. The people of a small country can certainly defeat aggression by a big country, if only they dare to rise in struggle, dare to take up arms and grasp in their own hands the destiny of their country. This is a law of history.

People of the world, unite and defeat the U.S. aggressors and all their running dogs!

APPENDIX II

Compiled by Douglas Sparks

Abbreviations

ARVN—Army of the Republic of Vietnam

COSVN—Central Office for South Vietnam

DRV—Democratic Republic of Vietnam (North Vietnam)

FUNK—Federation Unités Nationale Kampuchea

KKK—Khmer Kampuchea Krom

NLF—National Liberation Front, more precisely the National Front for the Liberation of South Vietnam (often referred to as the Vietcong)

NUFK—National United Front of Kampuchea (same as FUNK)

NVA—North Vietnamese Army

PRG—Provisional Revolutionary Government of South Vietnam

SEATO—South East Asia Treaty Organization

VPA—Vietnam People's Army (same as NVA)

Douglas Sparks is a graduate student in Asian Studies at the University of California, Berkeley.

Chronology

1863   A French protectorate is established over Cambodia.
        Siam takes control of Siem Reap and Battambang prov-
        inces, plus parts of Kompong Thom and Stung Treng prov-
        inces.

1864   Norodom assumes the Cambodian throne.

1867   Siam renounces claims of suzerainty over Cambodia; in
        return, France, acting on Cambodia's behalf, abandons
        Cambodian claims to Battambang and Siem Reap prov-
        inces. King Norodom protests this action.

1884   King Norodom refuses to participate in a customs union
        with Cochinchina and Annam. As a result, French troops
        and gunboats are sent to Phnom Penh, and King Noro-
        dom is forced to sign a convention making Cambodia a
        de facto colony of France.

1902   Siam signs first of three agreements returning annexed
        provinces to Cambodia (others signed 1904, 1907).

1904   King Norodom dies. French pass over his sons in favor
        of his brother, Sisowath.

1927   King Sisowath dies and is succeeded by his son, Monivong.
1940   French Vichy government agrees to Japanese occupation
        of Indochina.

1941   King Monivong dies. French pass over his son, Monireth,
        and choose as next king Norodom Sihanouk, whom they
        feel to be weaker and more accommodating.

        Thailand (Siam) again annexes Battambang and Siem
        Reap provinces, with Japanese assistance.

1945   Japanese evict French authorities and declare Indochina
        independent.

        Japan surrenders. Son Ngoc Thanh leads a coup, arrests
        all pro-French ministers, and declares himself Premier.

His actions are approved in a national referendum, but Thanh is soon arrested. Supporters flee to Thailand and form dissident nationalist movement, the Khmer Issarak.

1946   Cambodia becomes "autonomous state within the French union." An anti-French party wins elections, but Sihanouk favors gradual achievement of negotiated independence. Indochina War begins with Viet Minh attacks on French military positions.

Thailand returns Battambang and Siem Reap provinces to Cambodia by terms of Washington Conference of 1946.

1949   French sign a treaty stating France will transfer *de jure* independence to Cambodia; treaty provides for Cambodian control over its own army and police except in time of war. But French stipulate a continuing state of war.

1950   U.S. establishes diplomatic relations with Cambodia. Nationalist activity increases. Viet Minh name a "liberation government" for Cambodia. Sihanouk takes a stronger nationalist stance in the face of increased Viet Minh activity in Cambodia.

1952   Anti-government activity from both Communists and non-Communists increases; Sihanouk takes emergency powers.

1953   Sihanouk's "royal crusade for independence" seeks aid from U.S. to pressure the French, but U.S. refuses. Continued French presence causes many non-Communist elements to join insurgents. Sihanouk enters voluntary exile and declares intent to lead "holy war for independence."

French finally agree to independence in effort to prevent two-front war in Indochina. Sihanouk begins efforts to oust Viet Minh forces. U.S. offers aid.

1954   Geneva Conference agreement provides for evacuation of Viet Minh from Cambodia. Cambodia designated a protected state under September 1954 SEATO treaty (ratified U.S. Senate February, 1955).

Sihanouk announces Cambodia will remain unaligned and will conduct a neutral foreign policy.

1955   Sihanouk abdicates throne, competes in national elections.

His party wins overwhelming victory. Bandung conference produces understanding between Sihanouk and China for peaceful coexistence and no foreign bases in Cambodia. Sihanouk renounces SEATO protection.

1956 Thailand and South Vietnam impose blockade of Cambodia in retaliation for Sihanouk signature of aid agreement with China. U.S. suspends aid. Subsequent negotiations result in lifting of the blockade.

1958 South Vietnamese army units invade Cambodian border areas. Cambodia appeals to U.S. to restrain Saigon but U.S. refuses. Cambodia proposes diplomatic relations with China. U.S. considers cutting off aid as anti-Sihanouk move. Khmer Serei (Free Cambodia) movement organized, principally by Son Ngoc Thanh and Sam Sary, reportedly with CIA, Thai, and Vietnamese aid. Thailand begins anti-Cambodian campaign; Cambodia suspends diplomatic relations with Thailand.

1959 Bangkok Plot exposed. Plot called for anti-Sihanouk invasion from Thailand by foreign-supported Khmer Serei forces and creation of new opposition political party. U.S., Thailand, and South Vietnam implicated in plot. Eisenhower denies U.S. involvement; Thailand and South Vietnam cease provocative actions. Diplomatic relations with Thailand restored.

1960 National referendum gives near unanimous support to Sihanouk policies. (Anti-Communist opposition elements compromised by implication in Bangkok Plot.) Sihanouk made Chief of State for life.

Sihanouk calls for international conference on Laos.

1961 At Geneva Conference on Laos, Sihanouk proposes that neutralization of Laos be extended to Cambodia. Saigon persecution of Cambodian minority in Vietnam results in stream of refugees fleeing to Cambodia. Thais accuse Cambodia of giving sanctuary to Communist elements which seek to subvert the rest of Southeast Asia; Cambodia breaks diplomatic relations with Thailand.

1962 Sihanouk calls for new conference in Geneva, this time

to extend "international protection" to Cambodia; U.S. noncommittal. Sihanouk offers to accept international control in return for recognition of existing borders. South Vietnamese oppose this, carry out continued border violations.

1963   Cambodia protests continued Saigon repression of Vietnamese Buddhists and discrimination against Cambodian minority in Vietnam; diplomatic relations broken. Anti-Sihanouk activity by Khmer Serei resumes at new intensity; includes virulent propaganda from CIA-furnished transmitters in Thailand and South Vietnam. Sihanouk cancels U.S. aid agreements; Pentagon reacts by calling for intervention in Cambodia.

1964   Continuing border violations from South Vietnam (including at least one attack in mid-March by South Vietnamese unit with American advisers). USSR and France ask U.S. support for declaration of Cambodian neutrality. U.S. refuses unless Cambodia first resolves its differences with its neighbors.

April

Cambodia recalls its diplomatic mission from Washington. U.S. delegate in U.N. denies Cambodian charges about continuing U.S. involvement in border violations and states that U.S. is convinced "Vietnam has no aggressive designs toward Cambodia."

Sept.-Oct.

North Vietnam infiltrates first large force of regular troops through Cambodia, into Mekong Delta. U.S. requests negotiations with Cambodia.

Dec.

U.S. and Cambodia open talks in Cambodia; disagree over question of border determinations. Cambodia wants recognition of boundaries before international conference takes place. Talks broken off.

1965

April

Rusk indicates U.S. would participate in international conference on Cambodian neutrality.

May–Oct.

Cambodia severs diplomatic relations with U.S. Border

violations continue; U.S. planes attack two Cambodian border villages in May and napalm a third in October.

Nov.

Sihanouk's conditions for renewed U.S. relations: recognition of Cambodian territorial integrity; cessation of military incursions; indemnity for losses caused to life and property.

1966

Jan.

U.S. 14-point peace plan for Southeast Asia includes possibility of neutralization. Armed border violations continue. Rusk announces continued support for Cambodian neutrality, adds that Hanoi and Viet Cong have abused it. U.N. mediation of Thai-Cambodian border conflict fails; border attacks continue.

1967   U.S. hires members of Khmer Serei for covert missions in Cambodia (revealed at 1968 trial of Green Beret captain). U.S. informs Cambodia about Communist use of its territory.

April–May

Sihanouk sends army against Communist rebels and continues his military action to counter Khmer Serei attacks still being mounted from South Vietnam and Thailand. Sihanouk given full powers by national assembly. Lon Nol dropped as Premier after leftist pressures (and auto accident). Sihanouk refuses U.S. request for talks on use of Cambodia by North Vietnamese troops.

June

Cambodia establishes diplomatic relations with North Vietnam; offers to renew relations with Thailand if borders recognized.

July–Aug.

U.S.-sponsored Khmer Serei attacks continue into Cambodia and penetrate up to 12 miles.

Sept.-Oct.

Sihanouk accuses China of imperialism and internal interference in Cambodia and threatens to seek aid from the U.S. Sihanouk accuses Hou Youn, Hu Nim, and Khieu Samphan of being "leading Communist conspirators"; they are forced to flee Phnom Penh. Chau Sen and So Nem are labeled "lesser Communist conspirators."

Nov.

Reconciliation between Cambodia and Peking.

Nov.–Dec.

U.S. continues refusal to recognize existing borders; it considers this a matter for negotiations between Cambodia and its neighbors. U.S. upholds border incursions by U.S. army "in hot pursuit."

1968

Jan.

Bowles's mission to Cambodia; inconclusive in matter of reestablishing diplomatic relations. USSR condemns violation of Cambodian territorial integrity but opposes strengthening of International Control Commission. Sihanouk accuses Communist elements of fomenting civil war in northwestern Cambodia.

March–July

Sihanouk charges Communists support rebel activity in northeastern Cambodia. Sihanouk complains to U.S. of continuing U.S. and South Vietnamese border incursions in south.

Sept.

U.S. charges use of Cambodia for bases by Viet Cong and North Vietnamese forces in northeast Cambodia and Svay Rieng province has tripled.

Nov.–Dec.

Cambodia charges that U.S. air attacks killed 300 Cambodians in border villages; four captured American flyers released.

1969

April

Cambodia offers to reestablish diplomatic relations with U.S. in exchange for recognition of her territorial integrity. U.S. states that it "recognizes and respects sovereignty, independence, neutrality and territorial integrity" of Cambodia. U.S. planes bomb border regions.

May

Two U.S. helicopters downed in Cambodia. NLF mission in Cambodia raised to Embassy status.

Aug.

American Embassy reopened in Phnom Penh. Sihanouk

says new cabinet formed under General Lon Nol will re-examine issue of U.S. aid.

Oct.

Sihanouk alleges 40,000 Communist troops in Cambodia.

Oct.–Dec.

Sihanouk protests U.S. bombing of border provinces.

1970
Jan.

U.S. pays compensation for Cambodian losses resulting from continuing border clashes.

Mar. 11–13

While Sihanouk is in Europe, Premier Lon Nol and Cambodian army sanctions the sacking of North Vietnamese and NLF embassies by Cambodian youths in Phnom Penh; action termed a protest against Communist infiltration. Lon Nol's government orders Viet Cong and North Vietnamese troops out of Cambodia. Cambodian military reportedly backs continuing demonstrations against NLF and North Vietnamese.

March 18

Sihanouk ousted in coup led by Lon Nol and Sirik Matak. New regime begins campaign to destroy Sihanouk's prestige. Sihanouk plans government in exile. (U.S. says recognition of Cambodia unaffected by overthrow of Sihanouk.)

March 20–26

Cambodian army moves against pro-Sihanouk demonstrations. New leaders reaffirm Cambodian neutrality, but pledge to root out Communist troops in border sanctuaries. U.S. planes attack inside Cambodia. North Vietnam and NLF recall diplomats from Phnom Penh.

March 27

South Vietnamese troops launch first major attack against Cambodian sanctuaries, with U.S. helicopter support.

March 28

White House announces American troops may cross border in response to "enemy threats."

March 29–30

Pro-Sihanouk demonstrations in eastern provinces; North Vietnamese and Viet Cong troops move against government forces. Vietnamese residents in Cambodia flee to

South Vietnam as result of widespread persecution in eastern provinces.

March 30

Cambodia appeals for U.N. observers, asks for return of ICC.

April 1

Cambodia says it would accept U.S. military aid but not ground troops. France calls for general conference on Indochina.

April 4

The New York Times reports that authoritative Nixon administration sources say Viet Cong headquarters (COSVN) was moved in late March from Cambodia to South Vietnam.

April 9

Cambodian troops withdraw from Parrot's Beak area on border, abandoning it to virtual Viet Cong control. Continuing reports of Vietnamese civilians in Cambodia being massacred.

April 15

All diplomatic missions in Phnom Penh receive official request for arms and equipment to be used against Communist forces.

April 21

Reports say that Vietnamese Communists are in complete control of three Cambodian provinces (with partial control of three others) and are within 15 to 20 miles of Phnom Penh. News correspondents fail to find any evidence of troop movements in vicinity of Phnom Penh.

April 22

U.S. agrees to send captured arms from Vietnam to Cambodia. U.S. calls situation in Cambodia a "foreign invasion of a neutral country." South Vietnam sends delegation to Phnom Penh to discuss repatriation of Vietnamese civilians.

April 27

U.S. Senate Foreign Relations Committee states opposition to extension of military aid to Cambodia.

Chronology by Weeks

April 30–May 3

Nixon addresses American people; authorizes joint U.S.–South Vietnamese invasion into Cambodia. Conventional strike forces enter Cambodia accompanied by artillery, armor, and air cover. Resistance is light.

On May 2, U.S. resumes massive air strikes against North Vietnam. Agnew and Rogers term the attacks "re-inforced protective reaction," deny escalation of war.

U.S. troops discover first of North Vietnamese weapons and food caches.

Lon Nol "ponders" launching protest against U.S. invasion; also expresses approval. Sihanouk meets with Mao in Peking. Britain calls for talks on Indochina.

May 4–May 10

Pentagon terminates air raids over North Vietnam, but is prepared to resume them if U.S. reconnaissance planes are fired upon.

5,000 more U.S. troops enter northeastern Cambodia west of Pleiku. 1,500 more sent to Fishhook area on May 4. New front opened on May 5 with 6,000 new troops and B-52 strikes. U.S. troop strength in Cambodia raised to 25,000 on May 7. Nixon announces all U.S. troops will be out of Cambodia by June 30; U.S. field commanders express concern with statement. Possibility of air support for ARVN after June 30 not ruled out.

North Vietnamese drive to within 30 miles of Phnom Penh.

First real resistance encountered at rubber plantation town of Snoul, which is taken and destroyed by U.S. armored squadron. Plantation workers reported joining Khmer Rouge. Rubber plantation area of Mimot also destroyed. U.S. mistakenly announces capture of COSVN. In Vietnam, NLF–NVA attacks increase; U.S. casualty rate highest in 20 weeks.

Thieu regime closes all universities and schools in wake of massive demonstrations.

From Peking, Sihanouk announces formation of new exile government and Indochinese liberation front. Receives quick recognition from China, NLF, North Vietnamese. U Thant calls for new Geneva talks.

Thieu announces ARVN has "no time limit for withdrawal," reveals "agreement in principle" for ARVN operations with Lon Nol. South Vietnamese–Cambodian diplomatic relations restored (severed in 1963).

On May 10, 140-ship "flotilla" (110 South Vietnamese and 30 U.S. ships) begins Mekong River invasion of Cambodia. South Vietnamese forces accompanied by U.S. advisers. Capture ferry crossing at Neak Luong under fire.

May 11–May 17

U.S.–ARVN forces launch two new operations, in northeastern and southern Cambodia. South Vietnamese navy joins U.S. in blockade of Cambodian coast. U.S. announces build-up of carrier strike force in Gulf of Tonkin for first time since 1968 cessation of bombing of North Vietnam. White House officials announce ARVN will not pull out with U.S. troops. Pentagon reports highest U.S. death rate in Indochina in 8 months.

Pathet Lao and NVA step up attacks around Saravane and Pak Song (Laos) in rice-rich areas bordering Ho Chi Minh Trail. In Djakarta, South Vietnamese Foreign Minister Tran Van Lam announces that ARVN and U.S. advisers have been regularly operating in Laos. U.S. Secretary of Defense Laird confirms this, calls operations "protective reaction" raids.

9,000 refugees are moved by South Vietnamese ships from "assembly centers" in Phnom Penh as part of massive

relocation of Vietnamese living in Cambodia threatened
with massacre by Cambodian army. U.S. officials in Vietnam report that 47,000 refugees have already been pro-
cessed by South Vietnamese government.

Cambodian officials establish first liaison with U.S. military in Saigon. Lon Nol government also renews diplomatic ties with Thailand (broken in 1961). Sihanouk announces that three cabinet members of his exile government (Hu Nim, Hou Youn, Khieu Samphan, former
Khmer Rouge leaders) are in Cambodia organizing guerrilla forces.

Hanoi delegate to Paris talks leaves in protest of U.S.
action. USSR sends official to Peking in attempt to heal
Sino-Soviet split and unify Indochina policy, but later
in the week USSR harshly criticizes China (and Mao
by name).

May 18–May 24

U.S. Command again mistakenly announces capture of
COSVN. U.S.–ARVN forces launch thirteenth and four-
teenth operations in Cambodia. *AP* reports slowdown of
U.S. drive into Cambodia and "strengthening of resistance."
Monsoon rains hamper U.S.–ARVN forces. NLF, NVA,
and Khmer Rouge continue operations in area between
Phnom Penh and coast, cutting off main route from
capital to the sea.

Lon Nol reassures 600,000 Chinese living in Cambodia—
some of whom had been openly pro-Peking under Siha-
nouk—that they need not fear for their safety. South
Korea establishes relations with Lon Nol regime. Thai
Gen. Praphas Charusathien agrees to send U.S. weapons
and Thai advisers to Cambodian army. Ky calls for "anti-
Communist front line of Vietnam, Laos, Cambodia, and
Thailand."

Thieu regime decides to abandon "humanitarian evacuation" of some 70,000 ethnic Vietnamese still detained in
"assembly camps" by Cambodian government. Instead, Saigon plans to relocate these refugees in areas "stabilized" by
ARVN troops within Cambodia.

China calls off Warsaw talks with U.S. in protest to U.S. action in Cambodia. Mao Tse-tung makes rare public announcement from Peking calling for world revolution against "U.S. imperialism." On May 21, Sihanouk joins Mao at massive rally in Peking. Sihanouk later attacks USSR for delaying recognition of his Peking-based exile government.

May 25–May 31

Cambodian forces destroy and take town of Tonle Bet in northern front of war. U.S. jets hit North Vietnamese antiaircraft positions 100 miles north of DMZ in "protective reaction" raids. National United Front of Cambodia announces that northern provinces of Stung Treng, Mondolkiri, and Kratie are in rebel hands. Heavy resistance reported in Fishhook area, Prey Veng, and Kompong Cham. Route 6 between Phnom Penh and Angkor cut as rebel forces appear to be setting up Mekong River supply route to replace Ho Chi Minh Trail. *Le Monde* (Paris) reports Communists in control of 160 kilometers of Mekong from Lao border to Kompong Cham. In Laos, Royal Laotian Army retakes Phou Luang Noi near NVA-held city of Attopeu, and later claims to have cut Ho Chi Minh Trail near Saravane. U.S. Command mistakenly claims to have captured COSVN.

In Vietnam, NLF captures highland city of Dalat and hits 13 other posts in what *The New York Times* calls "the most serious attack since the Tet offensive." Next day, NLF sneaks through encircling ARVN force and escapes.

Soviet Ambassador to Cambodia makes ambiguous statement condemning U.S. invasion and accusing South Vietnam of trying to annex Cambodian territory. Sihanouk goes to Hanoi to woo Soviet support (USSR still recognizes Lon Nol regime) in attempt to prove neutrality in Sino-Soviet split. Hanoi announces new and larger Sino-Vietnamese aid agreement (last year's aid amounted to $200 million, roughly half of amount given by USSR).

Thailand declares alert along Cambodian border, agrees to send military and medical aid to Cambodia. *Agence France*

Presse reports Thai troops have participated in operations on Cambodian territory near Parrot's Beak area. Saigon and Phnom Penh regimes sign open-ended agreements to allow ARVN to remain in Cambodia; agreement also redraws border, giving two contested islands to South Vietnam. U.S. Special Forces reported to be recruiting ethnic Cambodians in South Vietnam for combat with ex-CIA Khmer Serei leader, under U.S. command. Lon Nol regime announces that ex-CIA Khmer Serei leader Son Ngoc Thanh will be appointed "counselor" to the government.

June 1–June 7

U.S. launches one of biggest attacks of Cambodian War from Vietnam into "free fire-zone" near Krasang. New rebel resistance reported at Kompong Thom, Setbo, and Siem Reap, where Communists cut only road to Thailand. Lomphat, capital of Rattanakiri province, falls to rebels. *The New York Times* reports that Communists now hold over half of Cambodia, mainly in the north and west. UPI reports Pathet Lao forces have joined NVA near Cambodia–Laos border in operations to keep Mekong supply routes open.

In Vietnam, NLF–NVA attacks continue. Thais announce they will send 1,200 ethnic Cambodian "volunteers" to defend Phnom Penh, also announce full border alert. Thais later change decision on troops, now say they will only "provide facilities" for "volunteers."

Former Green Beret Robert Marasco says in an NBC interview that U.S. was involved in intelligence operations in Cambodia more than a year before the invasion.

Sihanouk charges from Peking that Thais and South Vietnamese are trying to "steal" parts of Cambodia. Joint USSR–French statement decries "the foreign intervention that is prolonging the conflict in Indochina." USSR bitterly warns the Indochinese Communists that they court "defeat and destruction" if they permit their actions to be dictated by China.

Schools reopen in Saigon, but mass student strike against imprisonment of students, repression, torture, and the fail-

ing economy continue. Ky and South Vietnamese Minister
of State Phan Quang Dan arrive in Phnom Penh to discuss
military operations and "assembly camps," which Dan calls
"concentration camps." Ky assures Lon Nol that South
Vietnam seeks no territory from Cambodia. Thieu reported moving to curb Ky's newly developing rival power
in Cambodia, which *The New York Times* describes as
"something akin to a viceroy in eastern Cambodia."

June 8–June 14

Cambodian forces retake Siem Reap and Kompong Thom.
Fighting declines in Fishhook area but increases elsewhere.
Rebels reported to have taken Angkor Wat and to control
much of Kompong Som. Communist forces also attack
two key road-link towns: Kompong Speu on Sihanoukville
road, and Kompong Tralach on Thailand road. Pathet Lao
troops take provincial capital of Saravane, key city on
Communist infiltration route into southern Laos and
Cambodia.

AP reports Thai air forces will join South Vietnamese air
units in support of Cambodian troops. Thailand also
reported to have doubts about sending aid to Lon Nol
government and now hopes to avoid sending any troops
to Cambodia.

Evacuation of Vietnamese from Cambodia partially resumes; 75,000 Vietnamese still remain in "assembly camps"
outside of Phnom Penh.

Paris talks continue to be bogged down. Kosygin says
Russo-Chinese talks are stalled, but will continue. Brezh-
nev promises "all necessary help" to anti-American forces
in Indochina. North Vietnam and USSR conclude new
military and economic aid pact; wording indicates aid will
be used throughout Indochina. Ceylon announces intention
to recognize NLF Revolutionary Government.

U.S. casualties highest in 10 months. High Administration
officials reported in doubt U.S. can stop rebels in Cambodia; complain that White House has disregarded State
Department and CIA estimates of Communist response.
Thieu claims it will take "4 or 5 years to stabilize the

military situation." Says U.S. must continue to support
ARVN in Cambodia and to block Ho Chi Minh Trail in
Laos.

June 15–June 21

South Vietnamese and Cambodian forces retake Kompong
Speu amidst reports of looting by Vietnamese troops.
Communist forces cut and recut major highways and railroad lines throughout Cambodia. Fighting continues at
Kompong Thom, Kompong Cham, and Tonle Bet. Hanoi
radio accuses U.S. of firing on a number of North Vietnamese villages during past week; Pentagon officials deny
knowledge of any shelling. Royal Laotian troops blocked
on way to Saravane; last two Lao government bases in
area fall.

4,000 new South Vietnamese troops enter Cambodia. *The
New York Times* reports disclosure from Saigon officials
that U.S. planes and helicopters have been supporting
"allied" operations well beyond 21.7 mile limit set by
Nixon for two months. U.S. Command still expects withdrawal of ARVN soon after June 30; Thieu regime still
speaks of Vietnamese "pacification" program in Cambodia.
Thailand considers transferring some of its 12,000 Black
Panther force in Vietnam, sends Premier to South Vietnam
for inspection of troops and talks with Saigon. Thieu also
hopes for troops from Taiwan and South Korea despite
possible Chinese counteraction.

The New York Times reports urgent meetings in Washington, Saigon, and Bangkok on how to save Lon Nol regime.
Also reports that some embassies are reviewing evacuation
plans. China informs U.S. it is not ready for resumption
of talks because of present situation.

June 22–June 30

Lon Nol government abandons entire northeastern quadrant
(four provinces) of Cambodia to rebel forces. $7.9 million
in U.S. arms rushed to Cambodia, the total promised for
the fiscal year. Pentagon acknowledges U.S. planes are
striking as deep as 100 miles inside Cambodia, but only

in raids against enemy troop and supply lines; claims "no information" about eyewitness reports of direct support of Cambodian troops at Kompong Thom. Lon Nol issues "general mobilization" decree requiring everyone 18–60 to serve in military or perform some "service of national interest"; also makes all property and finances subject to government requisition.

The New York Times reports 90 percent of defoliants in Vietnam consists of 2,4,5–T, which is linked to fetal damage in animals and hazardous to women of child-bearing age. Previous reports had placed use of 2,4,5–T at 50 percent.

Reports from *The New York Times* correspondents indicate that events in Cambodia have not only brought Indochinese closer together, but also closer to China. Vietnam peace talks in Paris remain blocked, with both sides trading charges.

Lon Nol expresses hope that departing U.S. troops will return if military situation takes a drastic turn for the worse. Last U.S. troops leave Cambodia; question of U.S. air combat support for Cambodian and ARVN troops left vague. Military sources report at least 39,000 ARVN troops will remain in Cambodia indefinitely.

U.S. claims to have withdrawn all forces. South Vietnamese remain. Thais mobilize. North Vietnamese remain. NLF remains. National United Front of Cambodia remains. ". . . a brief surgical operation lasting no more than six to eight weeks." (White House aide, May 1, 1970).

Groups and Organizations

Khmer Issarak

Formed at the end of World War II, the Khmer Issarak (Free Khmer) was a loosely structured nationalist movement, composed of several different factions each with its own leader. The Issarak group's activity was directed against the French and the Cambodian governments, with some factions cooperating with the Viet Minh. Following independence in 1954, the Issarak movement faded.

Khmer Kampuchea Krom

Literally meaning ethnic Khmers from the Mekong Delta area of South Vietnam, the term Khmer Kampuchea Krom also refers to a mercenary force composed of these ethnic Khmers which has fought with U.S.–South Vietnamese troops in South Vietnam. Over 4,000 of the KKK have been transported to Cambodia to aid the Lon Nol government.

Khmer Loeu

Minority groups ethnically, culturally, and linguistically distinct from the Cambodians, the Khmer Loeu are groups of mountain tribesmen located mainly in the remote northeastern part of Cambodia. In the past few years, some of the Khmer Loeu have staged revolts against the Cambolian government, with some assistance from NLF cadres.

Khmer Rouge

The Khmer Rouge (Red Khmers) are the indigenous armed Communist opposition in Cambodia. Founded during the Indochina War against the French, they were deactivated after independence and remained largely quiescent until recent years, when they have renewed activity against the Cambodian government. They have remained active to the present and are now part of the National United Front of Kampuchea headed by Sihanouk.

Khmer Serei

A resistance movement against Sihanouk organized by Son Ngoc Thanh and Sam Sary, the Khmer Serei contains many former elements of the Khmer Issarak. The Khmer Serei has operated from Thailand and South Vietnam with reported CIA support; some members were also recruited to work with U.S. Special Forces in clandestine operations within Cambodia. There are some reports that elements of the Khmer Serei returned to Cambodia and entered the Cambodian army during the last year.

National Liberation Front

An organization of diverse political composition founded in December 1960 to oppose the Diem regime and the American presence in Vietnam. Much of the high-ranking leadership is affiliated with the Marxist-Leninist People's Revolutionary Party. However, the Front also has prominent representation from practically all religious, ethnic, and political sectors of South Vietnam. In 1968, it became a constituent part of the Provisional Revolutionary Government of South Vietnam.

Pathet Lao

The Pathet Lao are the indigenous armed Communist resistance in Laos. Headed by Prince Souphanouvong, the Pathet Lao were formed in 1950; they have participated in coalition governments, but have acted as a guerrilla force since the breakup of the government formed by the Geneva Accords of 1962. Since 1955 the formal name of their organization has been the Lao Patriotic Front (Neo Lao Hak Sat).

Biographical Sketches

Chang Heng

Now Chief of State in the Lon Nol government, Chang Heng was first elected to the Cambodian National Assembly in 1958, and was appointed Chairman of the Assembly in 1968. He is reputed to have amassed a personal fortune when he served as a director of a government import-export monopoly called SONEXIM. He has long been identified with a faction that was critical of Sihanouk's policies of nationalized rather than free enterprises.

Chau Seng

Chau Seng, an ethnic Vietnamese with pro-China leanings, is Sihanouk's Minister Charged with Special Missions in the exile government, and is presently Sihanouk's representative in Paris. He has been active in Cambodian politics since his election to the National Assembly in 1958; he has served at various times as a cabinet minister in the Departments of Education, Agriculture, and Information, and also was Sihanouk's Director of the Cabinet. He aroused Sihanouk's ire, though, when the newspaper *La Depeche,* of which Seng was a director, became involved in the dispute between Sihanouk and Peking in 1967. This led to Chau Seng's purge, after Sihanouk had labeled him a "lesser Communist conspirator." He resided in Paris at the time of the coup.

Ho Chi Minh

Ho Chi Minh was the founder of the Vietnamese revolutionary movement and is referred to by the Vietnamese as "Uncle Ho." He was President of North Vietnam from independence until his death on September 3, 1969.

Hou Youn

Hou Youn, often referred to as a "giant intellect," is at present the Minister of Interior, Communal Reforms, and Cooperatives in Sihanouk's exile government. He first gained wide attention in 1962 when he vociferously criticized the government's foreign policy, which he said was leading Cambodia into SEATO. His criticism later that year of Sihanouk and others' financial planning—receiving loans from the West—helped bring about the fall of that government. Youn was forced to flee Phnom Penh in 1967 after Sihanouk labeled him—as well as Hu Nim and Khieu Samphan—a "leading Communist conspirator." He then became a leader of the independent (from North Vietnam) Khmer Rouge in the western part of Cambodia. Hou Youn holds a Ph.D. in economics, Paris.

Hu Nim

Hu Nim, who holds the portfolio for Information and Propaganda in Sihanouk's government in exile, has served in previous cabinets. He was a member of the leftist group in the National Assembly until 1967 when he, along with Hou Youn and Khieu Samphan, was forced to flee Phnom Penh after being labeled a "leading Communist conspirator" by Sihanouk. Hu Nim has a doctorate in law, Phnom Penh.

Khieu Samphan

Formerly a member of the leftist opposition in the National Assembly, Khieu Samphan was forced to flee Phnom Penh in 1967 when he was charged—with Hou Youn and Hu Nim —with being a "leading Communist conspirator." He is now serving as Minister of National Defense in Sihanouk's exile government. He holds a Ph.D. in economics, Paris.

Queen Kossomak

Queen Kossomak is Sihanouk's mother and a member of the Sisowath branch of Cambodia's royal families. Following Sihanouk's abdication in 1955 and the death of his father in 1960, she has remained the official symbol of the Cambodian throne.

Lon Nol

One of the principal leaders of the coup which overthrew Prince Sihanouk on March 18, 1970, and the present Premier of Cambodia, Lon Nol's official career dates back to 1934. After serving in the administrative service he joined the army in 1952. At the time of the formation of the National

Assembly in 1955, he was the leader of the Khmer Renovation faction, of which Sirik Matak was also a member. Long associated with American military officials, Lon Nol has served, at various times since 1960, as Deputy Premier, Premier, and Defense Minister. During his first period as Premier (the second began in late 1969), he was rumored in late 1966 to be planning a right-wing coup against Sihanouk, but a severe auto accident forced him to resign.

Nguyen Cao Ky

Former Air Vice-Marshal, Nguyen Cao Ky is presently Vice-President of South Vietnam, a position he has held since the elections of September 1966. He was one of the principal leaders of the military junta, which included General Nguyen Van Thieu, that assumed power in June 1965. Ky held the office of Premier from that time until the elections in 1966.

Nguyen Huu Tho

Ngyen Huu Tho, chairman of the NLF Central Committee since its formation, has been active in Vietnamese politics and the revolutionary movement since 1949. He served as provisional chairman of the National Liberation Front before his election to the post of chairman of the Central Committee when that office was organized in 1960.

Nguyen Van Thieu

President of South Vietnam since 1966, General Nguyen Van Thieu is a Catholic from the North who has long been aligned with American military commanders. One of the principal members of the military junta which took power in June 1965, Thieu was Chief of State until he became President.

Prince Norodom Sihanouk

Prince Norodom Sihanouk, who is a member of both branches of the Cambodian royal families, the Norodom and the Sisowath, became king in 1941, and has symbolized Cambodia from the end of World War II until his overthrow on March 18, 1970. "Sihanouk," he has said, "is Cambodia. Cambodia is Sihanouk." His voluntary exile in 1953 helped force France to grant Cambodian independence and made him a hero in the eyes of the Cambodian people. In 1955, he abdicated in favor of his father in order to participate more directly in Cambodian politics; since 1960, he has held the title of Chief of State. An ardent nationalist, he has displayed amazing political agility and shrewdness in preserving Cambodia's integrity from its historical enemies, Vietnam and Thailand, and in preventing Cambodia from being drawn into the Vietnam War. His role in Cambodia's future remains to be seen; he is at present the head of a National United Front against the Lon Nol government.

Penn Nouth

Long one of Sihanouk's most trusted advisers, Penn Nouth is now serving in Sihanouk's exile government as Premier, a position he has held in various Cambodian governments over the last twenty years. A French-trained administrator, he first served in a colonial Cambodian government in 1940. He is best known for his role in the negotiations for independence from the French in the early 1950s.

Pham Hung

Pham Hung is the head of the Central Affairs Committee of COSVN, a post he has held since 1967. He is also a deputy premier of North Vietnam, as well as a member of both the Central Committee and the Secretariat of the North Vietnamese Communist Party.

Pham Van Dong

A member of the Vietnamese revolutionary movement for over thirty-five years, Pham Van Dong was one of Ho Chi Minh's closest friends and aides. He has served as Prime Minister of North Vietnam since independence; since Ho's death in September 1969, he has been the official head of North Vietnam.

Sam Sary

Sam Sary, one of the three delegates to the Geneva Conference on Indochina in 1954, was formerly a close and trusted adviser to Sihanouk. As a result of Sihanouk's patronage, he rose from the rank of police captain to secretary-general of the Sangkum (the party headed by Sihanouk), Minister of State, Deputy Premier, and ambassador to London. He is said to have fallen in Sihanouk's estimation when he became too openly involved in scandals. Implicated in a plot to overthrow Sihanouk in 1959, he fled to South Vietnam when news of his impending arrest reached him. He later joined Son Ngoc Thanh in Thailand where he helped organize the Khmer Serei.

Prince Sisowath Sirik Matak

Now Deputy Prime Minister in the Lon Nol government, Sirik Matak has long been active in Cambodian politics, having held the posts of Defense Minister and Foreign Minister in preindependence governments. After independence, he was identified with the Khmer Renovation faction when the National Assembly was founded in 1955; this group was led by Lon Nol and others like him who had begun successful official careers in the prewar colonial administration. Matak has also been Cambodia's ambassador to Peking and envoy to Tokyo. He is a member of the Sisowath branch of Cambodia's royal families.

Son Ngoc Thanh

Son Ngoc Thanh, of part-Cambodian, part-Vietnamese parentage, was an early Cambodian nationalist and founded the first Cambodian language newspaper (1937). In 1942, he fled to Bangkok and from there to Japan. Returning to Cambodia in 1945, he first served as Foreign Minister in the Japanese occupation government, then, on the eve of Japan's surrender, he staged a coup and declared himself Premier. He was quickly arrested by British and French troops and exiled. However, he returned in 1951, but soon fled to northern Cambodia where he tried to organize the several Issarak bands. Frustrated in this endeavor, he sought refuge in Thailand. Thanh was implicated in the abortive coup against Sihanouk in 1959 with Sam Sary, who later joined him in Thailand where they organized the Khmer Serei.

Vo Nguyen Giap

A top leader of the Viet Minh movement since its inception, Giap founded the North Vietnamese Army and commanded the victorious Viet Minh forces at Dienbienphu. He now holds the posts of Defense Minister of North Vietnam and Commander-in-Chief of the Vietnam People's Army.

Yem Sambaur

Yem Sambaur, Foreign Minister in the Lon Nol government until July 1970, has been a political figure in Cambodia for more than twenty years. Formerly a close adviser to Sihanouk—Sambaur was Premier of a preindependence government and headed a coalition party at Sihanouk's request for Cambodia's first independent elections—the two became estranged when they disagreed over constitutional reforms that Sihanouk proposed after victory in the first elections.

CAMBODIA

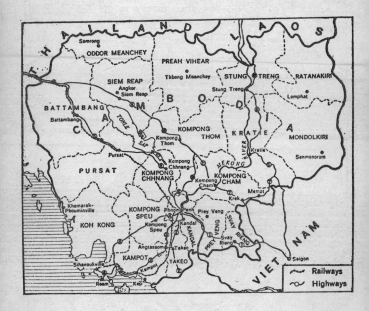

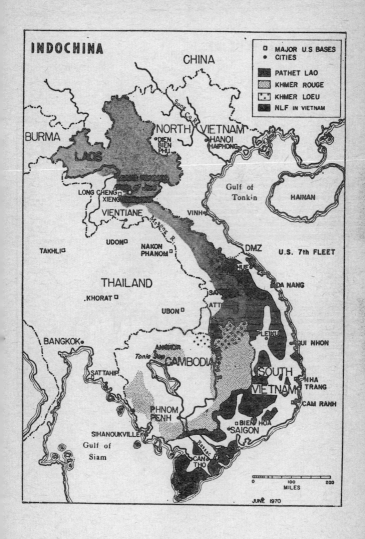

INDOCHINA

CHINA

☐ MAJOR U.S BASES
• CITIES
▨ PATHET LAO
▨ KHMER ROUGE
▨ KHMER LOEU
▨ NLF IN VIETNAM

BURMA

LAOS

NORTH VIETNAM
• DIEN BIEN PHU
• HANOI
HAIPHONG

Gulf of Tonkin

HAINAN

LONG CHENG ☐
XIENG
VIENTIANE

VINH

U.S. 7th FLEET

TAKHLI ☐

UDON ☐

NAKON PHANOM ☐

DMZ

HUE

THAILAND

DA NANG

KHORAT ☐

UBON ☐

ATTI

PLEIKU

QUI NHON

BANGKOK •

Tonle

CAMBODIA

SOUTH VIETNAM

NHA TRANG

SATTAHIP

PHNOM PENH

BIEN HOA ☐
SAIGON

CAM RANH

SIHANOUKVILLE

Gulf of Siam

CAN THO

0   100   200
MILES

JUNE 1970

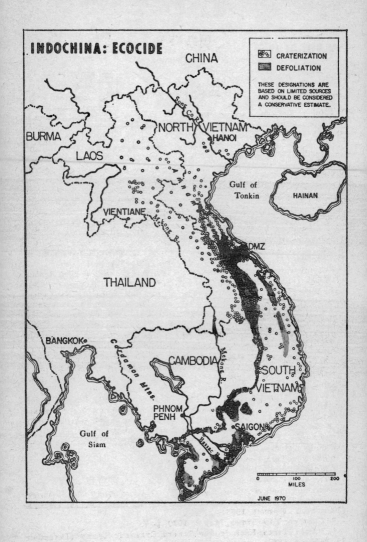

INDOCHINA: ECOCIDE

CRATERIZATION
DEFOLIATION

THESE DESIGNATIONS ARE BASED ON LIMITED SOURCES AND SHOULD BE CONSIDERED A CONSERVATIVE ESTIMATE.

CHINA

BURMA

NORTH VIETNAM

HANOI

LAOS

Song Coi R.

Gulf of Tonkin

HAINAN

VIENTIANE

Mekong R.

THAILAND

DMZ

BANGKOK

Cardamon Mtns.

CAMBODIA

Mekong R.

SOUTH VIETNAM

PHNOM PENH

SAIGON

Gulf of Siam

Bassac R.

0   100   200
MILES

JUNE 1970

NOTES

CHAPTER TWO

1 Robert Shaplen, a writer close to CIA sources, writes that "There is no evidence that the Americans participated in the [Cambodian] coup or that they were apprised of it until a few hours before it took place, although they were undoubtedly aware of what might happen and did nothing to try to prevent it" ("Letter from Indo-China," *New Yorker*, May 9, 1970, p. 139). This is disingenuous. Central in preparing for the March 18 coup were cadres of CIA-trained Khmer Serei guerrillas, who were infiltrated in from South Vietnam or Thailand at least ten days before the coup. They are said to have led the confrontations with the NLF on March 8 in the field (to which Shaplen alludes, p. 136), the assault on the embassies on March 11, and the subsequent slaughter of both Vietnamese and Cambodian civilians. Testimony in the Green Beret murder trial in December identified the Khmer Serei as "an organization which plans the political overthrow of the Cambodian Government in the future" (*The New York Times*, January 28, 1970, p. 9).

2 Cf. my warning against a similar escalation in *The New York Review of Books* ("Laos: The Story Nixon Won't Tell," April 9, 1970), p. 39: "The present period . . . offers disturbing parallels to the [Laotian] withdrawals of 1962 and 1964."

3 In private, the President went further. On April 28, the day of the Fishhook decision and two days before the public and Congress were informed, the President told a small group of visitors to the White House that the action he was soon to order against the Cambodian sanctuaries "was imperative if we were to escape the probability of total and humiliating defeat in Vietnam" (San Francisco *Examiner*, May 21, 1970, p. 1).

4 Shaplen, *op. cit.*, p. 146. Also see *The New York Times*, April 4, 1970; *Washington Post*, April 5, 1970, for similar reports.

5 Robert G. Kaiser, *Washington Post*, May 3, 1970, A18: "Pressed on this point, military analysts . . . could not point to any recent development of this kind." However, *The Wall Street Journal* of April 28, 1970, p. 1, said "Allied intelligence sources" had predicted a "surge of Red attacks in Viet Nam, as violent as those of the 1968 Tet offensive," especially "along the Cambodian border."

6 *The New York Times*, April 24, 1970, p. 3.

7 *Washington Post*, May 6, 1970, p. A1.

8 *The Christian Science Monitor*, May 14, 1970.

9 Chalmers Roberts, "The Day We Didn't Go to War," *The Reporter*, September 14, 1954, p. 35; reprinted in Marvin E. Gettleman, *Vietnam* (New York: Fawcett, 1965), p. 104.

10 *The New York Times*, May 2, 1970, p. 7.

11 Harold Munthe-Kaas, in *Far Eastern Economic Review* (December 25, 1969), p. 668.

12 *The New York Times*, April 24, 1970, p. 1.

13 Flora Lewis, *Newsday,* May 2, 1970.

14 *The New York Times,* April 4, 1970, p. 3.

15 *The New York Times,* April 27, 1970, p. 5.

16 *The New York Times,* April 21, 1970, p. 1.

17 Robert Shaplen, *op. cit.,* p. 132: "Some Americans have felt that a break in the Laotian situation now could produce some movement in the deadlocked peace talks in Paris, and perhaps bring to an end at least some of the fighting in Vietnam." For earlier phases of the recent diplomatic initiative over Laos, and their successive frustration by U.S.-backed escalations, see my article, *The New York Review of Books,* April 9, 1970, pp. 35ff.

18 Shaplen, *op. cit.,* p. 145.

19 Charles R. Smith, UPI correspondent in Hong Kong, Oakland *Tribune,* May 17, 1970.

20 San Jose *Mercury,* May 13, 1970.

21 For details on this and subsequent incidents, see Joseph Goulden, "Talks with China: The Military Saboteurs," *The Nation,* March 2, 1970, pp. 231–233.

22 *Ibid.,* p. 232.

23 *Ibid.,* p. 232.

24 Richard Nixon, "Cuba, Castro, and John F. Kennedy," *Reader's Digest* (November 1964), p. 291.

25 *The New York Times,* January 29, 1970, p. 12.

26 Samuel P. Huntington, "The Bases of Accommodation," *Foreign Affairs* (July 1968), p. 650; Noam Chomsky, "After Pinkville," *The New York Review of Books,* January 1, 1970, p. 4.

27 Townsend Hoopes, *The Limits of Intervention* (New York: David McKay, 1969), p. 214.

28 Richard Barnet, speech of May 20, 1970, to Business Executives Against the War, Washington.

29 San Francisco *Chronicle,* May 13, 1970.

30 *U.S. News and World Report,* September 22, 1969, p. 37. When Clark Clifford called for a withdrawal of *all* combat troops by the end of 1970, Nixon publicly expressed the hope that he could beat this schedule.

This was the first announced withdrawal of U.S. troops from the area since a similar announcement by the Kennedy Administration on October 2, 1963, concerning the probable withdrawal of 1,000 U.S. troops by the end of that year. The Kennedy withdrawals would have been implemented by the decisions of a top-level Honolulu Conference on November 20, 1963; but these decisions seem to have been secretly countermanded apparently at an unscheduled "emergency" meeting of Johnson and his top advisers on November 24, two days after the Kennedy assassination. (Cf. Council on Foreign Relations, *The United States in World Affairs,* 1963, Harper & Row, Publishers, 1964, p. 193. The number of U.S. "advisers" dropped for a while by about 500 to 15,500 but soon rose again.)

31 In February 1968, at the time of the Tet offensive and Johnson's response to it, there were 510,000 troops in Vietnam. When Nixon was elected in November 1968, there were 538,300. As of March 1, 1969, there were 541,500.

32 That escalation, like the present one, followed hard on the heels of developments that might have been construed as a "peace threat": the North Vietnamese Foreign Minister's hint of January 28, 1967, that there "could" be discussion between North Vietnam and the United States.

33 *The Wall Street Journal,* May 11, 1970, p. 1.

[34] In June 1958, South Vietnamese troops invaded Cambodia's Stung Treng Province: the United States then not only refused to condemn the invasion, it even reminded Sihanouk "that the arms he had received from us were meant for use only against the Communists" (Robert Shaplen, *Time Out of Hand* [New York: Harper & Row, Publishers, 1969], p. 311).

[35] San Francisco *Chronicle*, May 14, 1970, p. 43.

[36] Hoopes, *op. cit.*, p. 204.

[37] They must realize, furthermore, that such a course is not likely to be ratified by the electorate of 1972. Probably only a few of us were disturbed last fall when I. F. Stone reported that generals in Washington ". . . apparently have told dinner parties hereabouts that there would be no elections in 1972 because the military were going to end all this 'turmoil' by taking over" (*I. F. Stone's Weekly*, September 22, 1969, p. 1). Now even *The Wall Street Journal* sees fit to report that the RAND Corporation "is studying the idea of canceling the 1972 Presidential election if radicals threaten (sic) to disrupt it." It is hardly necessary to take such reports seriously, however. The prospects for the year ahead are grave enough.

CHAPTER THREE

[1] Cited by Jim Peck in an excellent discussion of postwar American Asian scholarship in the Spring 1970 *Bulletin of Concerned Asian Scholars*, (Vol. 2, No. 3 April–July, 1970) p. 54–70.

[2] Michael Leifer, "Rebellion or Subversion in Cambodia," *Current History*, February 1969, p. 92.

[3] *Is Cambodia Next?* (Washington, D.C.: Russell Press, 1967). An ABC television crew had also been unable to substantiate the American charges. Both groups were free to travel anywhere in Cambodia, and they checked locations specifically alleged to be base camps and transit routes.

[4] UN Document S/7820 15/3/67, quoted in *Is Cambodia Next?*

[5] T. D. Allman, "The Price of Neutrality," *Far Eastern Economic Review*, February 26, 1970, p. 26. Allman noted that the number has continued to rise and that not all such incidents are reported. More details are given in a Cambodian Government White Paper, January 3, 1970. The report also notes that not a single Viet Cong body has ever been found after U.S.-Saigon bombardments or ground attacks.

For evidence on American defoliation in Cambodia, see "Report on Herbicidal damage by the United States in Southeastern Cambodia," A. H. Westing, E. W. Pfeiffer, J. Lavorel, and L. Matarasso, December 31, 1969, Phnom Penh, in T. Whiteside (ed.), *Defoliation* (New York: Ballantine Books, 1970). They note, incidentally, that "despite a week of free and unhampered travel by automobile, on foot, and by low-flying aircraft along hundreds of kilometers of the border, we could find no evidence of Viet Cong activity in Cambodia; nor did our repeated conversations with Cambodians and Europeans living along the border suggest any such activity." But they do report extensive damage from defoliants, in direct and apparently deliberate overflights.

[6] Roger Smith, "Cambodia: Between Scylla and Charybdis," *Asian Survey*, January 1968, p. 77.

[7] Michael Leifer, "Cambodia," *Asian Survey*, January 1967.

8 This characterization of Songsak and Son Ngoc Thanh is given by Daniel Roy, "Le Coup de Phnom-Penh," *Le Monde diplomatique*, April 1970.

Those familiar with internal Cambodian politics regard the information that is available to Westerners as being of highly uncertain quality, and any effort at detailed interpretation must surely be taken with caution. CIA involvement with the Khmer Serei is not in doubt, however. Some details were publicly revealed during the recent appeal of Green Beret officer John J. McCarthy, Jr., who had been convicted for killing a member of Khmer Serei. See *The New York Times*, January 28, 1970.

9 Arthur H. Westing letter, *New Republic*, March 28, 1970, pp. 28–29.

10 T. D. Allman, "The Price of Neutrality," *Far Eastern Economic Review*, February 26, 1970, p. 25.

11 Speech to the closing session of the Summit Conference of Indochinese Peoples, at an unidentified location in South China, April 25, 1970, *Peking Review*, April 28, 1970, p. 32.

12 T. D. Allman, "The Price of Neutrality," *Far Eastern Economic Review*, February 26, 1970, p. 28.

13 T. D. Allman, "Sealing Their Own Doom?", *Far Eastern Economic Review*, April 2, 1970, p. 6.

14 *Ibid.*

15 T. D. Allman, "Anatomy of a Coup," *Far Eastern Economic Review*, April 9, 1970, p. 17.

16 John L. Hess, *The New York Times*, March 13, 1970.

17 Jean Chesneaux in *Le Monde diplomatique*, May 1970, p. 00. In the same issue, François Honti comments that "It is now certain that those who took it upon themselves to abandon [Sihanouk's policy of neutralism] received serious encouragement from American military circles hopeful of being able to count on Phnom Penh for a friendly government and to cut off the Viet Cong and North Vietnamese troops from their 'Cambodian sanctuary.' "

18 Roy, *op. cit.* Among the current American allies in Cambodia are also several thousand "semi-pirates, semi-mercenaries" of the Khmer minority in South Vietnam, organized in the "National Liberation Front of the Khmers of Kampuchea Khrom" (K.K.K.). They were "formed under the Japanese occupation, then mercenaries for the French during the first Indochina war, and of the Americans during the second. . . ." See Jean-Claude Pomonti, *Le Monde*, April 25, 1970.

The New York Times, May 3, states that 2,000 well-armed members were flown into Phnom Penh during the night of May 2. It is interesting that Premier Lon Nol requested the use of these troops from President Nixon directly. Obviously he understands very well who runs Indochina.

19 Jean-Claude Pomonti, *Le Monde Weekly Selection*, April 22, 1970.

20 *Ibid.*

21 *Ibid.*

22 T. D. Allman, "Honeymoon with Disaster," *Far Eastern Economic Review*, April 23, 1970, p. 32.

23 *Le Monde Weekly Selection*, April 22, 1970.

24 Michael Leifer, "Rebellion or Subversion in Cambodia," *Current History*, February, 1969, p. 113.

25 Roger Smith, "Prince Norodom Sihanouk," *Asian Survey*, June 1967, p. 362.

26 See *Le Monde*, April 23, 1970.

27 See Allman's article in this book, page 97.

28 Jean-Claude Pomonti, *Le Monde Weekly Selection*, May 16, 1970.

29 *Washington Post*, April 24, 1970.

30 Michael Field, *The Prevailing Wind* (Methuen, 1965).

31 A fact that leads to some weird contortions. For example, Ambassador William Sullivan, now Deputy Assistant Secretary of State for East Asian and Pacific Affairs, makes the absurd claim that the Truman Doctrine is a "parsing" of the UN Charter (Symington Subcommittee Hearings).

32 According to Pentagon sources, aerial bombardment of Indochina from 1965 through 1969 reached 4.5 million tons, nine times the total tonnage in the entire Pacific theater in World War II. This is about half of the total ordnance expended.

33 Robert G. Kaiser, *Washington Post–Boston Globe*, May 3, 1970.

34 T. D. Allman, "The Price of Neutrality," *Far Eastern Economic Review*, February 26, 1970, pp. 26–28.

35 *Ibid.*

36 *The New York Times*, May 3, 1970.

37 AP, *Boston Globe*, May 4, 1970.

38 CBS radio news, May 5, 1970.

39 P. F. Langer and J. J. Zasloff, *The North Vietnamese and the Pathet Lao*, RM-5935, September 1969.

40 For more extensive discussion, see my article "After Pinkville" in *The New York Review of Books*, January 1, 1970, pp. 3–14.

41 *The New York Times*, May 5, 1970.

CHAPTER FOUR

1 For details of this symbolism, see Georges Coedès, *pour mieux comprendre Angkor* (2d ed.; Paris: A. Maisonneuve, 1948), ch. v, and Bernard P. Groslier, with the collaboration of C. R. Boxer, *Angkor et le Cambodge au XVIe siècle d'après les sources portugaises et espagnoles* (Annales du Musée Guimet, Bibliothèque d'Etudes, vol. LXIII; Paris: Presses Universitaires de France, 1958), ch. iv.

2 Groslier, *Angkor et le Cambodge*, pp. 155–164.

3 The choice of city sites by the Khmer kings was dictated by the needs of the economy. The plain of Siem Reap, where Angkor is located, is an area of some 5 million hectares, and it had the two essential ingredients of wet rice culture: rich and flat land and water. The main problem (as it still is in Cambodia) was the disposition of water. It rained heavily four months of the year, but the water quickly ran off to the rivers and lake, leaving the people without adequate supplies for the rest of the year. The solution to this problem was found in the construction of a hydraulic network. Hundreds of large reservoirs and artificial lakes were built, including, for example, the Barai Occidental, which was 5 miles by 1.5 miles in area and held an estimated 30 million cubic meters of water. Water was distributed by a network of canals and ditches as needed by the system. According to one observer of the twelfth century, as many as four harvests a year were produced as a result. See Paul Pelliot, trans. and ed., *Mémoires sur les coutumes du Cambodge de Tcheou Ta-kouan* (Paris: A. Maisonneuve, 1951), p. 24.

4 Groslier, *Angkor et le Cambodge*, pp. 118–121; L. Palmer Briggs, *The Ancient Khmer Empire*, (Philadelphia: American Philosophical Society, 1951), pp. 258–261.

5 Siamese tutelage was imposed upon Cambodia in 1594. In 1673, Ang Non ascended to the Cambodian throne with Annamese support. Thereafter Annam, in competition with Siam, sought to exercise influence over Cambodia and began to colonize the provinces of Prey Kôr (Saigon), Kâmpéâp Srêkatrey (Bien Hoà), and Baria in the Mekong delta. These areas were officially annexed by Annam in the eighteenth century.

6 See R. Stanley Thomson, "The Establishment of the French Protectorate over Cambodia," *Far Eastern Quarterly*, IV, no. 4 (August 1945), 313–340, and "Siam and France, 1863–1870," *ibid.*, V, no. 1 (November 1945), 28–46.

7 France wished to consolidate its position on the peninsula and did not want to risk the Siamese government's falling more under British influence. The *faux pas* was rectified forty years later when Siamese violation of other treaties led France to reopen the issue. In return for concessions along the Mekong River, Siam abandoned its claims in Cambodia by conventions signed in 1902, 1904, and 1907. The northern provinces were again annexed by Siam at the beginning of the Second World War but were returned after the war.

8 According to one account of Thomson's meeting with Norodom, Kol de Monteiro, a descendant of a Portuguese adventurer who was the king's interpreter, told the king, "'Sire, this is not a convention which is proposed to Your Majesty; it is an abdication." See Paul Collard, *Cambodge et Cambodgiennes* (Paris: Société d'Editions Géographiques, Maritimes et Coloniales, 1925), p. 111. (This translation and others in this article were made by the author.) See also Protectorat du Cambodge, *Recueil des actes du gouvernement cambodgien* (Saigon, 1920), I, 63–65, for the text of the treaty.

9 For details of the colonial administration, see René Morizon, *Monographie du Cambodge* (Hanoi: Imprimerie d'Extrême-Orient, 1931), pp. 51–55, and A. Silvestre, *Le Cambodge administratif* (Phnom Penh, 1924), pp. 42–54.

10 Protectorat du Cambodge, *Recueil des actes*, pp. 83–84, 131–135.

11 The French justified their decision by pointing to a quarrel between the Norodom and Sisowath branches of the royal family over the throne and noting that Sihanouk, an offspring of both sides, would help to reconcile the dispute. See J. Decoux, *A la barre de l'Indochine: Histoire de mon gouvernement général, 1940–1945* (Paris: Plon, 1949), pp. 285–286. It must have been well known to the French, however, that Monireth was also the offspring of both branches. See Princess Yukanthor, "Personalité de S. M. Norodom Suramarit," *France-Asie* (Saigon), XII, no. 113 (October 1955), 242–247.

12 Son Ngoc Thanh was forced to flee from Cambodia in early 1942 following a demonstration of Buddhist monks against French authority which he was charged with having inspired. He took refuge in the Japanese Embassy in Bangkok and later was sent to Japan, where he spent the war studying Japanese and teaching Cambodian.

13 *Journal Officiel du Cambodge* (Phnom Penh), no. 1, March 22, 1945.

14 See *Mouvement Yuvan Kampuchéarat: Statuts* (Phnom Penh, 1944). The youth group was organized in 1943 by the French to combat what seemed to them to be increasing Japanese influence over the youth. Some of Cambodia's most prominent preindependence politicians and postindependence administrators were members of the group, including Son Sann, Sonn Vœunsai, Khim Tit, and Prince Sisowath Essaro.

15 *Le Cambodge* (Phnom Penh), August 15, 1945.

16 See text in *Journal Officiel de la Fédération Indochinoise* (Saigon),

March 21, 1946, pp. 78–81. See also Roger Lévy, *L'Indochine et ses traités* (Centre d'Etudes de Politique Etrangère, Section d'Information, Pub. no. 19; Paris, 1947), pp. 41–46.

[17] See King Sihanouk's message to the first Democrat government in *La Liberté* (Phnom Penh), February 21, 1948. See also Gouvernement Royal du Cambodge, *Livre Jaune sur les revendications de l'indépendance du Cambodge*, vol. I (Paris: Imprimerie Centrale Commerciale, 1953), passim. Hereafter cited as *Livre Jaune, I.*

[18] See Lévy, *L'Indochine et ses traités*, pp. 82–87. These provinces had been annexed by Thailand in 1941 with the assistance of Japan.

[19] See Sam Sary and Mau Say, *Bilan de l'œuvre de Norodom Sihanouk, pendant le mandat royal de 1952 à 1955* (Phnom Penh: Imprimerie Albert Portail, 1955), pp. 20–27. See also Southeast Asia Treaty Organization, Research Services Office, *Background Brief: Communism and Cambodia* (RSO/BB/25; Bangkok, December 31, 1959).

[20] *Le Cambodge,* January 14 and 15, 1953.

[21] Details of the Crusade are found in *Livre Jaune, I.* See also Sihanouk's own account in his *La monarchie cambodgienne et la croisade royale pour l'ndependance* (Phnom Penh: Imprimerie Rasmey, 1961), pp. 60–68.

[22] See *The New York Times*, April 18 and 19, 1953.

[23] See *Le Monde* (Paris), June 16, 1953. The news of the king's exile was received with great consternation in Paris. Its impact was enhanced by the almost simultaneous occurrence of another event of great significance—news of increased Chinese aid to the Viet Minh.

[24] See Gouvernement Royal du Cambodge, *Livre Jaune sur les revendications de l'indépendance du Cambodge*, vol. II (Phnom Penh: Imprimerie du Palais Royal, 1954), passim.

[25] See Great Britain, *Documents Relating to the Discussions of Korea and Indo-China at the Geneva Conference, April 27–June 15, 1954*, Cmd. 9186, Misc. no. 16 (London: H.M. Stationery Office, 1954; hereafter cited as *Cmd. 9186*), and *Further Documents Relating to the Discussion of Indo-China at the Geneva Conference, June 16–July 21, 1954*, Cmd. 9239, Misc. no. 20 (London: H.M. Stationery Office, 1954; hereafter cited as *Cmd. 9239*).

[26] See *Conférence de Genève de 1954: Compte rendu sténographique provisoire* (nonofficiel), F/I.C./PV.1 (May 8, 1954), and F/I.C./PV.3 (May 12, 1954). See also *Cmd. 9186*, pp. 107–114.

[27] Molotov apparently played a key role in resolving this difference. See *Memoirs of Anthony Eden: Full Circle* (Boston: Houghton Mifflin, 1960), pp. 130, 131–132, 136, and 140.

[28] *Conférence de Genève*, F/I.C./PV.4 (May 14, 1954); *Cmd. 9186*, pp. 116–118.

[29] *Conférence de Genève*, F/I.C. 17 (June 8, 1954), and F/I.C. 20 (June 9, 1954).

[30] Anthony Eden, *The Memoirs of Anthony Eden: Full Circle* (Boston: Houghton Mifflin, 1960) p. 158.

CHAPTER SEVEN

[1] "No Holds Barred," *Far Eastern Economic Review*, September 4, 1969, p. 613.

[2] Francois Nivolon, "Cross Purposes," *Ibid.*, March 14, 1963, p. 543.

3 *Ibid.*, September 4, 1969, p. 612.

4 The Khmer Serei is a group formed out of the remnants of the Khmer Issarak, which had been led by an early opponent of Sihanouk's, Son Ngoc Than, who was an anti-French nationalist, but also a Japanese collaborator. From the early sixties, the Khmer Serei, which was composed almost entirely of expatriated Cambodians living in the Mekong Delta in South Vietnam and eastern sections of Thailand, began actively trying to subvert the Sihanouk government. It is openly pro-American and has been both trained and equipped by the CIA, as well as getting support from the Thai government.

5 Roger Smith, "Between Scylla and Charybdis," *Asian Survey,* January 1968, p. 75.

6 Robert Shaplen, *Time out of Hand* (New York: Harper & Row, Publishers, 1970), p. 323.

7 Michael Leifer, "Rebellion or Subversion in Cambodia," *Current History,* February 1969, p. 91.

8 *Le Monde Weekly,* November 26, 1969. What is particularly curious about this entire affair is that in comparison with the CIA-supported activities of the Khmer Serei these incidents of Communist rebellion were quite minor. During the entire month of fighting in April, 19 rebels and 4 government troops had been killed and 100 locally manufactured rifles were discovered. In contrast, during the previous year, more than 300 border violations had been carried out by the Thai-based Khmer Serei in which 320 men had been killed or wounded. The Khmer Serei forces had even planted land mines throughout Battambang province. "In certain areas," Bernard Couret of *Le Monde* reported, "things are so insecure that jeep patrols have been suspended. At Kandol outpost the commander indicated that he could assure no responsibility for personnel outside a 100 metre range, indicating that a village woman had recently been killed by an anti-personnel mine less than 200 metres from the military camp." *Le Monde,* May 6, 1967. (This article also describes in some detail the extent of CIA support of the Khmer Serei.)

9 "The Next Domino," *Far Eastern Economic Review,* April 27, 1967, p. 153.

10 *Ibid.*

11 Roger Smith, "Between Scylla and Charybdis," p. 75.

12 T. D. Allman, "Cracking a Smile," *Far Eastern Economic Review,* February 26, 1970, p. 24.

13 *The New York Times,* March 14, 1968.

14 T. D. Allman, "And Nowhere Else To Go," *Far Eastern Economic Review,* February 5, 1970, p. 24.

15 *Ibid.* Sihanouk's statements are particularly noteworthy, since in February he had himself stated that the hill tribesmen were not interested in ideology, but were reacting to government enforced resettlement which would "permit them to enjoy the social achievements which the Sangkum offers." *Réalités Cambodgiennes,* February 16, 1968; cited Leifer, "Rebellion or Subversion in Cambodia," p. 112.

16 *The New York Times,* June 30, 1969.

17 *Le Sangkum,* October 1969, gives figures and geographical locations of the Khmer Rouge base areas.

18 *Far Eastern Economic Review,* September 4, 1969, p. 612, December 25, 1969, p. 668.

19 *Ibid.*, February 26, 1970, pp. 24–25.

20 *Ibid.*, September 4, 1969, p. 613.

21 "Thorns Each Side," *Ibid.*, January 15, 1970 p. 27.

22 *Ibid.*, February 26, 1970, p. 24.

23 *Ibid.*

24 *Ibid.* In the Parrot's Beak area, for instance, there were, as of February, no Vietnamese bases or sanctuaries and, as a matter of fact, hardly any Vietcong activity at all. According to one local Cambodian officer interviewed at the time: "There are no VC in Chantrea district. They never enter our territory more than 500 metres, even at night. Mostly they are passing. There are no camps here. No sanctuaries." "The Price of Neutrality," *Far Eastern Economic Review*, February 26, 1970, p. 27.

25 This is Allman's phrase.

26 *Kambuja Monthly Review*, April 15, 1968.

27 David Chandler, "Cambodia's Strategy of Survival," *Current History*, December 1969, p. 346.

28 For an authoritative report on U.S. defoliation in Cambodia, A. H. Westing, E. W. Pfeiffer, J. Lavoree, and L. Matarasso, "Report on Herbicidal Damage by the United States in Southeastern Cambodia," in Thomas Whiteside, *Defoliation* (New York: Ballantine Books, 1970).

29 W. Burchett, *The Guardian*, April 25, 1970.

30 *Washington Post*, March 19, 1970.

31 *Far Eastern Economic Review*, September 4, 1969, p. 612.

32 *Le Monde*, March 14, 1970.

33 *Ibid.*, March 15, 1970.

34 *Ibid.*

35 *Ibid.*

36 *Ibid.*, March 19, 1970.

37 San Francisco *Examiner*, March 29, 1970.

38 *Far Eastern Economic Review*, February 12, 1970, p. 23.

CHAPTER TEN

1 *Washington Post*, May 2, 1970; *The Christian Science Monitor*, May 4, 1970.

2 T. D. Allman, "When Khmers Kill Khmers," *Far Eastern Economic Review*, April 7, 1970, pp. 6–7.

3 T. D. Allman, *Far Eastern Economic Review*, April 16, 1970, p. 91.

4 *Washington Post*, March 29, 1970.

5 *The New York Times*, March 19, 1970.

6 T. D. Allman, "Honeymoon with Disaster," *Far Eastern Economic Review*, April 28, 1970, pp. 33–34.

7 *Le Monde*, March 18, 1970.

8 *The New York Times*, April 2, 1970.

9 San Francisco *Chronicle*, April 20, 1970.

10 San Francisco *Examiner*, March 29, 1970.

11 San Francisco *Chronicle*, March 31, 1970.

12 San Francisco *Chronicle*, March 29, 1970; *Le Monde*, March 31, 1970; *Far Eastern Economic Review*, April 9, 1970, p. 5.

13 San Francisco *Chronicle*, March 28, 1970.

14 *Le Monde*, April 8, 1970.

15 T. D. Allman, "The Cambodian Pogrom," *Far Eastern Economic Review*, May 7, 1970, p. 23.

16 San Francisco *Chronicle*, April 14, 1970.

17 *Le Monde Weekly*, April 22, 1970.

18 *Newsweek*, May 4, 1970, p. 25.

19 *The New York Times*, April 11, 1970.

20 *The New York Times*, April 27, 1970.

21 San Francisco *Chronicle*, April 22, 1970.

22 *The New York Times*, April 14, 1970.

23 San Francisco *Chronicle*, April 28, 1970.

24 *The New York Times*, May 11, 1970.

25 Associated Press, May 11, 1970.

26 *Newsweek*, May 25, 1970, p. 25.

27 *Guardian*, April 25, 1970.

28 *Le Monde*, March 24, 1970.

29 *Washington Post*, March 23, 1970.

30 San Francisco *Chronicle*, March 18, 1970.

31 San Francisco *Chronicle*, March 16, 1970.

32 Reuters, March 17, 1970; *Washington Post*, March 28, 1970; *The New York Times*, April 4, 1970.

33 *The New York Times*, March 30, 1970, April 1, 1970.

34 *The New York Times*, April 9, 18, 22, 1970; San Francisco *Chronicle*, April 9, 1970.

35 *The New York Times*, April 11, 1970.

36 T. D. Allman, "When Khmers Kill Khmers," *Far Eastern Economic Review*, April 7, 1970, p. 6.

37 T. D. Allman, "Better Dead Than Red," *Far Eastern Economic Review*, May 7, 1970.

38 *The New York Times*, June 8, 1970.

39 *The New York Times*, April 18, 1970.

40 T. D. Allman, *op. cit.*, p. 23; and *Newsweek*, May 4, 1970, p. 23B.

41 *The New York Times*, May 3, 1970.

42 *The Christian Science Monitor*, May 5, 1970.

43 *The New York Times*, May 13, 1970.

44 *The New York Times*, May 12, 1970.

45 *The New York Times*, May 28, 1970.

46 *The New York Times*, June 6, 1970.

47 *The New York Times*, May 24, 1970.

48 *The New York Times*, June 16, 1970.

49 *The New York Times*, May 21, 1970.

50 San Francisco *Chronicle*, May 6, 1970; *The Wall Street Journal*, May 11, 1970.

51 *The New York Times*, May 7, 1970.

52 *Le Monde*, May 5, 1970.

53 *The New York Times*, June 8, 1970.

54 Los Angeles *Times*, May 28, 1970.

55 *Le Monde*, June 5, 1970.

CHAPTER ELEVEN

1 *Le Monde*, April 7, 1970.

2 Wilfred Burchett, *Guardian*, June 6, 1970. Jean Lacouture in *Foreign Affairs*, July 1970, p. 627, says that there was solidarity at the conference, "but a solidarity sufficiently flexible not to have led . . . into creating a combat structure." Burchett's information, however, was based on an interview with Sihanouk.

³ *Peking Review*, May 8, 1970, p. 3.

⁴ *Daily Report: Asia and Pacific*, Foreign Broadcast Information Service, July 6, 1970.

⁵ *Le Monde*, March 25, 1970.

⁶ *Le Monde*, May 7, 1970. See also *Le Monde Diplomatique*, June 1970. "Also noteworthy is the wish of the authors of the program to get rid of the post colonial era in which Cambodia remains: Progressive Khmerization of education (already well in progress before the coup under Sihanouk's direction and the direction of a dynamic minister of education) and research on the national history 'often deformed by foreign authors'; discretely, this task has already been begun by certain progressive [Cambodian] intellectuals living in France."

⁷ *Le Monde Diplomatique*, June 1970.

⁸ *The New York Times*, May 9, 1970.

⁹ *The New York Times*, May 18, 1970, reports on the structure of the NUF: "Information from Peking has shown the existence of a classic Communist-style political apparatus in Prince Sihanouk's exiled 'royal government,' complete with a national front, a central committee, and a politburo."

¹⁰ Robert Shaplen, *Time out of Hand* (New York: Harper & Row, Publishers, 1970), pp. 323–324.

¹¹ T. J. S. George, "Charlie Khmer," *Far Eastern Economic Review*, June 11, 1970, p. 21.

¹² *Le Monde Diplomatique*, June 1970. Jacques Decornoy translates a Khmer Rouge document from the 1967 period which attacked the army, police, and government administration.

¹³ T. J. S. George, *op. cit.*

¹⁴ *Ibid.* George states that Sihanouk's wife's step-brother, Oum Mannorine, head of the provincial guard, was responsible for the repression after Lon Nol had taken the uprising lying down. Shaplen, on the other hand, credits Lon Nol with the repression of the peasant uprising in Battambang. Shaplen, *Time out of Hand*, p. 322.

¹⁵ T. D. Allman, "No Holds Barred," *Far Eastern Economic Review*, September 4, 1969.

¹⁶ T. J. S. George, *op. cit.*, p. 20.

¹⁷ *Le Monde Diplomatique*, June 1970.

¹⁸ *Le Monde Weekly*, March 25, 1970.

¹⁹ *Le Monde Diplomatique*, June 1970.

²⁰ T. J. S. George wrote in *Far Eastern Economic Review*, June 11, 1970, p. 19, concerning the lack of knowledge outside Cambodia of the Khmer Rouge: "The existence of an indigenous leftist movement in Cambodia—which was growing, not weakening, even before the present crisis started—never received the attention it deserved. For one thing, Prince Sihanouk's dominant personality shielded from the world's eyes all political activity in his country. For another, the many-splendoured crusaders of the American press started on the assumption that communism in Cambodia began with the Vietcong and ended with the North Vietnamese."

²¹ T. J. S. George, *op. cit.*, p. 21.

²² Wilfred Burchett, *Guardian*, June 13, 1970.

²³ *Peking Review*, May 22, 1970.

²⁴ T. D. Allman, "Better Dead Than Red," *Far Eastern Economic Review*, May 7, 1970, p. 21–24.

²⁵ Associated Press, May 4 and 7, 1970; *Le Monde*, June 7–8, 1970, reported that the Cambodian mercenaries were at best out of control

of their Cambodian generals, and at worst their units were rapidly dis-integrating.

26 Los Angeles *Times*, May 24, 1970.

27 *Le Monde*, June 7–8, 1970.

28 *The New York Times*, June 24, 1970.

29 *Le Monde*, April 12, 1970.

30 *Newsweek*, May 4, 1970.

31 Liberation Press Agency (NUF), June 29, 1970; reported in *Daily Report: Asia and Pacific*, Foreign Broadcast Information Service (U.S. Gov't.), July 2, 1970.

32 *Le Monde*, June 5, 1970.

33 *Ibid*. Jean Pomonti, in *Le Monde Weekly Selection*, June 3, 1970, reported that "Among the political clans who were opposed to Prince Sihanouk, only those belonging to the extreme right-wing have, for the moment, been willing to rally to the new government. The others are hesitating or, like the 'Red Khmer,' are already fighting it openly. . . . [Many] began gradually to make up their minds, and finally came out for the United Front."

34 *Le Monde*, June 25, 1970. Michael Morrow, a Dispatch News Service reporter who had been captured by the NUF, reported that "There was no doubt that the guerrillas were in complete control and in good rapport with the people," in the villages he traveled through on the way to his release (San Francisco *Chronicle*, June 27, 1970).

35 *Le Monde*, June 7–8, 1970.

CHAPTER TWELVE

1 The 1960 RAND study by Allen Whiting entitled *China Crosses the Yalu* has definitively exploded the myth that China was acting in an unprovoked or aggressive fashion in Korea. Two excellent brief intro-ductions to China's foreign policy of the past twenty years are John Gittings: "The Great Power Triangle and Chinese Foreign Policy," *The China Quarterly*, No. 39, July–September, 1969, pp. 41–54; and Lawrence Batistini: "Sino-American Confrontation: A Look At The Chinese Side," *Yale Review*, December, 1968, pp. 608–613.

2 Agence France Presse interview; translated in *Daily Report: Asia and Pacific*, Foreign Broadcast Information Service (Government Publi-cation), May 11, 1970.

3 *Ibid.*, July 6, 1970.

CHAPTER THIRTEEN

1 At his May 8th News Conference, Mr. Nixon said: "As Commander-in-Chief I alone am responsible for the lives of 425 or 430,000 Americans in Vietnam. That's what I've been thinking about and the decision that I made on Cambodia will save those lives."

2 The German reliance during the Nazi period upon fifth-column tactics to undermine the governing process in countries which were the targets of aggression should be recalled in the Cambodian context. "A Quisling regime" is one that operates in the name of a nation, but serves as an agent of its dismemberment and destruction. Vidkun Quisling was

the head of the Nationalist Party of Norway, a pro-Nazi group with no parliamentary representatives and little popular following; in April 1940, when Hitler invaded Norway, Quisling welcomed the German occupation of Norway and eventually obtained dictatorial powers from the Germans in Norway. The Quisling experience is an extreme case, but it usefully illustrates the undesirability of accepting a constituted regime as automatically empowered to act as the legitimate government of a country.

3 *The Congressional Record,* memorandum prepared by George McT. Kahin, "Cambodia: The Administration's Version and the Historical Record," pp. 57428–57431, at p. 57431.

4 For one persuasive analysis along these lines see Louis Henkin, "Force, Intervention, and Neutrality in Contemporary International Law," *Proceedings, American Society of International Law 1963,* pp. 147–162.

5 D. W. Bowett, *Self-Defense in International Law* (Manchester: Manchester University Press, 1958), p. 206, see also pp. 216–217.

6 *Ibid.,* p. 207; see also J. Stone, *Legal Controls of International Conflict* (Sydney, Australia: Maitland Publications, 1954), p. 245, especially the assertion that "under general international law, a State has no right of 'self-defense' in respect of an armed attack upon a third State."

7 Myres S. McDougal and Florentino P. Feliciano, *Law and Minimum World Public Order* (New Haven, Conn.: Yale University Press, 1962), p. 248; see generally pp. 244–253.

8 Stanley Hoffman has recently written that "Professor McDougal's theory . . . will remain an astounding testimony to the grip of the Cold War on American thought and practice." "Henkin and Falk: Mild Reformist and Mild Revolutionary," *Journal of International Affairs,* Vol. XXLV, 1970, pp. 118–126, at p. 120.

9 McDougal and Feliciano, *Law and Minimum World Public Order,* p. 251.

10 *Ibid.,* p. 67; the most widely relied-upon description of conditions appropriate for a claim of self-defense was given by Daniel Webster on April 24, 1841, in a diplomatic note to Canada. Mr. Webster, in his capacity as U.S. Secretary of State, wrote that there must be shown by the claimant government to be a "necessity of self-defense, instant, overwhelming, leaving no choice of means and no moment for deliberation." *British and Foreign State Papers,* p. 1129 (1840–1841).

11 The legal status of the invasion is not, of course, determined by the military success or failure of the operation. However, the reasonableness of a limited claim of self-defense depends on the proportionality of means and ends, and an assessment of military success or failure may give some insight into whether the force used was proportional to the end sought.

12 I have written a legal analysis of this earlier phase of the conflict. See Falk, ed., *The Vietnam War and International Law,* Vol. I (Princeton, N. J.: Princeton University Press, 1968), pp. 362–400, 445–508; see Vol. I and II for main legal positions in relation to the war.

13 Although there has been a steady erosion of this role under the pressure of geo-political and ideological considerations. Among the instances where this pressure has been resolved at the expense of legal restraints are Guatemala (1954), Lebanon (1958), Bay of Pigs (1961), Stanleyville Operation (1964), Dominican Republic (1965), as well as a number of less visible interventions in the affairs of foreign countries through the activities of the CIA.

14 Address by David Packard, Department of Defense News Release, May 15, 1970, p. 5.

15 See note from the *Columbia Law Review*, "International Law and Military Operations Against Insurgents in Neutral Territory," in Falk, *The Vietnam War*, Vol. II, pp. 572–593.

16 For an analysis of the compatibility between special claims to use force and international law (including the U.N. Charter) see Falk, "The Beirut Raid and the International Law of Retaliation," *American Journal of International Law*, Vol. 63, July 1969, pp. 415–443. Note that the Beirut Raid conducted by Israeli military units on December 28, 1968, was far more limited in scope, duration, and effects than has been the Cambodian Operation. It seems questionable whether a use of armed forces on the scale of the Cambodian Operation can ever be considered as a special claim falling outside the Charter, but must be justified, if at all, as an exercise of the right of self-defense.

17 Packard, Address, p. 6.

CHAPTER FOURTEEN

1 The pros and cons of urbanization as a means for bringing about the development of "Third World" countries is a very important debate. However, it is not the issue treated in this article. The authors' focus is on the inhumanity of the urbanization strategy developed in Indo-China by the U.S. military and civilian decision-makers in their attempt to realize military goals.

For purposes of this paper, "city" or "urban place" is used to refer to settlements of 20,000-plus inhabitants. The reader should also note that all figures used are approximate, not exact. However, the magnitudes, particularly in comparative context, are great enough to make them quite meaningful.

2 "The People and Cities of Indo-China," *Extreme Asie*, No. 77, August 1933, p. 368.

3 T. G. McGee, *The Southeast Asian City* (New York: Praeger, 1967), p. 81; F. P. Munson et al., *Area Handbook for Cambodia* (Washington, D.C.: U.S. Government Printing Office, 1968), p. 35.

4 Gerald Hickey, quoted in *The New York Times*, February 16, 1970, IV, p. 1; other sources converge on the 40 to 45 percent estimate.

5 From discussions of one of the authors with officials in Viet Nam, 1969; Samuel P. Huntingdon, "The Bases of Accommodation," *Foreign Affairs*, Vol. 64, No. 4 (July 1968), p. 648.

6 VIÉT-NAM NIÊN-GÍAM THÔNG-KÊ 1967–68, Vietnam Statistical Yearbook, Vol. Fourteenth 1968 (Saigon, Vietnam: National Institute of Statistics, Office of the Prime Minister, 1968), pp. 394, 399.

7 *Vietnam Guardian*, March 22, 1969.

8 Frances Fitzgerald, "The Tragedy of Saigon," *Atlantic Monthly*, December 21, 1966, pp. 62–63.

9 *Civilian Casualty and Refugee Problems in South Viet Nam*, Findings and Recommendations of the Subcommittee to Investigate Problems Connected with Refugees and Escapees of the Committee on the Judiciary, United States Senate (Washington, D.C.; U.S. Government Printing Office, 1968), p. 11.

10 U.S. Senate Refugee Subcommittee Findings, *Civilian Casualty*, p. 20.

[11] Informed source: former Mennonite volunteer refugee worker, Viet Nam, 1966–1969.

[12] U.S. Senate Refugee Subcommittee Findings, *Civilian Casualty*, p. 2.

[13] Donald Duncan, "Return to Vietnam," *Ramparts*, August 10, 1968, p. 12.

[14] American Friends Service Committee, *White Paper on Ending the War*, May 1969.

[15] U.S. Senate Refugee Subcommittee Findings, *Civilian Casualty*, p. 9; *The New York Times*, February 16, 1970, IV, p. 1.

[16] *Newsweek*, December 29, 1969, p. 38.

[17] *The New York Times*, June 23, 1968, p. 6.

[18] Don Luce, "Viet Nam: Life in a Sad Land," *Saturday Review*, June 1, 1968, p. 59.

[19] *Newsweek*, December 29, 1969, p. 38.

[20] Don Luce, "Viet Nam," p. 59.

[21] Frances Fitzgerald, "The Tragedy of Saigon," p. 64.

[22] *Newsweek*, December 29, 1969, p. 38.

[23] Quoted in: *Saigon Metropolitan Area, Urban Development Study Summary of Reports DOX–VNS–A1 to DOX–VNS–A7* (Athens: Doxiadas Associates, 1965), p. 10.

[24] *The New York Times*, April 14, 1968, IV, p. 18; Lt. Col. Dan C. Cavanaugh et al., "Some Observations on the Current Plague Outbreak in the Republic of Vietnam," *American Journal of Public Health*, Vol. 58, No. 4 (April 1968), p. 743, graph.

[25] *Bay Area Institute Newsletter*, No. 6, June 9, 1970, p. 4.

[26] It is quite difficult to obtain exact figures for the reductions in health assistance. One informed M.D. reports that USAID's budget for its Viet Nam public-health programs was cut from approximately $57 million for 1967 to $36 million for 1969. The statement of USAID's administrator, submitted to the Senate Judiciary's Subcommittee to Investigate Problems Connected with Refugees and Escapees, on June 24, 1969, notes that USAID's budget for Viet Nam public-health programs between mid-1965 and mid-1968 averaged approximately $29 million. For fiscal year 1970, USAID requested only $22 million. It should be noted that in 1965, before the tremendous increase in U.S. involvement, USAID's budget was quite small, thus the scale of the cut to the 1970 figure is disguised. Another example is the U.S. contributions to the cost of construction of Vietnamese health facilities: $339,000 in 1965, $3 million in 1967, $2 million in 1968.
The former U.S. medical adviser in Viet Nam who informed the authors of the cutback in military medical services to civilians, suggested that the reason for this was the military's decision that the civilian health problems presented little threat to U.S. personnel.

[27] *Newsweek*, June 15, 1970, p. 37.

[28] *The New York Times*, July 6, 1968, p. 6.

[29] *The New York Times*, March 23, 1970, p. 31.

[30] *Newsweek*, December 29, 1969, pp. 38, 39; *The New York Times*, July 6, 1968, pp. 1, 6.

[31] *The New York Times Magazine*, August 8, 1965, p. 12; Frances Fitzgerald, "The Tragedy of Saigon," p. 65.

[32] Samuel P. Huntington, "The Bases of Accommodation," pp. 649, 650.

[33] The Directorate's functions are to review all building and development plans, both public and private, and authorize the issuance of building permits by local governments; develop long- and short-range

plans for local governments; design and construct all public buildings for all ministries; and design and construct housing for civil servants and military personnel. Frank R. Pavich and Robert F. Moss, "Urban Planning in Vietnam," Office of Urban Reconstruction and Development, ADID/USAID/VIETNAM, Saigon, June 1968, p. 15.

34 *Ibid.*, p. 20.

35 *Ibid.*, pp. 21–25.

36 *Newsweek,* January 20, 1969, p. 32.

37 Frances Fitzgerald, "The Tragedy of Saigon," p. 61.

38 *Newsweek,* December 29, 1969, p. 39.

39 Informed sources: a former USAID planning official and a former Public Safety Adviser, Viet Nam, 1969–70. It would appear that one conspicuous exception to the cutbacks in USAID programs is in "public safety" training.

40 Frances Fitzgerald, "The Tragedy of Saigon," p. 66.

41 U.S. Senate Refugee Subcommittee Findings, *Civilian Casualty,* p. 27.

42 *Ibid.*, p. 30.

43 *Ibid.*

44 *Ibid.:* Operation Lincoln in Pleiku, Phu Bon, and Darlac provinces, April 8; major battle west of Quang Nai, April 21; first of four Paul Revere Operations west of Pleiku, May 10; operation Davy Crockett in Binh Dinh province, May 16; operation Birmingham in III corps, May 17; and operation El Paso II in Binh Long province, June 2, 1966.

45 *Ibid.*

46 Jonathan Schell, *The Military Half* (New York: Vintage Books, 1968), pp. 15–16.

47 *Life,* January 27, 1967, p. 26.

48 U.S. Senate Refugee Subcommittee Findings, *Civilian Casualty,* p. 4.

49 *The New York Times,* February 8, 1968. The most publicized case in the U.S. media was the city of Ben Tre (population of 35,000). In order to recapture the city "with the minimum loss of American lives," the U.S. troops resorted to massive fire power. According to one officer: "It became necessary to destroy the town to save it."

50 Melvin Gurtov and Konrad Kellen, "Vietnam: Lessons and Mislessons," Rand Corp., 1969, p. 16.

51 Irving Bengelsdorf, "Starvation as a Weapon," San Francisco *Sunday Examiner & Chronicle,* July 14, 1968, p. 20; for a detailed report on defoliation and its effects in Viet Nam see the following article in this book by Ngô Vinh Long.

52 Seymour Hersh, "My Lai 4: A Report on the Massacre and Its Aftermath," *Harper's,* May 1, 1970, p. 53–84; My Lai is not unique. A number of other cases have had limited coverage in the American press. One of the latest concerns the murder of 16 Vietnamese women and children in the Que San Valley by a U.S. "killer patrol" (Oakland *Tribune,* June 19, 1970). The French press is a superior source for information on these atrocities. The Provisional Government of South Viet Nam prepares and circulates reports of war crimes allegedly committed by ARVN, the United States, and mercenaries in South Viet Nam. They include date and location of incident; typically, numbers of men, women, and children killed, wounded, and tortured; houses and other structures burned down; crops destroyed. The specific military units involved in the action are often identified. One document, "U.S.—Puppet Massacres of the population in South Viet Nam (from 1965 to 1969)," December 1969, includes alleged massacres.

[53] U.S. Department of Defense press release, August 20, 1968.

[54] *The Nation,* April 21, 1969, p. 485.

[55] Jonathan Schell, *The Military Half,* p. 13.

[56] U.S. Senate Refugee Subcommittee Findings, *Civilian Casualty,* quoted in Pacific Studies Center, "Operation Total Victory," May 10, 1970, p. 5.

[57] *Newsweek,* January 20, 1969, p. 32.

[58] General Matthew B. Ridgeway, "Pull Out, All Out, or Stand Fast in Vietnam?" *Look,* April 5, 1966, p. 84.

[59] Samuel P. Huntington, "The Bases of Accommodation," p. 648.

[60] *Ibid.,* p. 653.

[61] *Ibid.,* p. 650.

[62] Noam Chomsky, "After Pinkville," *The New York Review of Books,* January 1, 1970, p. 4.

[63] H. Harding, "Refugees in Laos," Committee of Concerned Asian Scholars, Stanford, (unpublished manuscript), May 1970.

[64] *The New York Times,* October 1, 1969, p. 27.

[65] Noam Chomsky, "After Pinkville," p. 8.

[66] *Washington Post,* May 2, 1970.

[67] David Kale, "The Refugees of Laos," *The Nation,* January 26, 1970, pp. 76–77.

[68] *The New York Times,* January 27, 1968; *The New York Times,* November 1, 1969.

[69] David Kale, "The Refugees of Laos," p. 77.

[70] H. Harding, "Refugees in Laos."

[71] *Hearings of the Subcommittee on U.S. Security Agreements & Commitments Abroad, The Committee on Foreign Relations, U.S. Senate* (Washington, D.C.: U.S. Government Printing Office, October 20–22, 1969), p. 483.

[72] *Op cit.,* Richard L. Ottinger, speech delivered at Johns Hopkins University, School of Advanced International Studies, April 30, 1970; U.S. Senate Security Agreement, Subcommittee Hearings, p. 556.

[73] *Ibid.,* pp. 76–77.

[74] There are a number of sources, including: President Nixon's June 3, 1970 speech, *Newsweek,* June 15, 1970, p. 29; State Department spokesman (C. Bartch), *The New York Times,* June 27, 1970; Pentagon Officials, *Washington Post,* May 23, 1970.

[75] The United States is reportedly already giving the Lon Nol regime $7.9 million for the last months of this fiscal year, and the Pentagon is planning a new $50 million military aid program to begin July 1, 1970. *Los Angeles Times,* June 3, 1970.

[76] Frances Fitzgerald, "The Tragedy of Saigon," p. 61.

[77] *U.S. News & World Report,* June 17, 1968, p. 14.

[78] *The New York Times,* March 13, 1968, p. 16.

[79] Donald Duncan, "Return to Vietnam," p. 16.

[80] *Ibid.*

CHAPTER FIFTEEN

[1] According to an article entitled "Ravaging Vietnam," which appeared in *The Nation,* April 21, 1969, pp. 484–485, B-52 bombing had by 1968 produced an estimated 2.6 million craters of approximately 30 feet in

depth and 45 feet in diameter. Filled with water, these are said to be ideal breeding grounds for malarial mosquitoes.

2 W. A. Nighswonger, *Rural Pacification in Viet Nam* (New York: Praeger, 1966), p. 46.

3 Nguyễn Khac Nhân, "Policy of Key Rural Agrovilles," in *Asian Culture*, Vol. 3, July–December 1961, No. 3–4, p. 32; also W. A. Nighswonger, *Rural Pacification*.

4 Seymour M. Hersh, "Our Chemical War," *The New York Review of Books*, April 25, 1968, p. 32.

5 During my map-surveying expedition, I witnessed countless heart-breaking incidents. Here are but a few: In a village of central Viet Nam one day I saw a group of children chasing after one another toward an open fire which the corvee laborers (who had been recruited to build the fence and moats around the village) had made from uprooted grass. One boy threw a handful of something into the fire; the rest waited. As I was approaching them out of curiosity, one boy used a stick to get the things out of the fire and the rest swarmed over him, snatching them up. The "things" were baby rats! In near frenzy, the children began to pursue one another again, some tossed the hot rats between their two hands, others gulped them down whole. Another time, as I was approaching a village I saw a woman working in a rice-field with a small baby tied to her back by a piece of cloth, and a boy about four years old standing in the glaring sun at the border of the field and yelling out to her (his mother, I guessed). The baby cried. The woman switched the baby around to let it suck at her breast. The baby sucked as hard as it could, but was not able to draw any milk and began crying again. The woman looked around as if to see whether I was watching. When I pretended that I was looking in the direction of the boy, she spat into the mouth of the child in an attempt to silence it.

Hunger struck most of the strategic hamlets I visited. In the village of Karom in central Viet Nam, 200 persons, mostly children, died in a single month. Many people had not eaten anything decent in months, and as a result, their anal muscles had become so dilated that every time they ate or drank something, it would pass right through them in not more than a few minutes.

6 Seymour M. Hersh, "Our Chemical War," pp. 31–32.

7 W. A. Nighwonger, *Rural Pacification*, p. 64.

8 *Ibid.*, pp. 114–115.

9 See two excellent books on this subject by Jonathan Schell: *The Village of Ben Suc* (New York: Random House, 1967), and *The Military Half* (New York: Random House, 1968).

10 Seymour M. Hersh, "Our Chemical War," p. 33.

11 *Tien Tuyen*, July 4, 1969.

12 This was the proportion of abnormal fetuses per litter when the dosage of 2,4,5-T given was 113 mg. per kg. of body weight, administered subcutaneously in a solution of dimethylsulfoxide. When the same dosages were given the mice orally in a honey solution, the proportion of abnormal fetuses per litter was an even higher 54 per cent.

13 In the recent controversy over the use of cyclamates as food additives in the United States, it is to be noted that the Food and Drug Administration deemed the compound to be harmful to humans when maximum concentrations which might be consumed were only 1/50 those concentrations which showed negative results in experiments with laboratory test animals.

14 *The Nation*, April 21, 1969, p. 485.

15 A. H. Westing, E. W. Pfeiffer, J. Lavorel, and L. Matarasso, "Report on Herbicidal Damage by the United States in Southeastern Cambodia," in Thomas Whiteside, *Defoliation* (New York: Ballantine Books, 1970), pp. 117–132.

Selected Bibliography

*Denotes that a paperback edition is available.

I. SOUTHEAST ASIA AND INDOCHINA

*Bastin, J. and Benda, Harry. *History of Modern Southeast Asia* (Englewood Cliffs, N.J.: Prentice-Hall, 1968).

A concise history of the area.

Bulletin of Concerned Asian Scholars.

A political/scholarly quarterly on modern Asia. Many of the contributors to this volume are associated with the *Bulletin,* Suite 300, 9 Sutter St., San Francisco, Calif. 94104. ($6 per year, $4 for students.)

*Chomsky, Noam. *At War with Asia* (New York: Pantheon, 1970).

A collection of Chomsky's perceptive essays on America in Indochina. Includes a report of Chomsky's trip to Laos.

*Committee of Concerned Asian Scholars. *The Indochina Handbook* (New York: Bantam, 1970).

An excellent attempt to answer who, how, and why the U.S. is fighting in Indochina.

Hall, D. G. E. *A History of Southeast Asia* (New York: St. Martin's Press, 1968).

A detailed and well-documented historical outline of Southeast Asia from the earliest periods through the early 1960s.

*Hoopes, Townsend. *The Limits of Intervention: An Inside Account of How the Johnson Policy of Escalation in Vietnam was Reversed* (New York: David McKay, 1969).

A good account of U.S. policy debates by a former Undersecretary of the Air Force.

Kahin, George McT., ed. *Government and Politics of Southeast Asia,* 2nd ed. (Ithaca: Cornell University Press, 1964).

The standard text on the period from World War II to the present. The articles on Vietnam, Cambodia, Laos, Thailand, Indonesia, Burma, Malaysia, and the Philippines provide the reader with historical background as well as an analysis of recent trends in the respective countries. Specialized bibliographies follow each section and a general annotated bibliography offers the reader further suggestions.

*Kahin, George McT., and Lewis, John. *The United States in Vietnam,* rev. ed. (Ithaca: Cornell University Press, 1969).

The most complete account of American involvement in Vietnam. Written by two veteran scholars of Asia, it deals principally with the period since 1954 and carries the narrative down to mid-1969.

*Schurmann, Franz, Scott, Peter Dale, and Zelnick, Reginald. *The Politics of Escalation in Vietnam* (New York: Fawcett, 1966).

Documents how, under Johnson, every publicized "peace feeler" was accompanied by escalation of the war.

Scott, Peter Dale. *The Covert Origins of the Indochina War* (New York: Bobbs Merrill, 1971).

A study revealing how American escalations created an ever-larger war, with emphasis upon relevant U.S. economic and military institutions.

Selden, Mark, and Friedman, Edward, eds. *America's Asia* (New York: Pantheon, 1971).

Essays by the new generation of Asia scholars; excellent.

*Weisberg, Barry, ed. *Ecocide in Indochina: The Ecology of War* (New York: Harper & Row, 1970).

Documents the full complexity of the U.S. destruction of individuals, societies, and the landscapes of Indochina. The book deals with such issues as defoliation, craterization, refugees, antipersonnel weapons, and air power.

II. VIETNAM

*American Friends Service Committee. *Peace in Vietnam: A New Approach in Southeast Asia.* 1966.

A short book which illustrates the major issues in Vietnam; has extensive appendices plus bibliography.

*Chaliand, Gerard. *The Peasants of North Vietnam* (New York: Hill & Wang, 1969).

Chaliand, a French journalist, visited rural North Vietnam. In this book, he attempts to explain how and why the peasants of North Vietnam have continued their struggle despite massive American bombing.

Devillers, Philippe and Lacouture, Jean. *End of a War* (New York: Praeger, 1969).

Written by a team of French historians and journalists, this book is the best account of the Geneva Conference of 1954. It also deals with the French Indochina War and the period 1954–55 when France's involvement in Indochina was transferred to the U.S.

*Falk, Richard A. *The Vietnam War and International Law*. 2 vols. (Princeton: Princeton University Press, 1968).

Falk's work is the definitive study of this subject.

*Fall, Bernard. *The Two Vietnams: A Political and Military Analysis*, 2nd ed., rev. (New York: Praeger, 1967).

This is the best one-volume history of Vietnam available. Fall was one of the few competent Vietnam scholars in the English-speaking world and was widely quoted by both sides in the debate on Vietnam.

————. *Last Reflections on a War* (New York: Doubleday, 1967).

Published posthumously, this work includes the writings and tapes that Fall made during his last trip to Vietnam.

————, ed. *Ho Chi Minh on Revolution* (New York: Praeger, 1967).

Includes speeches, essays, poems, public messages, interviews, and letters of Ho from 1920 to 1966, and has an introduction by Fall.

*Gettleman, Marvin E., ed. *Vietnam* (Greenwich, Conn.: Fawcett, 1965).

This book contains selected writings of historians, statesmen, and journalists which illustrate the major events and epochs in the evolution of Indochina. It also includes policy statements, position papers, and analytic reports on the Vietnam War, as well as a good collection of basic documents.

*Lacouture, Jean. *Vietnam: Between Two Truces* (New York: Random House, 1966).

A very good, quite readable political analysis of Vietnam by an eminent French journalist.

————. *Ho Chi Minh: A Political Biography* (New York: Vintage, 1968).

The first in-depth biography of Ho Chi Minh.

*Lang, Daniel. *Casualties of War* (New York: McGraw-Hill, 1969).

An engrossing account of the war's dehumanization of the Vietnamese and brutalization of American soldiers.

Marr, David. *A History of Vietnamese Anti-Colonialism 1885–1925* (Berkeley & Los Angeles: University of California Press, 1970).

This work documents the historical roots of the modern Vietnamese struggle for independence and investigates the relations between this struggle and the antiforeigner and anticolonialism movements that began in the late nineteenth and early twentieth centuries. By one of the country's leading scholars of Vietnam.

McAlister, John. *Vietnam: The Origins of Revolution* (Berkeley & Los Angeles: University of California Press, 1969).

A sociological and historical account of the nature of revolution in Vietnam.

*Pike, Douglas. *Viet Cong* (Cambridge: M.I.T. Press, 1966).

A thorough if biased account of the NLF by a staunch anti-Communist. Nevertheless, as a foreign service officer in Vietnam, Pike had access to large numbers of captured NLF documents.

*Schell, Jonathan. *The Village of Ben Suc* (New York: Knopf, 1967).

Recounts a U.S. military operation in a single village of South Vietnam.

————. *The Military Half* (New York: Vintage, 1968).

A first-hand account of the U.S. air war and the destruction it is wreaking on the Vietnamese people and countryside.

*Zinn, Howard. *The Logic of Withdrawal* (Cambridge: Beacon, 1967).

The best of the books on the reasons for and the means of U.S. withdrawal from Vietnam.

III. LAOS

Dommen, Arthur. *Conflict in Laos* (New York: Praeger, 1964).

A very good outline of the complicated political situation leading to American involvement in Laos. Despite its pro-American bias, his facts are generally well-documented for the period after 1958. Nevertheless, Dommen fails to distinguish between the Pathet Lao and the North Vietnamese.

Fall, Bernard. *Anatomy of a Crisis: The Laotian Crisis of 1960–61* (New York: Doubleday, 1969).

> Fall focuses on the various minority groups in Laos, pointing out their particular cultural, economic, and political affinities and analyzing the Pathet Lao.

Halpern, Joel. *Economy and Society of Laos: A Brief Survey* (New Haven: Southeast Asian Monograph Series, No. 5, 1964).

> A good descriptive work.

*McCoy, Al and Adams, Nina, eds. *Laos: War and Revolution* (New York: Harper & Row, 1970).

> An excellent collection of articles on the background and impact of the American war in Laos.

Toye, Hugh. *Laos: Buffer State or Battleground* (New York: Oxford University Press, 1968).

> Toye provides an excellent descriptive historical background. This ex-British intelligence officer in Laos is academically critical of American involvement. Although his account is more objective than that of Dommen, Toye also fails to analyze the connection between the Pathet Lao and the North Vietnamese.

IV. CAMBODIA

*Armstrong, John. *Sihanouk Speaks* (New York: Walker, 1964).

> Contains extracts from Sihanouk's articles and speeches. Armstrong, in addition to translating Sihanouk's works, also introduces the various selections.

Lacouture, Jean. *The Demi-Gods* (New York: Knopf, 1970).

> A quarter of the book is devoted to a discussion of Sihanouk as a charismatic leader.

Leifer, Michael. *Cambodia: The Search for Security* (New York: Praeger, 1967).

> Leifer looks at Cambodia from an American point of view. He is less sanguine than Smith (below) about Sihanouk's ability to hold Cambodia together as a sovereign nation committed to a policy of neutralism.

Munson, F. P., et al. *Area Handbook for Cambodia* (Washington, D.C.: U.S. Government Printing Office, 1968).

> A basic survey of Cambodia, its people, and their culture, society, politics, and economics.

Smith, Roger. *Cambodia's Foreign Policy* (Ithaca: Cornell University Press, 1965).

This is a reliable account of Cambodia's policy of neutralism. This observer of Cambodian politics is a sympathetic admirer of Sihanouk.

Index